How to Use the
UNIFORM RESIDENTIAL
APPRAISAL REPORT

Third Edition

Martha R. Williams, JD • William L. Ventolo, Jr.

Dearborn
Real Estate Education

This publication is designed to provide accurate and authoritative information in regard to the subject matter covered. It is sold with the understanding that the publisher is not engaged in rendering legal, accounting, or other professional service. If legal advice or other expert assistance is required, the services of a competent professional person should be sought.

President: Roy Lipner
Vice-President of Product Development and Publishing: Evan M. Butterfield
Associate Publisher: Louise Benzer
Development Editor: Elizabeth Austin
Director of Production: Daniel Frey
Typesetter: Janet Schroeder
Creative Director: Lucy Jenkins

Published by Dearborn™ Real Estate Education,
a division of Dearborn Financial Publishing, Inc.®
30 South Wacker Drive
Chicago, IL 60606-7481
(312) 836-4400
http://www.dearbornRE.com

Printed in the United States of America.

06   07   08   10   9   8   7   6   5   4   3   2   1

CONTENTS

How to Use the Uniform Residential Appraisal Report is designed to assist both new and experienced appraisers. The new appraiser must learn how real estate appraisal theory relates to appraisal practice techniques. The experienced appraiser may want a "refresher" in this vital area. *How to Use the Uniform Residential Appraisal Report* serves both these needs and is also an easy-to-use reference for the field or the office.

The newly recognized importance of real estate appraisal education has highlighted the need for learning materials that cover the basics as they related to the "real world" of practice. *How to Use the Uniform Residential Appraisal Report* meets that need by having the reader do more than just read about what must be done to complete a URAR form. The reader practices filling out each form section as it is discussed. As a final project, the reader has the opportunity to complete an entire sample appraisal.

In short, whether used alone or as part of a course, this book helps bridge the gap between the world of the observer and the world of the participant.

ACKNOWLEDGMENTS

Preparation of *How to Use the Uniform Residential Appraisal Report* was greatly aided by the comments and encouragement received from those who reviewed the manuscript. Corina D. Rollins, CRPA/R, Marin Community College, reviewed the manuscript of both the first and second editions. Additional reviews of the first edition were provided by Dean Bishop, I.F.S., Omaha School of Real Estate, and Ronald D. Oslin, President, Tennessee Real Estate Educational Systems, Inc., and Oslin Mortgage Company. Reviews for the third edition were provided by James E. Jacobs, Grayson College; Hal London, Key Appraisals; David L. Shoemaker, Montana Real Estate Institute; Dennis Tosh, FNC, Inc; and Terrence M. Zajac.

Special thanks go to Software for Real Estate Professionals, Inc., in Baton Rouge, Louisiana, for providing the AppraiseIt software, used to complete the forms in this book.

Thanks also go to Rick Anderson and his staff at U.S. Forms, Inc., Grafton, Massachusetts, who provided the copies of the URAR form used in earlier editions of this book, and to Dick McKissock, Dater Systems, who provided the software used to complete the forms in the second edition.

Production of this book would not have been possible without the encouragement of Evan Butterfield, Vice-President of Product Development and Publishing, and the capable assistance of his staff, including Elizabeth Austin, Development Editor, and Daniel Frey, Director of Production. Production of the first edition was aided by Acquisitions Editors Wendy Lochner and Margaret M. Maloney, and Project Editor Timothy Taylor. Our sincere thanks to all of them.

Last (as usually is the case), but certainly not least, go our thanks for the patience and understanding of our long-suffering spouses, who must share the tribulations of writing a book without ever fully realizing the pleasure that comes from the accomplishment.

Martha R. Williams, JD, RCE
William L. Ventolo, Jr.

INTRODUCTION

Most residential real estate loans now are placed on the secondary mortgage market, and many federal and quasi-federal agencies are involved in these and related transactions. The most prominent include the following, which are referred to throughout this book by the following:

Fannie Mae	Formerly the Federal National Mortgage Association
FHA	Federal Housing Administration
Freddie Mac	Formerly the Federal Home Loan Mortgage Corporation
Ginnie Mae	Formerly the Government National Mortgage Association
HUD	Department of Housing and Urban Development
RHS	Rural Housing Service, formerly the Farmers Home Administration
VA	Department of Veterans Affairs

Over the years, the need for standardized appraisal documentation became apparent and resulted in creation of the Uniform Residential Appraisal Report (URAR). The URAR has become the key reporting tool for appraisers of single-family residences. Appraisers must learn how to use this tool to its maximum advantage, always keeping in mind the client's requirements as well as those of the agency receiving the form.

How to Use the Uniform Residential Appraisal Report is designed for maximum clarity as well as maximum ease of use.

The text begins with a brief overview of real estate appraisal and the history of the URAR form. Each section of the URAR form is then explained, and the relevant agency criteria are provided. Next, the reader has the opportunity to examine how the technique explained can be carried out in actual practice. Finally, the reader has the opportunity to apply what has been learned.

Sections of the form are covered in the same order in which they appear in the form. In addition, all discussion of a particular topic, including agency criteria, appears in the same part of the book. In this way, the reader need not search through the book to find explanations, agency requirements, or form samples. It is important to note that, while the agency criteria presented in this book, including the Fannie Mae criteria, were current as of the date this book was written, all criteria are subject to revision at any time, particularly following the release of a new edition of the form. Readers are referred to the Web sites *www.efanniemae.com* and *www.hud.gov* for press releases and other information on updates to the URAR form and guidelines for using the URAR form. Copies of the URAR and other forms are available at *www.efanniemae.com*. A paid

WEB@LINK

W E B @ L I N K

subscription service that provides all requirements for FHA, VA, Fannie Mae, Freddie Mac, Ginnie Mae, RHS, and others is available at *www.allregs.com.*

For ease of reference, a heading at the top of each right-hand page of this book shows the section that is discussed on that page. An Answer Key and topic Index are located at the back of the book. With all of these features, *How to Use the Uniform Residential Appraisal Report* takes the reader through a three-step learning process of

1. discussion,
2. examination, and
3. application.

Step One: Discussion

The URAR form is broken down into its component sections. Each section is presented, and the information required for each entry in that section is explained. The order of presentation follows the order in which topics appear on the form, even when the logical progression of the appraiser's work dictates a different order. For instance, the section on reconciliation (the final part of the appraisal process) comes before discussion of the cost and income approaches because this is the sequence in which the information appears on the form. In practice, if the cost or income approach is used, the appraiser will complete that analysis before beginning the process of reconciliation.

The URAR is intended for a national marketplace. To the extent that it can accomplish this formidable task, it can be labeled a *generic* document. To use the form effectively, however, the appraiser must know and recognize the diversity of properties and regional marketplaces in which it will be used. As often as possible, the authors point out local variables that will require special attention.

Specific agency criteria are presented immediately following the relevant discussion. Agency criteria are not lumped together in a series of appendixes, and they are *not* simply quoted without commentary. The authors have attempted to present and explain agency criteria in clear, uncomplicated language. The criteria are always placed in the context of the form itself.

Note: Always double-check individual agency requirements. The stated requirements can be ambiguous and may not cover every type of information that must be supplied in completing the URAR. The appraiser always must investigate local needs and preferences, which no "national" form (or text) could ever adequately cover.

Step Two: Examination

How to Use the Uniform Residential Appraisal Report is a practice manual as well as a reference book. The discussion of each section of the form is followed by a sample completed version of that section, identified as **Appraisal 1,** and the background data that led to the entries shown. The reader thus has an example of how the form can be used in practice. Because the example comes immediately after the text discussion, it reinforces the information just learned.

Step Three: Application

After each URAR form section is discussed and a completed version of that section examined, the reader is asked to complete a blank copy of the form section, identified as **Appraisal 2,** using the information supplied. This step provides the ultimate reinforcement of hands-on application of what has been learned.

The book concludes with a problem, **Appraisal 3,** which calls on the reader to make use of all the information learned to complete the first three pages of the URAR form, which provide information on the subject property, the appraiser's opinion of value, and supporting data.

Of course, there is a comprehensive Answer Key at the back of the book for the reader to check the completed Appraisal 2 and Appraisal 3 form sections against the suggested responses.

How to Use This Book

The easiest way to use this book is to begin with Part One, which gives an overview of real estate appraisal. Part Two opens with a brief look at development of the URAR form. Experienced appraisers may choose to skip this introductory material and go directly to Part Three, the discussion of the URAR form.

In Part Three, the reader is led through the URAR form by the process of discussion, examination, and application explained in this Introduction. Any material that is not completely understood can be reread before proceeding. It is recommended that answers to the exercises always be checked against the Answer Key at the back of the book before proceeding to the next text discussion.

By the time the reader gets to Part Four, "Putting It All Together," completing the URAR form should be a familiar and nonthreatening task.

Conclusion

The most important point for an appraiser to remember about the URAR form is that it is a reporting tool, not an end in itself. No form—even with legal descriptions, maps, photographs, and a variety of other attachments—can ever contain all the information an appraiser relied on to form a stated opinion of market value. The best an appraiser can hope to accomplish with a form is to have a convenient tool with which to summarize the data that had the most influence on the valuation decision. The best the appraiser's client or form recipient can hope for is to have the necessary appraisal data presented in terms that are readily understood and consistent with those used in other appraisals.

This book is intended to help ensure that the Uniform Residential Appraisal Report is completed properly and used productively.

## PART ONE

What Is a Real Estate Appraisal?

■ THE REAL ESTATE MARKETPLACE

Real estate, real property, land, terra firma. No matter what it's called, it's an inescapable part of our daily lives. With the exception of the extraordinary work performed by astronauts, every human activity takes place on some form of real estate.

Over the centuries, fortunes both vast and modest have been made through real estate ownership. The last few years have been no exception. With favorable financing at record low interest rates, seemingly unstoppable property appreciation, and unpredictable results from the stock market, more investors than ever are looking to real estate for its profit potential. Only in recent decades, however, has research been launched on components of the real estate marketplace and questions raised about underlying assumptions that, among other things, have helped establish our national housing policy.

Residential Property

In 1949, Congress acknowledged in the National Housing Act that decent, safe, and sanitary housing is a right of every citizen of the United States. Over more than a half century, federal, state, and local governments have attempted to bring decent, safe, and sanitary housing to all citizens by a variety of building construction, financing, and related programs. Direct funding, bond programs, tax credits, and relaxation of zoning constraints are only some of the methods used to meet this priority.

There are many other ways government has imposed itself on the real estate marketplace, of course. Interest rates paid by property owners and investors reflect the prime rate set by the Federal Reserve System and charged by member institutions to their best-rated commercial borrowers. Federally insured and guaranteed home and farm mortgages have helped popularize the benefits of real property ownership and investment. So have similar state programs and the enormous secondary mortgage market.

1

The availability of affordable financing has resulted in the highest rate of homeownership ever recorded in the United States, and record price appreciation and property values. In most parts of the country, prospective first-time homebuyers can choose among a variety of low- and no-down-payment loan programs. Interest-only loans have proven attractive to owner-occupants as well as investors. But in areas of the country where appreciation has been highest, such as California, Hawaii, Nevada, and Florida, first-time homebuyers in urban areas have difficulty financing the down payment and/or monthly payments for a "starter" home. Incomes have simply failed to keep up with housing prices.

How long will the current situation last? It is difficult to predict, but there will inevitably come a time when prices level off, and there is always the possibility that other economic factors will reduce demand, creating an oversupply of properties and a resulting downturn of values.

Commercial Property

In many parts of the country the commercial real estate marketplace has been even more volatile than the housing market. Demand for commercial properties, though much improved in recent years, is still much more susceptible to economic conditions than the demand for housing. More and more, the commercial real estate marketplace is becoming a national one, with local and state governments involved in proposals to attract businesses of all types, from manufacturing, assembly, and distribution facilities to office, hotel, and educational complexes. Ironically, the strong demand for housing has helped save some commercial areas. Downtown areas that were once blighted have seen a resurgence of residential development in the form of new high-rise condominiums and conversions of commercial and industrial buildings to residential use. These new urban homes have, in turn, created demand for grocery stores and other services, bringing a new surge of business opportunities.

■ APPRAISAL REGULATION

Historically, appraisers were subject to few legally mandated rules and regulations, but the massive federal bailout effort required to salvage or rescue hundreds of failed financial institutions in the 1980s led to new regulations for appraisers and appraisals. As of January 1, 1993, most appraisals of property involved in federally related transactions must be performed only by appraisers licensed or certified by the state in which the property is located. A federally related transaction is any real estate-related financial transaction (any sale, lease, purchase, investment, exchange, refinancing, or other use of real property as security for a loan or investment) involving a federal financial institution and requiring an appraisal. Federal institutions include the Comptroller of the Currency, Federal Deposit Insurance Corporation, Federal Reserve System, and National Credit Union Association.

A certified appraiser always is required for an appraisal of property valued at $1 million or more. The decision as to whether to use a certified or a licensed appraiser for an appraisal of property valued at less than $1 million (normally based on a transaction's complexity) must be made by the federal agency or lending institution involved. Typically, the appraiser is responsible for recognizing a "complex" appraisal and notifying the client (usually a lender), who then decides whether a certified appraiser is required.

Appraisals must be conducted in the fashion prescribed by the state, in conformance with federal law. Each state must require of appraisers a combination of experience and education that at least meets the minimum established by the Appraisal Foundation's Appraiser Qualifications Board. Appraisal standards must meet the minimum level established by the Appraisal Foundation's Appraisal Standards Board.

Although a large majority of mortgage loans (such as those made by federally insured banks) ultimately involve a federal agency, a substantial segment of the mortgage market is handled by nonfederal lenders such as insurance companies and others. Such lenders are free to set their own standards for appraisers and the information required in an appraisal; however, the federally mandated requirements are generally followed even by those lenders.

■ THE LANGUAGE OF APPRAISAL

An appraiser is one who provides an opinion of value. An appraisal is the process by which a determination of value is made. Most often the value sought by a real estate appraiser is market value.

For many years market value generally was defined as the highest price a property could be expected to bring in an arm's-length transaction occurring under normal market conditions. In an arm's-length transaction all parties have full knowledge of the property's assets and defects, the parties are unrelated, and no party is acting under duress. Normal market conditions include a reasonable marketing time and financing terms that are customary for similar properties in the area.

The assumption of market value as the *highest* price a property can command may be acceptable in a time of continuing price appreciation. During a time of declining prices, or even stagnant prices, a property owner may have little hope of attaining an optimum price. Because so many real estate markets throughout the United States have proven to be highly volatile, Freddie Mac and Fannie Mae define market value as the *most probable* price that a property should bring in a competitive and open market under all conditions requisite to a fair sale, with the buyer and seller each acting prudently and knowledgeably, and assuming the price is not affected by undue stimulus. This definition takes into account the fact that an appraiser's research and analysis typically result in a range of values and the highest value in that range is not necessarily an accurate indication of market value.

Because the requirements of Fannie Mae must be met in most transactions, the definition of market value that relies on a "most probable price" finding will be used in this book. Appraisers are not fortune-tellers, of course. No one can absolutely guarantee the accuracy of an appraisal. What an experienced and capable appraiser can do, however, is to learn as much as possible about the property being appraised and the pertinent market factors that influence value and apply that knowledge with skill and sound judgment to provide a justifiable opinion of value.

FIGURE 1
Appraisal Flowchart

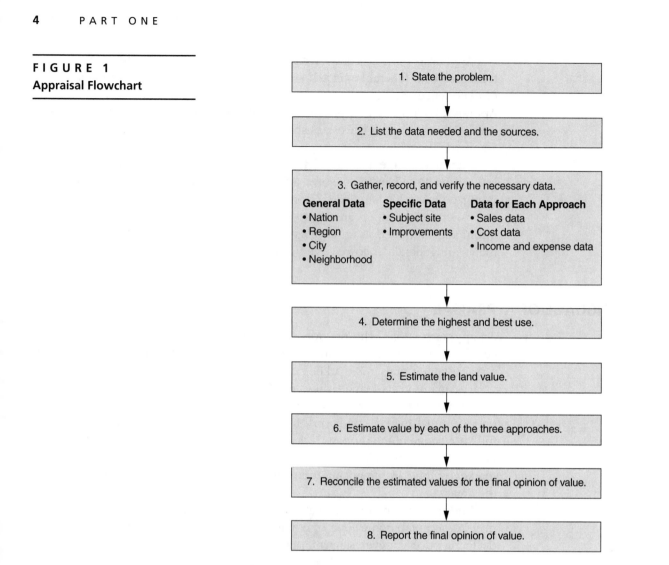

■ THE APPRAISAL PROCESS: A FLOWCHART

The process by which an appraisal is carried out is shown in the flowchart in Figure 1. The basic process generally is the same, regardless of the purpose of the appraisal or the type of property being appraised. The steps are described next.

1. State the appraisal problem; that is, identify the property being appraised and the purpose of the appraisal. Most often the appraisal will be conducted to determine market value for purposes of a sale, loan refinancing, or exchange.

2. Determine the kinds of data required and the sources from which they are to be collected.

3. Gather and verify the necessary data in the most efficient manner.

4. Determine the property's highest and best use. A valuation based on the current use will be meaningless if the property is not being used to its maximum potential.

5–6. Estimate the land value and then estimate the value of the improvements on the property, using any or all of the three approaches to estimating value (discussed below).

7. Make a final opinion of value that most accurately reflects the value of the subject property. The appraiser's final opinion of value is not an average but an opinion based on the type of property being appraised, the results of the research compiled, and the valuation techniques used.

8. Report the final opinion of value in one of the formats described under "How an Appraisal Is Communicated," later in this part.

METHODS OF APPRAISAL

The sales comparison approach is the most widely used appraisal method and the easiest to understand. The appraiser finds recently sold properties that are comparable to the subject property. Based on sales prices of the comparables ("comps"), the appraiser determines an equivalent price for the subject property. The mathematical formula for the sales comparison approach is:

$$\text{Sale Price of Comparable Property} \pm \text{Adjustments} = \text{Indicated Value of Subject Property}$$

The appraiser makes adjustments to the sale price of a comparable by adding the value of features that are present in the subject but not the comp and subtracting the value of features that are present in the comp but not the subject. In the cost approach, the present cost to construct the building(s) or other improvements being appraised is first reduced by the amount by which the improvements have depreciated, then added to the property's land value. The formula for the cost approach is:

$$\text{Cost of Improvements New} - \text{Depreciation on Improvements} + \text{Site Value} = \text{Property Value}$$

In the income capitalization approach, the net annual income, or investment return, that the property can be expected to produce determines the property's value as an investment. The formula for the income capitalization approach is:

$$\frac{\text{Net Operating Income}}{\text{Rate of Return}} = \text{Property Value}$$

Each valuation technique will be explained in more detail later in this book as you learn how it is used.

HOW AN APPRAISAL IS COMMUNICATED

USPAP recognizes three types of appraisal reports. The first is the *self-contained report*, which is a thorough presentation of the data, analyses, and reasoning that has led to the appraiser's opinion of value. Also called a *narrative appraisal report*, this is the most complete type of appraisal. In perhaps 30 to 100 or more pages, the appraiser summarizes important background research and presents all relevant data for each appraisal method that contributed to the final opinion of value. A number of exhibits may be attached, including photographs of the subject property and comparables, as well as maps showing demographic, topographical, soil, and other analyses of the subject and comparables.

FIGURE 2
Fannie Mae Appraisal Report Forms

Appraisal Update and/or Completion Report (Form 1004D)
Desktop Underwriter Property Inspection Report (Form 2075)
Exterior-Only Inspection Individual Condominium Unit Appraisal Report (Form 1075)
Exterior-Only Inspection Individual Cooperative Interest Appraisal Report (Form 2095)
Exterior-Only Inspection Residential Appraisal Report (Form 2055)
Individual Condominium Unit Appraisal Report (Form 1073)
Individual Cooperative Interest Appraisal Report (Form 2090)
Manufactured Home Appraisal Report (Form 1004C)
Single-Family Comparable Rent Schedule (Form 1007)
Small Residential Income Property Appraisal Report (Form 1025)
Uniform Residential Appraisal Report (Form 1004)

The self-contained appraisal report, being the most thorough, also is the most expensive report to prepare, but it is an important and frequently necessary tool in the valuation of complex properties, particularly for establishing value as part of a legal proceeding. Being the most detailed, the self-contained appraisal report makes the most convincing presentation; for the same reason, it is the most difficult type of report to attack.

The second type of report recognized by USPAP is the *summary report*. Although the summary report is not as complete as the self-contained report, it must provide sufficient information to lead the client to the appraiser's opinion of value. The URAR form, which is six pages plus addenda, is a summary report. Use of a form report provides an efficient, uncomplicated, and consistent way to present a survey of background research and data on the subject property and comparables.

In the past it was not unusual for particular institutions to develop their own appraisal forms. Over the years, however, as more properties have become involved in government-related transactions, the use of agency-mandated forms has become the rule. In addition to the URAR form, the subject of this book, other forms have been developed to expedite real estate appraisals. Figure 2 lists some of the forms currently available from Fannie Mae. Computerized forms and electronic data submission have cut the time needed both to prepare an appraisal form and to transmit it to the client. The appraiser should always verify the client's requirements as to both the type of form and accepted method of transmission.

The last type of appraisal report recognized by USPAP is the *restricted use report*, which is made for a specific client and for a stated limited purpose. Because it contains virtually none of the information the appraiser used to arrive at the opinion of value, the restricted use report is rarely used.

■ COMPLIANCE WITH USPAP

As client/agency requirements have become better defined, so have the requirements of the Uniform Standards of Professional Appraisal Practice. The Supplement Standards Rule states that, if a client imposes requirements beyond those of USPAP, and the appraiser certifies that they have been followed, the appraiser is bound to do so. The Supplemental Standards Rule appears below. The reader is advised to obtain a copy of the latest draft of USPAP from *www.appraisalfoundation.org* for study and reference of all applicable sections.

WEB@LINK

USPAP Supplemental Standards Rule

USPAP provides the common basis for all appraisal practice. Supplemental standards applicable to assignments prepared for specific purposes or property types may be issued (i.e., published) by government agencies, government sponsored enterprises, or other entities that establish public policy. An appraiser and client must ascertain whether any such published supplemental standards in addition to USPAP apply to the assignment being considered.

Comment: The purpose of the Supplemental Standards Rule is to provide a reasonable means to augment USPAP with requirements that add to the requirements set forth by USPAP.

Supplemental standards cannot diminish the purpose, intent, or content of the requirements of USPAP.

Upon agreeing to perform an assignment that includes acceptable supplemental standards, an appraiser is obligated to competently satisfy those supplemental standards, as well as applicable USPAP requirements.

An appraiser who represents that an assignment is or will be completed in compliance with agreed-upon supplemental standards and who then knowingly fails to comply with those supplemental standards violates the Ethics Rule, or who then inadvertently fails to comply with those supplemental standards violates the Competency Rule. (See the Ethics Rule and the Competency Rule.)

## PART TWO

The Uniform Residential Appraisal Report

■ **AN OVERVIEW**

At a time when subdivisions of similarly styled and built homes are the norm for new construction, it may be hard to believe that until the 1930s the custom home predominated. A prospective homeowner who failed to find a suitable existing house in the desired area typically would purchase a building lot and then hire an architect and builder. Methods of financing construction or purchase loans fell far short of the convenient long-term vehicles now available. Mortgages were typically for no more than 50 percent of property value, with part payable in installments over a relatively short term—perhaps five years—and the entire balance due at the end of that term.

The large number of residential loan foreclosures during the Great Depression was surely due, at least in part, to the onerous terms that borrowers were forced to accept. The collapse and subsequent restructuring of the nation's banking system by the federal government in the early 1930s helped place homebuyers on a more equal footing with lenders. Federal programs that guaranteed repayment of home mortgage loans provided lenders with the incentive they needed to expand their services in this growing market.

The Postwar Housing Boom

In the years to come, the demand for housing soon exceeded available supply. Encouraged by the extraordinary pent-up demand for residential construction that followed World War II, builders and developers learned to make use of economies of scale and standardization in residential construction. Such economies, which included quantity purchases of building materials and application of assembly-line construction techniques, were possible only with homes that offered little individualization.

Levittown, on Long Island in New York, was the first large single-family home tract development. Although Levittown's initial appearance may have struck some as unimaginative, its design and execution enabled thousands of families to

9

become homebuyers. The homes were small, but they were built on ample lots (at least by today's standards) and provided room for homeowners to remodel and expand over the years as needs demanded and finances allowed.

In both home construction and financing, the move toward standardization broadened the desirability and availability of home ownership. The sheer volume of home loans processed by lenders provided the incentive for finding a way in which to perform the necessary property appraisals as efficiently as possible while providing the information required to make a loan decision.

The Secondary Mortgage Market

The final push toward developing a standard appraisal form came with the emergence of the secondary mortgage market. Prior to 1938 lenders typically retained their mortgage loans in their own portfolios. The risk involved in purchasing mortgage loans meant that few buyers were willing to invest in mortgages on properties outside their immediate area. That risk was reduced markedly, however, by the development of government-insured loans and the creation in 1938 of the Federal National Mortgage Association, now called simply Fannie Mae, to serve as a secondary market for such loans.

In 1968 Fannie Mae was converted partly to private ownership. The secondary market was boosted further with the creation of the Government National Mortgage Association, now known as Ginnie Mae. The Federal Home Loan Mortgage Corporation, or Freddie Mac, was created in 1970 as part of the Federal Home Loan Bank System to serve as a secondary mortgage market for savings and loan associations and mortgage bankers. As a result of these readily available public and quasi-public secondary market sources, many lenders now prefer to transfer the risk of holding mortgages by selling them, even though the lender might retain the tasks (and fees) related to servicing the loans (overseeing payment collections, impound accounts, and so on).

Because the majority of today's residential mortgage loans will become part of the secondary mortgage market, the needs of the agencies involved have dictated the manner in which property appraisals are conducted and reported at the time of loan origination. This is not just an instance of "the tail wagging the dog," however. Federal mandates on appraiser qualifications and licensing that took effect in 1993 have highlighted the importance of accurate appraisals.

The extent to which faulty appraisals may have contributed to the collapse of so many financial institutions will probably never be known. What is known, however, is that a properly researched and documented appraisal is crucial to both the making and guaranteeing of loans secured by the appraised property.

Several years of record low interest rates have created a housing boom throughout the country, particularly in urban areas. In a trend eerily reminiscent of the Depression years, many current borrowers are opting for interest-only loans (some of them with an adjustable interest rate) that culminate in a five- or seven-year balloon payment. What will be the future of the real estate marketplace as those loans escalate in cost with the inevitable rise in interest rates, and particularly when the balloon payments come due? Only time will tell, but the best hope for a stable real estate market in the next decade most likely will be the projected increase in demand for housing.

Development of the URAR

A residential appraisal report appropriate for single-family residential property appraisals was created by Fannie Mae and Freddie Mac in the 1970s and revised in 1975 and 1979. The next version of the Uniform Residential Appraisal Report (URAR) was issued by Fannie Mae and Freddie Mac in October 1986 following input from other government agencies and field testing. In May 1987 the URAR became the required form for single-family residential appraisals performed for the Department of Housing and Urban Development (HUD) and the Department of Veterans Affairs (VA). VA appraisal report requirements appear in Figure 3. The URAR became the required form of the Farmers Home Administration (now the Rural Housing Service, or RHS) in June 1987.

FIGURE 3
VA Appraisal Report Requirements

Every VA appraisal report must include
- A properly completed appraisal report form on either
  - Uniform Residential Appraisal Report (URAR), Freddie Mac Form 70/Fannie Mae Form 1004, unless the property is a condominium unit or is income-producing (more than one living unit);
  - Individual Condominium Unit Appraisal Report, Freddie Mac Form 465/Fannie Mae Form 1073, if the property is a condominium unit; or
  - Small Residential Income Property Appraisal Report, Freddie Mac Form 72/Fannie Mae Form 1025, if the property has two to four living units.
- The Statement of Assumptions and Limiting Conditions that is included in the URAR form. No limiting conditions can be made in addition to those on the URAR form, Freddie Mac Form 70/Fannie Mae Form 1004. Additional certifications required by State law or related to continuing education or membership in appraisal organizations, etc., can be made on a separate form or page, provided they do not conflict with the language on the URAR form or any VA policy.
- A location map, showing the location of the subject and each comparable.
- A building perimeter sketch showing the "footprint" of the improvements. The calculation for the square foot size of the property must also be shown either here or in the "Comments on Cost Approach" section of the URAR.
- Photographs must be included as specified below.
  - In proposed construction cases, a front view photograph of each comparable is required, but photographs of the subject property are not required if there are no improvements under construction.
  - If the property is in a condominium more than three units high, no photographs of the comparables are required, provided they are located in the same project as the subject property and are substantially identical to the subject property.
  - In all other cases, each appraisal report requires:

    One set of original photographs of the subject property (two sets in LAPP cases) showing a front and back view (preferably including a different side view in each photograph) and the street scene; and

    One set of original photographs of each comparable. Only a front view of the comparables is required.
- Any additional appraisal or repair-related information that may be needed to support the fee appraiser's conclusions. (The appropriate areas on a computer-generated URAR can be expanded to include such information, provided the standard sequence of the URAR instructions, information entries, etc., does not change and the "Sales Comparison Analysis does not appear on two separate pages.)
- The appraisal request (VA Form 26-1805) provided by the appraisal requester. The appraiser must confirm, and correct if necessary, all information provided by the appraisal requester that is pertinent to the value estimate.

The appraiser must send two fully completed appraisal reports with all related exhibits (one original and one copy, each with a set of original photographs) to either VA or the LAPP Staff Appraisal Reviewer, as appropriate.

Appraisers may transmit VA appraisal reports electronically, with an electronically affixed signature, in accordance with USPAP Statement #8.

The URAR was revised again in June 1993. The changes to the form recognized the Uniform Standards of Professional Appraisal Practice as the minimum standards of the appraisal industry. After months of input from various sources, the final version of the current URAR became available in March 2005 and was mandated for use in Fannie Mae appraisals as of November 1, 2005. Certain types of single-family properties, such as condominiums and units in planned unit developments (PUDs), may require special appraisal forms or addenda for certain purposes.

■ SAMPLE FORM AND ATTACHMENTS

Appraisal 1, a sample completed Uniform Residential Appraisal Report and the attachments that accompany it, appears in Figure 4 on pages 14–24.

Form Design and Organization

The URAR is designed to record the data collected by the appraiser and to present a summary of the appraiser's findings and final conclusion of value. The current URAR, similar in format to the earlier one, makes use of a combination of checklists and fill-ins that are supplemented by applicable exhibits.

The current URAR form has six pages where the previous version had only two; however, the last three pages of the current form deal with standard explanations and disclaimers, such as definitions, assumptions, limiting conditions, and appraiser certifications. In the previous version of the form, this information was included in a separate document (Fannie Mae Form 1004B) and attached as an exhibit. Below is a page-by-page breakdown of the current URAR form.

Page 1 includes the following sections:

- **Subject:** basic information about the subject property and its sale
- **Contract:** analysis of the subject property's sales contract
- **Neighborhood:** location of subject property; space is provided for comments on trends and other factors that affect the subject property and its neighborhood
- **Site:** data for property under appraisal
- **Improvements:** description of property under appraisal, including **room list** (number, use, and types of rooms); **interior specifications** (including surface finishes and equipment); and **exterior descriptions** (including types of walls, roof surface, and window types)
- **Comments:** appraiser's remarks regarding additional features of property, condition of property improvements, and adverse environmental conditions

Page 2:

- **Sales comparison approach analysis,** including itemization of factors contributing to price differences between the subject property and comparable properties
- **Reconciliation statement,** explaining how appraiser correlated values derived by the appraisal approaches used to arrive at a single final opinion of market value

Page 3:

- **Additional comments** section for the appraiser's use for further explanation
- **Cost approach analysis,** including a breakdown of reproduction or replacement cost figures
- **Income approach analysis,** using the gross rent multiplier method
- **PUD** project information

Page 4:

- Describes the **scope of work** to be performed
- Identifies the **intended use** of the appraiser's opinions and conclusions
- Identifies the **client** and other intended users
- Defines **market value**
- Lists the appraiser's **assumptions and limiting conditions**

Page 5:

- Lists the appraiser's **certification**

Page 6 contains:

- A category where the appraiser signs the report and records other personal information
- A category where the supervisory appraiser (if applicable) signs the report and records other personal information

Like earlier versions of the URAR, the appraiser must include the necessary maps, floor plans, and photos of the subject property and comparables as exhibits.

FIGURE 4
Appraisal 1

Complete Appraisal Analysis - Summary Appraisal Report

Uniform Residential Appraisal Report   File # 05070001

The purpose of this summary appraisal report is to provide the lender/client with an accurate, and adequately supported, opinion of the market value of the subject property.

SUBJECT

Property Address 456 Cherry Hill Road	City Sarasota	State FL	Zip Code 34200

Borrower Arturo Mendez   Owner of Public Record Robert Travis   County Sarasota

Legal Description Lot 308 Bent Tree Village Subdivision, recorded in Book 12, Page 12, Sarasota County

Assessor's Parcel # BT 308   Tax Year 04-05   R.E. Taxes $ 3,524

Neighborhood Name Bent Tree Village   Map Reference G58   Census Tract 14

Occupant [X] Owner [ ] Tenant [ ] Vacant   Special Assessments $ None   [ ] PUD   HOA $ [ ] per year [ ] per month

Property Rights Appraised [X] Fee Simple [ ] Leasehold [ ] Other (describe)

Assignment Type [X] Purchase Transaction [ ] Refinance Transaction [ ] Other (describe)

Lender/Client Murphy Mortgage Company   Address PO Box 134, Serra, FL 34224-1347

Is the subject property currently offered for sale or has it been offered for sale in the twelve months prior to the effective date of the appraisal? [X] Yes [ ] No

Report data source(s) used, offering price(s), and date(s). Property listed for sale August 1, 2005, at $454,500.

CONTRACT

I [X] did [ ] did not analyze the contract for sale for the subject purchase transaction. Explain the results of the analysis of the contract for sale or why the analysis was not performed. No unusual financing or sales concessions noted.

Contract Price $ 450,000   Date of Contract 8-27-05   Is the property seller the owner of public record? [X] Yes [ ] No   Data Source(s) Lender

Is there any financial assistance (loan charges, sale concessions, gift or downpayment assistance, etc.) to be paid by any party on behalf of the borrower? [ ] Yes [X] No

If Yes, report the total dollar amount and describe the items to be paid:

NEIGHBORHOOD

Note: Race and the racial composition of the neighborhood are not appraisal factors.

Neighborhood Characteristics	One-Unit Housing Trends	One-Unit Housing	Percent Land Use %
Location [ ] Urban [X] Suburban [ ] Rural	Property Values [X] Increasing [ ] Stable [ ] Declining	PRICE $(000) AGE (yrs)	One-Unit 100 %
Built-Up [X] Over 75% [ ] 25-75% [ ] Under 25%	Demand/Supply [ ] Shortage [X] In Balance [ ] Over Supply	400 Low New	2-4 Unit %
Growth [ ] Rapid [X] Stable [ ] Slow	Marketing Time [X] Under 3 mths [ ] 3-6 mths [ ] Over 6 mths	550 High 15	Multi-Family %
		425 Pred. 8	Commercial %
			Other %

Neighborhood Boundaries On North by Bee Ridge Rd, on East by Bee Ridge extension, on South by Proctor Rd, on West by Sara Lane.

Neighborhood Description The subject neighborhood is 100% built-out, with mature landscaping. Values have increased annually due to proximity to downtown business district, schools and services, and highway access.

Market Conditions (including support for the above conclusions) Employment has risen steadily in metropolitan area due to business expansion and development. Area population has increased approximately 5% per year for the last five years, bolstering the housing market. Despite new-home development in the overall area, existing home sales have been strong.

SITE

Dimensions 68Fx160LSx75Rx139RS   Area 10726 +/- sq. ft.   Shape Irregular   View Residential

Specific Zoning Classification RSF-1   Zoning Description Residential Single-Family

Zoning Compliance [X] Legal [ ] Legal Nonconforming (Grandfathered Use) [ ] No Zoning [ ] Illegal (describe)

Is the highest and best use of the subject property as improved (or as proposed per plans and specifications) the present use? [X] Yes [ ] No If No, describe

Utilities	Public	Other (describe)		Public	Other (describe)	Off-site Improvements--Type	Public	Private
Electricity	[X]		Water	[X]		Street Asphalt	[X]	
Gas			Sanitary Sewer	[X]		Alley None		

FEMA Special Flood Hazard Area [ ] Yes [X] No   FEMA Flood Zone   FEMA Map No. 1251440170   FEMA Map Date 5/95

Are the utilities and off-site improvements typical for the market area? [X] Yes [ ] No. If No, describe

Are there any adverse site conditions or external factors (easements, encroachments, environmental conditions, land uses, etc.)? [ ] Yes [X] No If Yes, describe

IMPROVEMENTS

General Description	Foundation	Exterior Description materials/condition	Interior materials/condition
Units [X] One [ ] One with Accessory Unit	[X] Concrete Slab [ ] Crawl Space	Foundation Walls Concrete/good	Floors Hdwd/cpt/good
# of Stories	[ ] Full Basement [ ] Partial Basement	Exterior Walls Cedar/stucco/good	Walls Drywall/good
Type [ ] Det. [ ] Att. [ ] S-Det./End Unit	Basement Area sq. ft.	Roof Surface Asphalt shingle/good	Trim/Finish Wood/good
[X] Existing [ ] Proposed [ ] Under Const	Basement Finish %	Gutters & Downspouts Aluminum/good	Bath Floor Cer/good
Design (Style) Ranch/Typical	[ ] Outside Entry/Exit [ ] Sump Pump	Window Type Single-hung/good	Bath Wainscot Cer/good
Year Built 1994	Evidence of [ ] Infestation	Storm Sash/Insulated	Car Storage [ ] None
Effective Age (Yrs) 5-7	[ ] Dampness [ ] Settlement	Screens Yes/good	[ ] Driveway # of Cars
Attic [X] None	Heating [X] FWA [ ] HWBB [ ] Radiant	Amenities	Driveway Surface Asphalt
[ ] Drop Stair [ ] Stairs	[ ] Other Fuel	[X] Fireplace(s) # 1 [X] Fence	[X] Garage # of Cars 2
[ ] Floor [ ] Scuttle	Cooling [X] Central Air Conditioning	[X] Patio/Deck [X] Porch	[ ] Carport # of Cars
[ ] Finished [ ] Heated	[ ] Individual [ ] Other	[ ] Pool [ ] Other	[X] Att. [ ] Det. [ ] Built-in

Appliances [X] Refrigerator [X] Range/Oven [X] Dishwasher [X] Disposal [ ] Microwave [X] Washer/Dryer [X] Other (describe) Dryer

Finished area above grade contains: 7 Rooms   3 Bedrooms   2.00 Bath(s)   2,120 Square Feet of Gross Living Area Above Grade

Additional features (special energy efficient items, etc.) Ceiling fans in every room; roof vent; high-efficiency heating and cooling system

Describe the condition of the property (including needed repairs, deterioration, renovations, remodeling, etc.) Improvements overall are up-to-date and in good condition, typical of this neighborhood; depreciation is thus no more than approximately 10% of reproduction cost; no immediate repairs to major systems or structure are indicated.

Are there any physical deficiencies or adverse conditions that affect the livability, soundness, or structural integrity of the property? [ ] Yes [ ] No If Yes, describe

A routine inspection was made and no hazardous substances or detrimental environmental conditions were found on or near the subject property.

Does the property generally conform to the neighborhood (functional utility, style, condition, use, construction, etc.)? [X] Yes [ ] No If No, describe

FIGURE 4
Appraisal 1 (continued)

Uniform Residential Appraisal Report   File # 05070001

There are _____ comparable properties in the subject neighborhood ranging in price from $ _____ to $ _____

There are _____ comparable sales in the subject neighborhood within the past twelve months ranging in sale price from $ _____ to $ _____

FEATURE	SUBJECT	COMPARABLE SALE # 1	+(-)$ Adjustment	COMPARABLE SALE # 2	+(-)$ Adjustment	COMPARABLE SALE # 3	+(-)$ Adjustment
Address	456 Cherry Hill Road	403 Bent Tree Lane		475 Cherry Hill Road		191 Forest Trail	
	Sarasota	Sarasota		Sarasota		Sarasota	
Proximity to Subject		1/4 mile N/W		Same block		1 mile N/E	
Sale Price	$ 454,500	$ 445,000		$ 424,250		$ 430,000	
Sale Price/Gross Liv. Area	$ 214.39 sq. ft.	$ 210.40 sq. ft.		$ 223.76 sq. ft.		$ 250.29 sq. ft.	
Data Source(s)		Sales Agent		Sales Agent		Sales Agent	
Verification Source(s)		Public Records		Public Records		Public Records	
VALUE ADJUSTMENTS	DESCRIPTION	DESCRIPTION	+(-)$ Adjustment	DESCRIPTION	+(-)$ Adjustment	DESCRIPTION	+(-)$ Adjustment
Sale or Financing		Conv. mort.		Conv. mort.		Conv. mort.	
Concessions		No concess.		No concess.		No concess.	
Date of Sale/Time		8-10-05		7-15-05		4-8-05	
Location	Suburban	Sub/equal		Sub/equal		Busy street	+8,000
Leasehold/Fee Simple	Fee Simple	Fee Simple		Fee Simple		Fee simple	
Site	10726 sf/Gd	11,200 sf/Gd		8,250 sf/Avg	+5,000	10,000 sf/Gd	
View	Residential/Gd	Residential/Gd		Residential/Gd		Residential/Gd	
Design (Style)	Ranch/Typical	Ranch/Equal		Ranch/Equal		Ranch/Equal	
Quality of Construction	Good	Good		Good		Good	
Actual Age	11	11		10		5	-5,000
Condition	Good	Good		Good		Good	
Above Grade	Total / Bdrms. / Baths	Total / Bdrms. / Baths		Total / Bdrms. / Baths		Total / Bdrms. / Baths	
Room Count	7 / 3 / 2.00	7 / 3 / 2		7 / 3 / 2.5	-4,000	7 / 3 / 2	
Gross Living Area	2,120 sq. ft.	2,115 sq. ft.		1,896 sq. ft.	+5,500	1,718 sq. ft.	+8,500
Basement & Finished							
Rooms Below Grade	None	None		None		None	
Functional Utility	Good	Good		Good		Good	
Heating/Cooling	FWA/CAC	FWA/CAC		FWA/CAC		FWA/CAC	
Energy Efficient Items	H/C Syst/Fans	H/C Syst/Fans		H/C Syst/Fans		H/C Syst/Fans	
Garage/Carport	Gar 2 attached	Gar 2 attached		Gar 2 attached		Gar 2 attached	
Porch/Patio/Deck	Enclosed porch	Encl porch		Encl p/smaller	+4,500	Encl p/smaller	+4,500
Fireplace	Stone 1	Stone 1		None	+8,500	Stone 1	
Pool	Caged	Caged/smaller	+5,500	Caged/similar		Caged/similar	
Fence	Wood	Wood		Wood		Wood	
Net Adjustment (Total)		X + / - $	5,500	X + / - $	19,500	X + / - $	16,000
Adjusted Sale Price		Net Adj. 1.20 %		Net Adj. 4.60 %		Net Adj. 3.70 %	
of Comparables		Gross Adj. 1.20 % $	450,500	Gross Adj. 6.50 % $	443,750	Gross Adj. 6.00 % $	446,000

I [X] did [ ] did not research the sale or transfer history of the subject property and comparable sales. If not, explain

My research [ ] did [X] did not reveal any prior sales or transfers of the subject property for the three years prior to the effective date of this appraisal.

Data Source(s) County Assessor's Office

My research [ ] did [X] did not reveal any prior sales or transfers of the comparable sales for the prior year to the date of sale of the comparalbe sale.

Data Source(s) County Assessor's Office

Report the results of the research and analysis of the prior sale or transfer history of the subject property and comparable sales (report additional prior sales on page 3).

ITEM	SUBJECT	COMPARABLE SALE # 1	COMPARABLE SALE # 2	COMPARABLE SALE # 3
Date of Prior Sale/Transfer				
Price of Prior Sale/Transfer				
Data Source(s)				
Effective Date of Data Source(s)				

Analysis of prior sale or transfer history of the subject property and comparable sales

Summary of Sales Comparison Approach   All three comparable sales are located within the same neighborhood. Comparable 1 was given the most weight in the final analysis because it required the fewest adjustments and is most similar to the subject overall. All reported sales of comparable properties occurred within one to three months of listing; sale prices were within 98% of listing prices.

Indicated Value by Sales Comparison Approach $ 450,500

Indicated Value by: Sales Comparison Approach $ 450,500   Cost Approach (If developed) $ 452,900   Income Approach (If developed) $ _____

Because there are few rentals, the income approach is not considered applicable for properties in this area. There are no special financing considerations. The final value opinion is based on the sales comparison approach--a reasonable and supportable method for this type of property. The cost approach strongly suppports this opinion of value.

This appraisal is made [X] "as is," [ ] subject to completion per plans and specifications on the basis of a hypothetical condition that the improvements have been completed, [ ] subject to the following repairs or alterations on the basis of a hypothetical condition that the repairs or alterations have been completed, or [ ] subject to the following required inspection based on the extraordinary assumption that the condition or deficiency does not require alteration or repair:

Based on a complete visual inspection of the interior and exterior areas of the subject property, defined scope of work, statement of assumptions and limiting conditions, and appraiser's certification, my (our) opinion of the market value, as defined, of the real property that is the subject of this report is $ 450,500 , as of 9-12-05 , which is the date of inspection and the effective date of this appraisal.

FIGURE 4
Appraisal 1 (continued)

Uniform Residential Appraisal Report   File #   05070001

ADDITIONAL COMMENTS

COST APPROACH TO VALUE (not required by Fannie Mae)

Provide adequate information for the lender/client to replicate the below cost figures and calculations.

Support for the opinion of site value (summary of comparable land sales or other methods for estimating sale value)

Site value was determined by analyzing the most recent sale prices of comparable sites in neighborhoods similar to the subject neighborhood in location and physical characteristics.

ESTIMATED [X] REPRODUCTION OR [ ] REPLACEMENT COST NEW	OPINION OF SITE VALUE............................=$	90,000
Source of cost data Local builders	Dwelling 2,120 Sq. Ft. @ $ 147 =$	311,640
Quality rating from cost service Effective date of cost data	Entry 60 Sq. Ft. @ $ 50 =$	3,000
Comments on Cost Approach (gross living area calculations, depreciation, etc.)	Extras (porch, pool, fence)	38,450
See sketch for measurement analysis. Living area: 2120 SF. The	Garage/Carport 525 Sq. Ft. @ $ 30 =$	15,750
depreciation estimate reflects observed effective age. Cost	Total Estimate of Cost-New =$	368,840
estimates are supported by builders in the area. Land value is	Less Physical	Functional	External	
based on area land sales. The land/value ratio of the subject	Depreciation 18,000 N/A N/A =$(	18,000)
property is supported by those for comparable properties.	Depreciated Cost of Improvements............=$	350,840
	'As-is' Value of Site Improvements..................=$	12,020
	............................=$	
Estimated Remaining Economic Life (HUD and VA only) 54 Years	Indicated Value By Cost Approach..................=$	452,860

INCOME APPROACH TO VALUE (not required by Fannie Mae)

Estimated Monthly Market Rent $ N/A   X Gross Rent Multiplier   = $ Indicated Value by Income Approach

Summary of Income Approach (including support for market rent and GRM)

PROJECT INFORMATION FOR PUDs (if applicable)

Is the developer/builder in control of the Homeowners' Association (HOA)?   [ ] Yes   [ ] No   Unit type(s)   [ ] Detached   [ ] Attached

Provide the following information for PUDs ONLY if the developer/builder is in control of the HOA and the subject property is an attached dwelling unit.

Legal name of project

Total number of phases   Total number of units   Total number of units sold

Total number of units rented   Total number of units for sale   Data Source(s)

Was the project created by the conversion of existing building(s) into a PUD?   [ ] Yes   [ ] No   If Yes, date of conversion

Does the project contain any multi-dwelling units?   [ ] Yes   [ ] No   Data Source(s)

Are the units, common elements, and recreation facilities complete?   [ ] Yes   [ ] No   If No, describe the status of completion.

Are the common elements leased to or by the Homeowners' Association?   [ ] Yes   [ ] No   If Yes, describe the rental terms and options.

Describe common elements and recreational facilities

Freddie Mac Form 70 March 2005   Page 3 of 6   Fannie Mae Form 1004 March 2005

FIGURE 4
Appraisal 1 (continued)

Uniform Residential Appraisal Report

File # 05070001

This report form is designed to report an appraisal of a one-unit property or a one-unit property with an accessory unit; including a unit in a planned unit development (PUD). This report form is not designed to report an appraisal of a manufactured home or a unit in a condominium or cooperative project.

This appraisal report is subject to the following scope of work, intended use, intended user, definition of market value, statement of assumptions and limiting conditions, and certifications. Modifications, additions, or deletions to the intended use, intended user, definition of market value, or assumptions and limiting conditions are not permitted. The appraiser may expand the scope of work to include any additional research or analysis necessary based on the complexity of this appraisal assignment. Modifications or deletions to the certifications are also not permitted. However, additional certifications that do not constitute material alterations to this appraisal report, such as those required by law or those related to the appraiser's continuing education or membership in an appraisal organization, are permitted.

SCOPE OF WORK: The scope of work for this appraisal is defined by the complexity of this appraisal assignment and the reporting requirements of this appraisal report form, including the following definition of market value, statement of assumptions and limiting conditions, and certifications. The appraiser must, at a minimum: (1) perform a complete visual inspection of the interior and exterior areas of the subject property, (2) inspect the neighborhood, (3) inspect each of the comparable sales from at least the street, (4) research, verify, and analyze data from reliable public and/or private sources, and (5) report his or her analysis, opinions, and conclusions in this appraisal report.

INTENDED USE: The intended use of this appraisal report is for the lender/client to evaluate the property that is the subject of this appraisal for a mortgage finance transaction.

INTENDED USER: The intended user of this appraisal report is the lender/client.

DEFINITION OF MARKET VALUE: The most probable price which a property should bring in a competitive and open market under all conditions requisite to a fair sale, the buyer and seller, each acting prudently, knowledgeably and assuming the price is not affected by undue stimulus. Implicit in this definition is the consummation of a sale as of a specified date and the passing of title from seller to buyer under conditions whereby: (1) buyer and seller are typically motivated; (2) both parties are well informed or well advised, and each acting in what he or she considers his or her own best interest; (3) a reasonable time is allowed for exposure in the open market; (4) payment is made in terms of cash in U. S. dollars or in terms of financial arrangements comparable thereto; and (5) the price represents the normal consideration for the property sold unaffected by special or creative financing or sales concessions* granted by anyone associated with the sale.

*Adjustments to the comparables must be made for special or creative financing or sales concessions. No adjustments are necessary for those costs which are normally paid by sellers as a result of tradition or law in a market area; these costs are readily identifiable since the seller pays these costs in virtually all sales transactions. Special or creative financing adjustments can be made to the comparable property by comparisons to financing terms offered by a third party institutional lender that is not already involved in the property or transaction. Any adjustment should not be calculated on a mechanical dollar for dollar cost of the financing or concession but the dollar amount of any adjustment should approximate the market's reaction to the financing or concessions based on the appraiser's judgment.

STATEMENT OF ASSUMPTIONS AND LIMITING CONDITIONS: The appraiser's certification in this report is subject to the following assumptions and limiting conditions:

1. The appraiser will not be responsible for matters of a legal nature that affect either the property being appraised or the title to it, except for information that he or she became aware of during the research involved in performing this appraisal. The appraiser assumes that the title is good and marketable and will not render any opinions about the title.

2. The appraiser has provided a sketch in this appraisal report to show the approximate dimensions of the improvements. The sketch is included only to assist the reader in visualizing the property and understanding the appraiser's determination of its size.

3. The appraiser has examined the available flood maps that are provided by the Federal Emergency Management Agency (or other data sources) and has noted in this appraisal report whether any portion of the subject site is located in an identified Special Flood Hazard Area. Because the appraiser is not a surveyor, he or she makes no guarantees, express or implied, regarding this determination.

4. The appraiser will not give testimony or appear in court because he or she made an appraisal of the property in question, unless specific arrangements to do so have been made beforehand, or as otherwise required by law.

5. The appraiser has noted in this appraisal report any adverse conditions (such as needed repairs, deterioration, the presence of hazardous wastes, toxic substances, etc.) observed during the inspection of the subject property or that he or she became aware of during the research involved in performing this appraisal. Unless otherwise stated in this appraisal report, the appraiser has no knowledge of any hidden or unapparent physical deficiencies or adverse conditions of the property (such as, but not limited to, needed repairs, deterioration, the presence of hazardous wastes, toxic substances, adverse environmental conditions, etc.) that would make the property less valuable, and has assumed that there are no such conditions and makes no guarantees or warranties, express or implied. The appraiser will not be responsible for any such conditions that do exist or for any engineering or testing that might be required to discover whether such conditions exist. Because the appraiser is not an expert in the field of environmental hazards, this appraisal report must not be considered as an environmental assessment of the property.

6. The appraiser has based his or her appraisal report and valuation conclusion for an appraisal that is subject to satisfactory completion, repairs, or alterations on the assumption that the completion, repairs, or alterations of the subject property will be performed in a professional manner.

FIGURE 4
Appraisal 1 (continued)

Uniform Residential Appraisal Report

File # 05070001

APPRAISER'S CERTIFICATION: The Appraiser certifies and agrees that:

1. I have, at a minimum, developed and reported this appraisal in accordance with the scope of work requirements stated in this appraisal report.

2. I performed a complete visual inspection of the interior and exterior areas of the subject property. I reported the condition of the improvements in factual, specific terms. I identified and reported the physical deficiencies that could affect the livability, soundness, or structural integrity of the property.

3. I performed this appraisal in accordance with the requirements of the Uniform Standards of Professional Appraisal Practice that were adopted and promulgated by the Appraisal Standards Board of The Appraisal Foundation and that were in place at the time this appraisal report was prepared.

4. I developed my opinion of the market value of the real property that is the subject of this report based on the sales comparison approach to value. I have adequate comparable market data to develop a reliable sales comparison approach for this appraisal assignment. I further certify that I considered the cost and income approaches to value but did not develop them, unless otherwise indicated in this report.

5. I researched, verified, analyzed, and reported on any current agreement for sale for the subject property, any offering for sale of the subject property in the twelve months prior to the effective date of this appraisal, and the prior sales of the subject property for a minimum of three years prior to the effective date of this appraisal, unless otherwise indicated in this report.

6. I researched, verified, analyzed, and reported on the prior sales of the comparable sales for a minimum of one year prior to the date of sale of the comparable sale, unless otherwise indicated in this report.

7. I selected and used comparable sales that are locationally, physically, and functionally the most similar to the subject property.

8. I have not used comparable sales that were the result of combining a land sale with the contract purchase price of a home that has been built or will be built on the land.

9. I have reported adjustments to the comparable sales that reflect the market's reaction to the differences between the subject property and the comparable sales.

10. I verified, from a disinterested source, all information in this report that was provided by parties who have a financial interest in the sale or financing of the subject property.

11. I have knowledge and experience in appraising this type of property in this market area.

12. I am aware of, and have access to, the necessary and appropriate public and private data sources, such as multiple listing services, tax assessment records, public land records and other such data sources for the area in which the property is located.

13. I obtained the information, estimates, and opinions furnished by other parties and expressed in this appraisal report from reliable sources that I believe to be true and correct.

14. I have taken into consideration the factors that have an impact on value with respect to the subject neighborhood, subject property, and the proximity of the subject property to adverse influences in the development of my opinion of market value. I have noted in this appraisal report any adverse conditions (such as, but not limited to, needed repairs, deterioration, the presence of hazardous wastes, toxic substances, adverse environmental conditions, etc.) observed during the inspection of the subject property or that I became aware of during the research involved in performing this appraisal. I have considered these adverse conditions in my analysis of the property value, and have reported on the effect of the conditions on the value and marketability of the subject property.

15. I have not knowingly withheld any significant information from this appraisal report and, to the best of my knowledge, all statements and information in this appraisal report are true and correct.

16. I stated in this appraisal report my own personal, unbiased, and professional analysis, opinions, and conclusions, which are subject only to the assumptions and limiting conditions in this appraisal report.

17. I have no present or prospective interest in the property that is the subject of this report, and I have no present or prospective personal interest or bias with respect to the participants in the transaction. I did not base, either partially or completely, my analysis and/or opinion of market value in this appraisal report on the race, color, religion, sex, age, marital status, handicap, familial status, or national origin of either the prospective owners or occupants of the subject property or of the present owners or occupants of the properties in the vicinity of the subject property or on any other basis prohibited by law.

18. My employment and/or compensation for performing this appraisal or any future or anticipated appraisals was not conditioned on any agreement or understanding, written or otherwise, that I would report (or present analysis supporting) a predetermined specific value, a predetermined minimum value, a range or direction in value, a value that favors the cause of any party, or the attainment of a specific result or occurrence of a specific subsequent event (such as approval of a pending mortgage loan application).

19. I personally prepared all conclusions and opinions about the real estate that were set forth in this appraisal report. If I relied on significant real property appraisal assistance from any individual or individuals in the performance of this appraisal or the preparation of this appraisal report, I have named such individual(s) and disclosed the specific tasks performed in this appraisal report. I certify that any individual so named is qualified to perform the tasks. I have not authorized anyone to make a change to any item in this appraisal report; therefore, any change made to this appraisal is unauthorized and I will take no responsibility for it.

20. I identified the lender/client in this appraisal report who is the individual, organization, or agent for the organization that ordered and will receive this appraisal report.

FIGURE 4
Appraisal 1 (continued)

Uniform Residential Appraisal Report   File # 05070001

21. The lender/client may disclose or distribute this appraisal report to: the borrower; another lender at the request of the borrower; the mortgagee or its successors and assigns; mortgage insurers; government sponsored enterprises; other secondary market participants; data collection or reporting services; professional appraisal organizations; any department, agency, or instrumentality of the United States; and any state, the District of Columbia, or other jurisdictions; without having to obtain the appraiser's or supervisory appraiser's (if applicable) consent. Such consent must be obtained before this appraisal report may be disclosed or distributed to any other party (including, but not limited to, the public through advertising, public relations, news, sales, or other media).

22. I am aware that any disclosure or distribution of this appraisal report by me or the lender/client may be subject to certain laws and regulations. Further, I am also subject to the provisions of the Uniform Standards of Professional Appraisal Practice that pertain to disclosure or distribution by me.

23. The borrower, another lender at the request of the borrower, the mortgagee or its successors and assigns, mortgage insurers, government sponsored enterprises, and other secondary market participants may rely on this appraisal report as part of any mortgage finance transaction that involves any one or more of these parties.

24. If this appraisal report was transmitted as an "electronic record" containing my "electronic signature," as those terms are defined in applicable federal and/or state laws (excluding audio and video recordings), or a facsimile transmission of this appraisal report containing a copy or representation of my signature, the appraisal report shall be as effective, enforceable and valid as if a paper version of this appraisal report were delivered containing my original hand written signature.

25. Any intentional or negligent misrepresentation(s) contained in this appraisal report may result in civil liability and/or criminal penalties including, but not limited to, fine or imprisonment or both under the provisions of Title 18, United States Code, Section 1001, et seq., or similar state laws.

SUPERVISORY APPRAISER'S CERTIFICATION: The Supervisory Appraiser certifies and agrees that:

1. I directly supervised the appraiser for this appraisal assignment, have read the appraisal report, and agree with the appraiser's analysis, opinions, statements, conclusions, and the appraiser's certification.

2. I accept full responsibility for the contents of this appraisal report including, but not limited to, the appraiser's analysis, opinions, statements, conclusions, and the appraiser's certification.

3. The appraiser identified in this appraisal report is either a sub-contractor or an employee of the supervisory appraiser (or the appraisal firm), is qualified to perform this appraisal, and is acceptable to perform this appraisal under the applicable state law.

4. This appraisal report complies with the Uniform Standards of Professional Appraisal Practice that were adopted and promulgated by the Appraisal Standards Board of The Appraisal Foundation and that were in place at the time this appraisal report was prepared.

5. If this appraisal report was transmitted as an "electronic record" containing my "electronic signature," as those terms are defined in applicable federal and/or state laws (excluding audio and video recordings), or a facsimile transmission of this appraisal report containing a copy or representation of my signature, the appraisal report shall be as effective, enforceable and valid as if a paper version of this appraisal report were delivered containing my original hand written signature.

APPRAISER	SUPERVISORY APPRAISER (ONLY IF REQUIRED)
Signature *James Havlic*	Signature *Todd Simpson*
Name James Havlic	Name Todd Simpson
Company Name	Company Name
Company Address 756 Man Hwy Sarasota, FL 34200	Company Address
Telephone Number	Telephone Number
Email Address	Email Address ToddSimpson@ChauncyRealtyAppraisal.com
Date of Signature and Report 9-12-05	Date of Signature 9-13-05
Effective Date of Appraisal 9-12-05	State Certification # 56789-0011
State Certification #	or State License #
or State License # 12345-0022	State Florida
or Other	Expiration Date of Certification or License 12-31-06
State Florida	
Expiration Date of Certification or License 12-31-06	SUBJECT PROPERTY

ADDRESS OF PROPERTY APPRAISED
456 Cherry Hill Road
Sarasota, FL 34200
APPRAISED VALUE OF SUBJECT PROPERTY $ 450500
LENDER/CLIENT
Name   Mr. Charles O. Murphy
Company Name   Murphy Mortgage Company
Company Address   PO Box 134
Serra, FL 34224-1347
Email Address   CharlesOMurphy@MurphyMortgage.com

SUBJECT PROPERTY

[ ] Did not inspect subject property
[X] Did inspect exterior of subject property from street
Date of Inspection   9-12-05
[ ] Did inspect interior and exterior of subject property
Date of Inspection

COMPARABLE SALES

[ ] Did not inspect exterior of comparable sales from street
[X] Did inspect exterior of comparable sales from street
Date of Inspection   9-12-05

FIGURE 4
Appraisal 1 (continued)

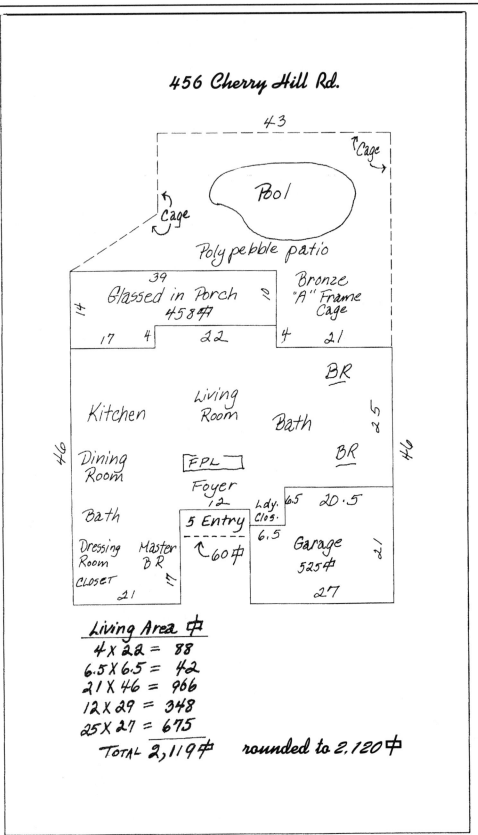

FIGURE 4
Appraisal 1 (continued)

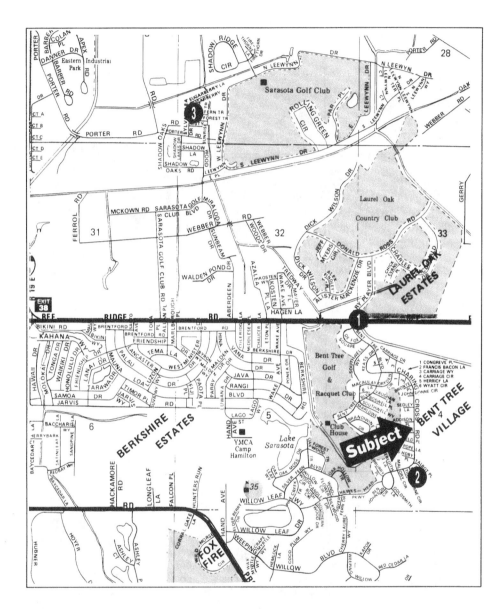

FIGURE 4
Appraisal 1 (continued)

Subject Front

Subject Rear

FIGURE 4
Appraisal 1 (continued)

Subject Street

Comparable 1

F I G U R E   4
Appraisal 1 (continued)

Comparable 2

Comparable 3

## PART THREE

The Uniform Residential Appraisal Report: A Closer View

SECTION 1: SUBJECT

Uniform Residential Appraisal Report

File #

The purpose of this summary appraisal report is to provide the lender/client with an accurate, and adequately supported, opinion of the market value of the subject property.

Property Address	City	State	Zip Code
Borrower	Owner of Public Record	County	
Legal Description			
Assessor's Parcel #	Tax Year	R.E. Taxes $	
Neighborhood Name	Map Reference	Census Tract	
Occupant ☐ Owner ☐ Tenant ☐ Vacant	Special Assessments $	☐ PUD HOA $	☐ per year ☐ per month
Property Rights Appraised ☐ Fee Simple ☐ Leasehold ☐ Other (describe)			
Assignment Type ☐ Purchase Transaction ☐ Refinance Transaction ☐ Other (describe)			
Lender/Client	Address		
Is the subject property currently offered for sale or has it been offered for sale in the twelve months prior to the effective date of this appraisal? ☐ Yes ☐ No			
Report data source(s) used, offering price(s), and date(s).			

Every appraisal begins in the same way. The appraiser defines the appraisal problem.

Complete this section of the URAR form by following these steps:

- Give the full street address of the subject property.

- Identify the borrower, the owner of public record, the lender/client, and the nature of the assignment.

- Provide the complete legal description of the subject property and property tax information.

- Indicate the property rights being appraised.

- Indicate any listing or sale of the property within the last year and identify data source(s).

▶ **Fannie Mae** It is essential that the lender obtain an independent, disinterested examination and valuation of the property that secures a mortgage it intends to sell to us. In fact, we hold the lender responsible for the accuracy of both the appraisal and its assessment of the marketability of the property. Therefore, the lender must select the appraiser and order and receive the appraisal report, rather than the homebuyer, seller, real estate broker, or other party who has an interest in the transaction.

▶ **VA** No new appraisal can be requested on property that already has a valid VA value determination.

Property is ineligible for VA appraisal if any party of interest to the transaction, other than the purchaser, is debarred government-wide, or otherwise excluded, from participation in the Loan Guaranty program due to a VA-imposed sanction for substantially prejudicing a veteran by either

- failing to correct justified construction complaint items,

- violating VA Minimum Property Requirements,

- deviating from plans and specifications without VA approval,

- failing to honor other contractual obligations on houses previously built and sold with VA financing, or

- using a sales contract or marketing method or practice with VA considered to be unfair or unduly prejudicial to the veteran involved.

The purpose of this summary appraisal report is to provide the lender/client with an accurate, and adequately supported, opinion of the market value of the subject property.

The URAR form contains a statement of the purpose of the appraisal in its first line. The URAR form is used most often as a summary appraisal report. Under specifically allowed circumstances, it may be used in a restricted report, or to provide a summary of data that is expanded upon in a self-contained report.

The URAR is defined as a summary appraisal report intended to provide an opinion of market value. Even if the report is used to determine property value for a refinance or other nonsale transaction (such as a marital dissolution or condemnation proceeding), the appraiser will still be interested in the reaction of the marketplace to the subject property as if it were for sale.

▶ **Fannie Mae** Market value is the most probable price that a property should bring in a competitive and open market under all conditions requisite to a fair sale, with the buyer and seller each acting prudently and knowledgeably, and assuming the price is not affected by undue stimulus. Implicit in this definition is the consummation of a sale as of a specified date and the passing of title from seller to buyer under conditions whereby:

1. buyer and seller are typically motivated;

2. both parties are well informed or well advised, and each acting in what he considers his own best interest;

3. a reasonable time is allowed for exposure in the open market;

4. payment is made in terms of cash in U.S. dollars or in terms of financial arrangements comparable thereto; and

5. the price represents the normal consideration for the property sold unaffected by special or creative financing or sales concessions granted by anyone associated with the sale.

‣ **VA**   For VA loan guaranty purposes, the reasonable value of a property is the figure that represents the amount a reputable and qualified appraiser, unaffected by personal interest, bias, or prejudice, would recommend to a prospective purchaser as a proper price or cost in the light of prevailing conditions.

VA considers reasonable value and market value to be synonymous. VA's definition of market value is consistent with that used by Fannie Mae, Freddie Mac, and major appraisal organizations.

File No.

The lender or agency involved may require that its file number be supplied in this space at the top right of each page of the form.

‣ **HUD/FHA**   Enter FHA case number.

‣ **RHS**   Enter RHS case number. An appraisal is required when the debt to be secured exceeds $15,000 or whenever RHS determines that it is necessary to establish the adequacy of the security. The appraisal must be made in accordance with the Uniform Standards of Professional Appraisal Practice. When other real estate is taken as additional security, it will be appraised if it represents a substantial portion of the security for the loan.

Property Address

Enter street address, if there is one, or rural route number. Enough information must be provided to locate the property.

‣ **Fannie Mae**   Use a complete property address. A post office box number is *not* acceptable. If the property has no house number, indicate the nearest intersection.

‣ **RHS**   Do *not* use a post office box number. If necessary, attach a map to the report showing the property location.

City

Enter the name of the city within which the property is located or, if the property is outside the city limits, where the post office serving the property address is located.

State

Enter the full name or the two-letter postal abbreviation of the state within which the property is located. If the property is located in more than one state, all states should be named.

Zip Code

Enter the U.S. Postal Service five- or nine-digit delivery zone code.

Borrower

Enter the name of the person obtaining funds from the lender.

Owner of Public Record

Identify the present legal owner of the property.

County

Enter the name of the county(ies) in which the property is located.

Legal Description

Fill in the property description found in the grant deed to the present owner. If the deed in the owner's possession cannot be examined, examine a copy of it at the county recorder's office or office of register of deeds. If the legal description is lengthy, it may be included in a separate attachment.

> ▸ **Fannie Mae**   If the legal description is too long to fit the space on the form, include it as an addendum to the form or refer to the public records where the legal description can be found.

> ▸ **RHS**   Attach a full legal description of the property to the form, indicating any restrictions, easements, or reservations.

Assessor's Parcel

Enter the property's parcel number assigned by the assessor's office.

Tax Year

Enter the tax year for which information is supplied.

R.E. Taxes $

Enter the total annual property tax due and whether the tax is paid on a current basis (for the current tax year) or in arrears (for the preceding tax year). If any amount is past due, it should be entered with the notation **PAST DUE.** The tax amount can be found by examining the seller's tax bill or contacting the county tax assessor's or treasurer's office. It may also appear on the preliminary title report. In some areas (such as California), property is reassessed for tax purposes at the time of sale. For California property, enter the current total annual tax rate charged by the community in which the property is located. There will be very little difference among communities, however, because the base tax rate is set by state law.

Neighborhood Name

Enter the name of the neighborhood subdivision or project in which the subject property is located.

Map Reference

Identify a commonly used map of the local area and enter the map reference points showing the location of the subject property. Attach a copy of the portion of the map showing the subject's location as an addendum.

Census Tract

The United States is divided into numbered areas that are used for reference when census data are compiled. Enter the one- to six-digit census tract number. This number is found on the census tract map. If the property is within a rural area that does not have a designated tract number, enter **N/A.**

Census tract maps showing the tract numbers can be obtained from the Superintendent of Documents, Government Printing Office, Washington, DC 20402, (202) 783-3238, or the Data User Services Division, Customer Services (Publications), Bureau of the Census, Washington, DC 20233, (301) 763-4100.

For more complete identification, list the four-digit Standard Metropolitan Statistical Area (SMSA) number in this space, before the census tract number. SMSA numbers are available from regional offices of the Bureau of the Census.

Occupant

Check the appropriate box to indicate whether the subject property was owner-occupied, tenant-occupied, or vacant at the time of the inspection.

Special Assessments $

Enter the dollar amount of any special assessment taxes still owed on the property.

PUD

This classification is checked if the property is a single-family residence in a planned unit development (PUD) that includes a shared interest in recreational or open space, clubhouse, or sports or other facilities.

> ▸ **Fannie Mae** The URAR form can be used for single-family properties, including PUDs. Specific information about a PUD project must be provided in the PUD section of the URAR. For condominium appraisals, use Appraisal Report—Individual Condominium or PUD Unit (Form 1073). The URAR (Form 1004) can be used in appraisals of detached condominium units, however, if the condominium project does not contain any common area improvements (other than greenbelts, private streets, and parking areas) and the appraiser includes an adequate description of the project and information about the homeowners' association fees and the quality of the project maintenance.

> ▸ **VA** You may use this form with any kind of PUD.

HOA $

If the property includes shared ownership of common areas under the authority of a homeowners' association, the amount charged per year or per month for association fees should be entered here. Association fees typically are used to pay for landscaping and other exterior maintenance, upkeep of any shared buildings or other facilities (such as a clubhouse, swimming pool, or tennis court), and administration expenses. If the amount charged seems too high or too low for the area, note that fact. Specific information about the project should be entered in the PUD section of the URAR form.

> ▸ **VA**   The appraisal report must
>
>   ■ show the amount of the current monthly assessment;
>
>   ■ for condominiums, indicate which utilities are/are not included; and
>
>   ■ comment on the adequacy of the monthly assessment, based upon the appraiser's opinion of the adequacy of the project's budget and a comparison to competitive projects. If the assessment is considered inadequate, a "fair" or "market" assessment must be recommended.

Property Rights Appraised

Identify the property rights being appraised, as described below.

Fee Simple

The highest right of ownership, also called *fee simple absolute.* Although most residential property is owned in fee simple, this does not mean that the property will be entirely free of easements, encroachments, deed reservations and restrictions, and the like. Any such encumbrance or reservation of an ownership right should be noted as specified on the appraisal form, in the COMMENTS block of the SITE section, or on the attached legal description. In oil states, conveyance of residential property with a reservation of mineral (oil and gas) rights in a former owner is common.

> ▸ **RHS**   Acceptable full fee ownership is evidenced by a fully marketable title with a deed vesting a fee interest in the property to the applicant.
>
> ▸ **VA**   Property involving less than fee simple ownership (for example, leaseholds, cooperatives, and ground rental arrangements) is not eligible for appraisal without prior VA approval of the specific legal arrangement or project. Submissions to VA Central Office (262A) must include
>
>   ■ details of the ownership arrangement,
>
>   ■ copies of leases or other instruments creating the estate, and
>
>   ■ recommendations of the VA office of jurisdiction.

Leasehold

Leasehold is the right of one who has possession but not ownership. A leasehold interest is what is transferred when the owner of a fee simple interest in real estate enters into a ground lease with a lessee. The lessee (the holder of the leasehold interest) pays the lessor (the holder of what is then termed the *leased fee interest*) a ground rent for the right to use the land, subject to the terms of the underlying lease agreement. When the lease terminates, there is a reversion of the real estate to the holder of the leased fee, who is then once again in possession of a fee simple interest. Any improvements that the lessee made to the property may be surrendered to the lessor, depending on the terms of the lease.

Leasehold interests are used most often with commercial developments. As a general rule, leasehold interests in single-family residential real estate are not common and thus are rarely valued. An exception to the rule occurs in the state of Hawaii, where a number of multi-unit residential projects, including condominiums and cooperative apartments, as well as units in PUDs, have been developed as leasehold interests.

> ▸ **RHS**   To secure a leasehold interest, a written lease is required. For loans, the unexpired portion of the lease must not be less than two years beyond the term of the promissory note. For grants, the remaining lease period must be at least five years. A leasehold for mutual help housing financed by HUD on Indian lands requires no minimum lease period and constitutes acceptable ownership.

Other (describe)

Other forms of property interest include a cooperative project, a life estate, and an undivided co-ownership (such as a tenancy in common).

> ▸ **Fannie Mae**   A cooperative project is a multi-unit property in which those who purchase units are actually buying shares in the ownership of the project as a whole. When you are evaluating a cooperative unit, you are developing an opinion of the market value of the cooperative interest, or the shares, that are assigned to the individual unit. Since this type of ownership has unique features, it is important to use one of our appraisal report forms designed for individual cooperative projects.
>
> An important part of your appraisal is how acceptable housing cooperatives are in the market area. Finding comparable data for similar cooperative units will help you determine the level of acceptance. When your research indicates a preference for condominium units over cooperative units in the market area, you should make adjustments in the comparables accordingly.

> ▸ **RHS**   To be acceptable, a life estate interest must provide the applicant with rights of present possession, control, and beneficial use of the property. For secured loans, persons with any remainder interests generally must be signatories to the mortgage. All of the remainder interests need not be included in the mortgage to the extent that one or more of the persons holding remainder interests are not legally competent (and there is no representative who can legally consent to the mortgage) or cannot be located, or if the remainder interests are divided among such a large number of people that it is not practical to obtain the signatures of all of the remainder interest. In such cases, the loan may not exceed the value of the property interests owned by the persons executing the mortgage.
>
> An **undivided interest** is acceptable if there is no reason to believe that the applicant's position as an owner-occupant will be jeopardized as a result of the improvements to be made, and (1) in the case of unsecured loans or grants if any co-owners living or planning to live in the dwelling sign the repayment agreement; or (2) in the case of a secured loan, when one or more of the co-owners are not legally competent (and there is no representative who can legally consent to the mortgage) or

cannot be located, or the ownership interests are divided among so large a number of co-owners that it is not practical for all of their interests to be mortgaged, their interests not exceeding 50 percent may be excluded from the security requirements. In the latter case, the loan may not exceed the value of the property interests owned by the persons executing the mortgage.

Other acceptable forms of ownership include **possessory rights** on an American Indian reservation or state-owned land and the interest of an American Indian in land held in severalty under trust patents or deeds containing restrictions against alienation, provided that land in trust or restricted status will remain in trust or restricted status.

Assignment Type

Purchase Transaction, Refinance Transaction, or Other (describe)
Indicate the purpose of the appraisal assignment. If a sale of the property is pending, indicate that it is a purchase transaction. If the current owner is refinancing an existing loan, indicate that it is a refinance transaction. An appraisal may also be required in a variety of other cases, such as a loan assignment, transfer of loan servicing, property exchange, bid at a foreclosure sale, property tax appeal, marital dissolution, estate distribution, or other asset valuation.

Lender/Client

If the appraiser is performing the appraisal for a lender, enter the lender's name and address. If the appraiser is being paid by anyone else, indicate that person by name and status (such as **OWNER** or **BUYER**).

WEB@LINK

▸ **HUD/FHA**   Property flipping, which is prohibited, is a practice whereby recently acquired property is resold for a considerable profit with an artificially inflated value, often abetted by a lender's collusion with the appraiser. The procedures for obtaining approval to participate in FHA mortgage insurance programs are contained in 24 CFR 202.10 et seq. Handbook 4060.1, *Mortgage Approval,* provides additional guidance for these regulations with specific procedures for obtaining approval. Program details are available on **HUD's** Web site at *www.hud.gov* or from the Office of Lender Activities and Program Compliance.

▸ **RHS**   If the report is to be used for loan-making purposes, enter the loan applicant's name. If the report is to be used for loan-servicing purposes, enter the borrower's name or advice number.

▸ **VA**   If the lender fails to exercise due diligence in determining appraisal eligibility, VA may deny or reduce payment on a future claim based on the ineligibility of the property.

Address

Enter the mailing address of the Lender/Client.

Is the subject property currently offered for sale or has it been offered for sale in the twelve months prior to the effective date of this appraisal? Yes or No. Report data source(s) used, offering price(s), and date(s).

The listing history of the subject property can be the strongest indicator of its acceptance in the marketplace. If a sales contract is pending, what is the difference between the asking price and the contract price? If the property has listed earlier in the past year, how has the asking price changed over that time? A large discrepancy between the contract price and previous offering prices may serve as a red flag to the lender of possible fraud.

APPRAISAL 1

Uniform Residential Appraisal Report

The purpose of this summary appraisal report is to provide the lender/client with an accurate, and adequately supported, opinion of the market value of the subject property.	

SUBJECT

Property Address 456 Cherry Hill Road   City Sarasota   State FL   Zip Code 34200

Borrower Arturo Mendez   Owner of Public Record Robert Travis   County Sarasota

Legal Description Lot 308 Bent Tree Village Subdivision, recorded in Book 12, Page 12, Sarasota County

Assessor's Parcel # BT 308   Tax Year 04-05   R.E. Taxes $ 3,524

Neighborhood Name Bent Tree Village   Map Reference G58   Census Tract 14

Occupant [X] Owner [ ] Tenant [ ] Vacant   Special Assessments $ None   [ ] PUD   HOA $ ___ [ ] per year [ ] per month

Property Rights Appraised [X] Fee Simple [ ] Leasehold [ ] Other (describe)

Assignment Type [X] Purchase Transaction [ ] Refinance Transaction [ ] Other (describe)

Lender/Client Murphy Mortgage Company   Address PO Box 134, Serra, FL 34224-1347

Is the subject property currently offered for sale or has it been offered for sale in the twelve months prior to the effective date of the appraisal? [X] Yes [ ] No

Report data source(s) used, offering price(s), and date(s). Property listed for sale August 1, 2005, at $454,500.

In Appraisal 1 the subject property is located at 456 Cherry Hill Road, Sarasota, Sarasota County, Florida. The census tract number is 14. The assessor's office identifies the property as "parcel No. BT308." The property's legal description is Lot 308, Bent Tree Village Subdivision, as recorded in Book 12, Page 12 of maps, Sarasota County.

The owner and present occupant of the property is Robert Travis. The borrower's name is Arturo Mendez. The map reference number is G58. The property was listed for sale on August 1, 2005, with a list price of $454,500, according to the listing agent. There was no other offering of the property in the last 12 months. The real estate taxes for the tax year 2004–2005 are $3,524.00. There are no special assessments due on this property.

The appraisal is being performed by James Havlic, 756 Main Highway, Sarasota, FL 34200, for Mr. Charles O. Murphy of the Murphy Mortgage Company, P.O. Box 134, Serra, Florida 34224-1347, the buyer's lender. The subject property is a single-family detached residence in a subdivision where there is a community-shared golf course, but membership is voluntary. A fee simple interest in the property is being sold.

EXERCISE: APPRAISAL 2

Uniform Residential Appraisal Report   File

The purpose of this summary appraisal report is to provide the lender/client with an accurate, and adequately supported, opinion of the market value of the subject property.				
Property Address		City	State	Zip Code
Borrower	Owner of Public Record		County	
Legal Description				
Assessor's Parcel #		Tax Year	R.E. Taxes $	
Neighborhood Name		Map Reference	Census Tract	
Occupant ☐ Owner ☐ Tenant ☐ Vacant	Special Assessments $	☐ PUD HOA $	☐ per year ☐ per month	
Property Rights Appraised ☐ Fee Simple ☐ Leasehold ☐ Other (describe)				
Assignment Type ☐ Purchase Transaction ☐ Refinance Transaction ☐ Other (describe)				
Lender/Client	Address			
Is the subject property currently offered for sale or has it been offered for sale in the twelve months prior to the effective date of this appraisal? ☐ Yes ☐ No				
Report data source(s) used, offering price(s), and date(s).				

Complete the blank URAR SUBJECT section provided above for Appraisal 2, using the following information. When you have finished, check your work against the completed Appraisal 2 in the Answer Key.

The subject property is a single-family detached residence located at 1053 Locust Lane, Pleasantown, Sunnyside County, Anystate. The census tract number is 4499. The assessor's parcel number is AL6857. The property's legal description is Lot 5 of Block 32, Meadow Green Subdivision, as shown on page 997 of book 438, records of Sunnyside County.

Frank and Mildred Justice, a married couple, own a fee simple interest in the property and occupy it themselves. They have accepted a purchase offer made to them by Jack Morris and Hope Temple, a married couple. The property is assessed at 25 percent of market value, and taxed at a combined tax rate of .0845, which includes property, school, and transportation district taxes typical for this metropolitan area. The most recent tax year for which property owners have been billed is 2004, and no taxes are past due. The property taxes of $4,344 for 2005 will be due in June 2006. The property is part of a planned unit subdivision that is governed by the homeowners and managed by an outside company; homeowners' association dues are $80 per month to cover maintenance of common areas.

This appraisal is being made at the request of the buyers' lender, State Savings Bank, 4312 State Street, Pleasantown, Anystate 42555. The listing agent reports that the property was listed for sale for $369,900 on September 30, 2005. MLS records verify this and indicate no other listings of the property in the last 12 months

SECTION 2: CONTRACT

C O N T R A C T	I ☐ did ☐ did not analyze the contract for sale for the subject purchase transaction. Explain the results of the analysis of the contract for sale or why the analysis was not performed.
	Contract Price $ Date of Contract Is the property seller the owner of public record? ☐Yes ☐No Data Source(s)
	Is there any financial assistance (loan charges, sale concessions, gift or downpayment assistance, etc.) to be paid by any party on behalf of the borrower? ☐ Yes ☐ No If Yes, report the total dollar amount and describe the items to be paid.

Most appraisals are requested because property is being purchased with borrowed money and the property is being used as security for the loan. It is most often the lender who orders the appraisal and is thus the appraisal client, even when the purchaser/borrower pays for the appraisal and is entitled under federal law to receive a copy of the appraisal report.

I did or did not analyze the contract for sale for the subject purchase transaction. Explain the results of the analysis of the contract for sale or why the analysis was not performed.

The price that the purchaser is willing to pay for the property and the terms under which the sale is being made are two additional factors that the appraiser should take into account when analyzing the current real estate market. Because the purchaser is interested in paying as low a price as possible and should have investigated both the subject property and available comparable properties in order to make an informed decision, the purchaser's opinion of value, expressed in the final, accepted offer, should be considered by the appraiser.

Contract Price $

If a sale of the property is pending, enter the amount of the sales price stipulated in the contract of sale. If the sales price information comes from another source, identify that source. If the transaction is a property exchange, enter **EXCHANGE.** If the appraisal is being made as part of a loan refinancing, enter **REFINANCE.** If no sale or other transaction is pending, enter **N/A** or **NONE.**

> ▸ **Fannie Mae** The lender must provide the appraiser with a copy of the sales contract and any other pertinent information known to the lender.

Date of Contract

If a sale of the property is pending, enter the date on which the contract was signed by the parties and not the date on which the sale is to close. For any other transaction, enter **N/A** and the type of transaction; for example, **N/A (REFINANCE).**

Is the property seller the owner of public record? Yes or No.

Check the box to indicate whether or not the property seller is the owner indicated by an examination of the latest documents on file in the county recorder's office. This information will also be part of the preliminary title report issued by the title insurance company.

▸ **HUD/FHA**   To be eligible for a mortgage insured by FHA, the property must be purchased from the owner of record and the transaction may not involve any sale or assignment of the sales contract. This requirement applies to all FHA purchase money mortgages regardless of the time between resales. The mortgage lender must obtain documentation verifying that the seller is the owner of record and submit this to HUD as part of the insurance endorsement binder. This documentation may include, but is not limited to, a property sales history report, a copy of the recorded deed from the seller, or other documentation, such as a copy of a property tax bill, title commitment, or binder, demonstrating the seller's ownership of the property and the date it was acquired.

Data Source(s)

List the source(s) of the contract information, such as the lender.

Is there any financial assistance (loan charges, sale concessions, gift or downpayment assistance, etc.) to be paid by any party on behalf of the borrower? Yes or No. If Yes, report the dollar amount and describe the items to be paid.

The amount of any financial assistance to be paid by anyone on behalf of the borrower should be entered here. This information will be revealed by inspecting the contract of sale, which the lender should provide to the appraiser. If the appraiser's information comes from any other source (such as the broker, buyer, seller, or lender), that source should be indicated.

There may be documents other than the contract of sale that should be examined, such as those required by programs sponsored by organizations like Nehemiah and American Dream. In such a program, the seller makes a gift of an agreed-upon part of the purchase price (say, 6 percent) to the organization involved, which in turn provides a similar amount to the buyer to be used as a down payment on the seller's property. While the seller receives the full purchase price at the closing, the amount the seller receives is effectively reduced by the amount of the gift. The seller will also pay a fee to the organization involved for the service. Even though the seller has made a gift equivalent to a percentage of the sale price, the advantage to the seller is that the property is sold. The seller also may benefit from a tax deduction in the amount of the gift.

▸ **Fannie Mae**   Enter the total dollar amount of any loan charges and/or concessions to be paid by the seller or any other party with a financial interest in the sale or financing of the subject property. The charges and/or concessions should be described briefly. If the appraisal is for purposes of a refinancing, that fact should be noted. Examples of loan charges and other concessions include:

■   settlement charges,

■   loan fees or charges,

- discounts to the sales price,

- payment of condominium or PUD fees,

- interest rate buydowns or other below-market-rate financing,

- refunds or credits,

- absorption of monthly payments,

- assignment of rent payments, and

- nonrealty items included in the transaction.

▸ **VA**   The appraiser is not required to investigate and complete this information but should supply it, if known, and its source. Otherwise enter **NONE KNOWN.**

APPRAISAL 1

C O N T R A C T	I [X] did [ ] did not analyze the contract for sale for the subject purchase transaction. Explain the results of the analysis of the contract for sale or why the analysis was not performed. No unusual financing or sales concessions noted.
	Contract Price $ 450,000 Date of Contract 8-27-05 Is the property seller the owner of public record? [X] Yes [ ] No Data Source(s) Lender
	Is there any financial assistance (loan charges, sale concessions, gift or downpayment assistance, etc.) to be paid by any party on behalf of the borrower? [ ] Yes [X] No
	If Yes, report the total dollar amount and describe the items to be paid:

In Appraisal 1, the sales price of the property is $450,000, and the date of the sales contract is August 27, 2005. There are no loan charges or concessions to be paid by the seller or anyone else on the buyer's behalf, and the financing will be typical for properties of this type. The seller is the property owner of record.

EXERCISE: APPRAISAL 2

C O N T R A C T	I [ ] did [ ] did not analyze the contract for sale for the subject purchase transaction. Explain the results of the analysis of the contract for sale or why the analysis was not performed.
	Contract Price $ Date of Contract Is the property seller the owner of public record? [ ]Yes [ ]No Data Source(s)
	Is there any financial assistance (loan charges, sale concessions, gift or downpayment assistance, etc.) to be paid by any party on behalf of the borrower? [ ] Yes [ ] No If Yes, report the total dollar amount and describe the items to be paid.

Complete the blank URAR CONTRACT section provided above for Appraisal 2, using the following information. When you have finished, check your work against the completed Appraisal 2 in the Answer Key.

The appraiser, Mary Ford, examined the sales contract, which is dated November 15, 2005, and found no unusual financing terms or concessions to be paid by the seller or anyone else. The contract price is $365,000. The seller is the property owner of record.

SECTION 3: NEIGHBORHOOD

Note: Race and the racial composition of the neighborhood are not appraisal factors.							
Neighborhood Characteristics			**One-Unit Housing Trends**			**One-Unit Housing**	**Present Land Use %**
Location ☐ Urban ☐ Suburban ☐ Rural			Property Values ☐ Increasing ☐ Stable ☐ Declining			PRICE AGE	One-Unit %
Built-Up ☐ Over 75% ☐ 25–75% ☐ Under 25%			Demand/Supply ☐ Shortage ☐ In Balance ☐ Over Supply			$ (000) (yrs)	2-4 Unit %
Growth ☐ Rapid ☐ Stable ☐ Slow			Marketing Time ☐ Under 3 mths ☐ 3–6 mths ☐ Over 6 mths			Low	Multi-Family %
Neighborhood Boundaries						High	Commercial %
						Pred.	Other %
Neighborhood Description							
Market Conditions (including support for the above conclusions)							

Study of the neighborhood is the starting point in gathering factual information, because anything that affects the neighborhood also affects the property being appraised. What exactly defines a *neighborhood?* In practice, it is the area within which any change has an immediate and direct influence on the value of the subject property.

Neighborhood boundaries are often established by natural barriers such as rivers, lakes, and hills, or by man-made barriers such as streets, highways, and rail lines. Boundaries also may be created by differences in land use, the income level of residents, the average value of homes, city limits, census tracts, political divisions, school districts, and so on. A neighborhood may consist of a single subdivision, perhaps due to the large size of the subdivision or its geographic isolation, but this is a rare occurrence. Most often, a neighborhood will consist of at least several subdivisions. Whatever the neighborhood's size, the appraiser should understand the reasons for selecting neighborhood boundaries and be prepared to explain them in the report.

A residential neighborhood is constantly undergoing changes throughout its life cycle. A neighborhood's life cycle usually involves the following stages, varying only in intensity and duration:

- Development and growth
- Stability
- Transition
- Decline

Because neighborhood analysis is so important, most appraisers include, as an addendum to the URAR, a neighborhood map showing neighborhood boundaries, the location of the subject property, and the location of comparable properties used in the sales comparison approach. An example of a neighborhood map used in Appraisal 1 appears on page 21. Complete this section of the URAR form by following these five steps:

1. Define the local market area—the neighborhood—in terms of property supply and demand factors.

2. Describe available housing ownership and price levels.

3. Analyze present and likely future land uses.

4. Note any other neighborhood factors likely to affect market value.

5. Provide support for conclusions related to the trend of property values, demand/supply, and marketing time.

Note: Race and the racial composition of the neighborhood are not appraisal factors.

The neighborhood's racial composition must never be a factor in an appraisal.

▸ **Fannie Mae** A neighborhood analysis considers the influence of social, economic, government, and environmental forces on property values in the subject neighborhood. Be specific and impartial in describing favorable or unfavorable factors. Avoid using subjective terms or phrases, such as "pride of ownership."

The racial composition of a neighborhood is never a reliable appraisal factor. Fannie Mae does not designate certain areas as acceptable or unacceptable, a practice called *redlining.* Locational factors may be considered if based on a realistic perception of risk in a given neighborhood but may not be based on improper factors such as race. Factors that serve as a "proxy for race" are "equally impermissible." Fannie Mae's guidelines are not intended to foster redlining in any form.

In urban areas currently undergoing redevelopment, block-by-block underwriting and appraisal analysis are acceptable in considering either the block in which the subject property is located or facing blocks. The appraiser must demonstrate that local conditions support the appropriateness of the analysis used and that all essential factors have been considered.

■ NEIGHBORHOOD CHARACTERISTICS

Location

Determine whether the subject property is in an urban, suburban, or rural neighborhood and check the appropriate box.

▸ **Fannie Mae** Fannie Mae purchases only those mortgages secured by property that is residential in nature. The determination of whether property is residential is based on consideration of the description of the subject property, zoning, and present land use.

Properties in resort or vacation areas are acceptable only if they are suitable for year-round use. *Any property not suitable for year-round occupancy—regardless of location—is unacceptable.*

▸ **RHS Loans** may be made only in rural areas designated by RHS. If an area designation is changed to nonrural:

1. New conditional commitments will be made and existing conditional commitments will be honored only in conjunction with an applicant for a section 502 loan who applied for assistance before the area designation changed.

2. REO property sales and transfers with assumption may be processed.

3. Subsequent loans may be made either in conjunction with a transfer with assumption of an RHS loan or to repair properties that have RHS loans.

Urban

An urban area tends to dominate the communities around it. Lack of land suitable for development in the urban core tends to produce greater population density and higher land values, provided the overall economy is good.

▸ **Fannie Mae**   An *urban* location is one that relates to a *city.*

Suburban

Development will gradually expand the area that may be considered suburban; that is, the area influenced by its proximity to a metropolitan area. Controlled highway access and, particularly, the availability of public transportation will tend to dictate the path of development and the desirability of housing areas that may be considered suburban, even though they are many miles from the city center.

▸ **Fannie Mae**   *Suburban* relates to the *area adjacent to a city.*

Rural

Rural areas are typically characterized by distance from the nearest city and very low population density. Minimum lot sizes by themselves are not necessarily an indication of a rural area. A minimum buildable lot size measured in acres is not uncommon in luxury suburban "estate" developments. Land usage, such as described by Fannie Mae below, may be the most obvious and reliable indicator of a rural area.

▸ **Fannie Mae**   *Rural* relates to the *country* or *anything beyond the suburban area.*

Fannie Mae does not purchase mortgages on agricultural-type properties (such as farms, orchards, or ranches), undeveloped land, or land development-type properties.

The presence of significant outbuildings such as a silo, barn, or other animal storage facility must be reviewed with great care by the lender, whether or not they contribute to appraised value, because they may indicate property that is agricultural in nature. On the other hand, outbuildings that are typical for residential properties in the area, such as a small barn or stable, and that are relatively insignificant in terms of their effect on property value, are acceptable.

All properties must be readily accessible by roads that meet local standards. All properties must have adequate utilities available and in service. Present or anticipated future uses of any adjoining property that may adversely affect the value or marketability of the subject property must be considered.

Built-Up

This section indicates the percentage of available land in the neighborhood that has been improved. Land reserved for parks and other public uses is not included.

Over 75%

Check this box if more than 75 percent of the available land in the neighborhood has been improved.

25–75%

Check this box if between 25 percent and 75 percent of the available land in the neighborhood has been improved.

Under 25%

Check this box if less than 25 percent of the available land in the neighborhood has been improved. If the "Under 25%" box is checked, the appraiser should comment on the reason for the low percentage of development and the neighborhood's future direction.

> ‣ **Fannie Mae**   Areas that are less than 25 percent developed are not acceptable for maximum financing.
>
> In an area that is less than 25 percent developed, site values may not exceed 30 percent of total appraised value *unless* the higher site value is typical of comparable properties in the area. For example, if zoning, highest and best use, and the present land use allow a two-acre lot size and this size is typical for the area, the site may warrant a higher proportion of total value.

Growth

Indicate the rate of development within the subject neighborhood in relation to normal market factors. For example, a neighborhood that is 50 percent built up and is between three and five years old may be experiencing normal growth, but a 10-year-old neighborhood that is 50 percent built up may be suffering some form of stagnation. A neighborhood's growth can be checked by contacting the local building department and asking for building permit statistics for the past several years and the year to date. Large numbers of permits can be translated into rapid growth.

Rapid

Check this box if the neighborhood is developing at a faster rate than comparable neighborhoods.

Stable

Check this box if the neighborhood is developing at about the same rate as comparable neighborhoods or if the neighborhood is fully developed.

Slow

Check this box if the neighborhood is developing at a slower rate than comparable neighborhoods. If the Slow box is checked, the appraiser should explain the possible effect on the marketability and value of the subject property.

■ ONE-UNIT HOUSING TRENDS

Property Values

The appraiser must indicate the current trend in market prices for single-family homes. Although some price fluctuations will be seasonal and are to be expected, year-to-year price changes for comparable properties should be charted to determine the overall trend of the market.

Note that, even though this category is described as Property Values, it refers to actual selling prices rather than estimated or appraised market values. Property sellers may feel they have "lost" value when a period of rapid appreciation is followed by a period of slower appreciation and high value expectations (asking prices) are not met, when in fact property values have increased overall though at a slower rate in some periods.

> ▸ **Fannie Mae**   Maximum financing is acceptable when property values are stable or increasing. If values are declining, comment on the reason for the decline and its effect on the property's marketability. Properties in such areas must be reviewed with great care. The reasons for a decline in values and the probability of its continuance are key considerations in the property's acceptability. The lender must not consider the use of maximum financing in any instance in which property values are declining.

Increasing

Check this box if property values have increased over the past year.

Stable

Check this box if property values have varied only slightly over the past year.

Declining

Check this box if property values have declined over the past year. Explain any decline in the Market Conditions part of this section.

> ▸ **HUD/FHA**   When both the *Urban* and *Declining* boxes are checked, consider recommending that "the mortgage encumbering the property be insured pursuant to Section 223(e)."
>
> Property values will rise as demand increases and/or supply decreases. In the ideal market, supply and demand are in balance—there are enough homebuyers relative to the number of houses on the market to keep prices stable. In reality, however, a perfect market is rare, and at any given time a neighborhood is likely to have a seller's market (not enough suitable, well-priced houses for sale to satisfy demand) or a buyer's market (many more houses for sale than demand warrants). The demand/supply relationship in a neighborhood can be determined by analyzing the
>
> ■ number of days houses have been on the market,
>
> ■ changes in sales prices over a period of time, and
>
> ■ number of sales versus the number of listings.

Demand/Supply

How many buyers are looking for housing in relation to the number of properties on the market? Too few buyers will result in lower prices, and too many may create a surge in prices that could prove to be temporary (a "bubble"). To prevent a downturn of property values, a moderate shortage of properties or a balance is preferred.

> ▸ **VA**   In every case, the appraiser must consider the supply and demand for available housing in the subject market area, and report, either in the NEIGHBORHOOD section of the URAR or in an addendum, the average listing price to sale price ratio for the subject market area. Professional judgment must be used to estimate that ratio if it cannot be determined from available data sources.

Shortage

Check this box if market data show a shortage of properties for sale, relative to demand. One key indicator of a shortage of properties for sale is the length of marketing time, which is covered in the next part of the NEIGHBORHOOD section of the URAR. The shorter the marketing time, the more likely it is that there are more prospective buyers than properties available.

In Balance

Check this box if market data show that demand/supply is in balance; that is, the number of sales has kept pace with the number of listings.

Over Supply

Check this box if the market data show an oversupply of properties for sale relative to demand. If the Over Supply box is checked, comment on the reason for the excess and its probable effect on the value of the subject property.

> ▸ **Fannie Mae**   An oversupply of housing is undesirable, because it will result in property selling slowly. An oversupply may be neighborhood-wide or citywide. In either case, comment on the reason for the oversupply and its effect on property value.

Marketing Time

Indicate the average time it takes to sell a reasonably priced property from the date it is first listed. The key phrase here is reasonably priced. An overpriced house may linger on the market indefinitely, undergoing an excruciating (to the seller) round of price reductions before finally attracting a buyer. On the other hand, an underpriced property may receive several purchase offers the first day it is listed. Neither situation may be an accurate reflection of the overall market.

A strong interrelationship exists among supply and demand, marketing time, and property values. For example, a lengthy marketing time indicates a buyer's market (low demand and high supply) and often declining values. A relatively short marketing period suggests a seller's market (high demand and low supply), often resulting in rapidly increasing property values. Information relating to marketing time can be obtained from a local multiple listing service (MLS).

> ▸ **VA**   In every case, the appraiser must consider the marketing time trend (increasing or decreasing) in the subject market area, and report, either

in the NEIGHBORHOOD section of the URAR or in an addendum, the extent of increase or decrease in the average marketing time (listing period) in that market area (for example, "In the last three months, the listing period in the subject's market area decreased from 180 to 90 days.")

Under 3 mths

Check this box if the average property in the neighborhood sells in less than three months. There is a great deal of leeway within this category. A marketing time of two to three months may indicate a stable market in a suburb, but a housing shortage in a rural area in which properties typically remain on the market for a much longer time.

3–6 mths

Check this box if the average property in the neighborhood sells within three to six months.

Over 6 mths

Check this box if the average property in the neighborhood takes over six months to sell.

▸ **Fannie Mae**   When marketing time in a particular area is more than six months, comment on the reason why, as well as the effect the extended marketing period may have on the property's value.

◼ ONE-UNIT HOUSING

Record the range of values and ages of neighborhood houses based on available market data. Isolated extremes at either end of the price or age range should be disregarded.

Price $ (000)

Enter the low and high values, excluding extremes.

▸ **Fannie Mae**   A property with a sales price (or value) above the upper price range is considered an "overimprovement" for the neighborhood. An overimprovement may indicate that loan terms generally should be more conservative because the property may not be acceptable to typical purchasers. Property in an urban area that is being renovated should not be regarded as an overimprovement by the lender as long as market demand for such properties, as indicated by the existence of comparable properties, is strong.

A property with a sales price (or value) that is less than the lower price range is considered an "underimprovement."

Explain the effect on value of either overimprovement or under-improvement, as reflected in the SALES COMPARISON APPROACH adjustment grid on page 2 of the URAR.

▸ **RHS**   Enter the predominant low and high prices within the neighborhood, after excluding the extremes.

Age (yrs)

Enter the low and high numbers, excluding atypical extremes.

> ▸ **Fannie Mae**   Isolated high and low extremes should be excluded from the price or age range.

Pred.

Enter the predominant (the most common or most frequently found) price to the left and the predominant age to the right.

> ▸ **Fannie Mae**   The predominant price can be stated as a single figure or, if more appropriate, as a range. The predominant age also can be recorded as a single figure or, if more appropriate, as a range.

▨ PRESENT LAND USE %

Estimate the current use of available land in the subject neighborhood, in the categories listed. If land in the neighborhood is used for purposes other than those indicated on the form, the appraiser should specify the property type and its percentage of use in the space provided in this section for comment on neighborhood boundaries and characteristics.

In the past, homogenous neighborhoods (those with very similar types of properties) tended to have the highest value. At a time of increasing energy costs and ever more demands on residents' busy schedules, mixed-use neighborhoods featuring a variety of services and other amenities within walking distance have proven their desirability anew, so much so that some suburban developments now take advantage of the "new town" concept to include a wide range of property uses. The decline of many industrial areas with their proximity to city centers, waterfront, and/or transportation has actually been a boon for developers seeking to respond to demand for housing in urban areas offering little or no vacant land. Conversion of existing buildings to apartment or condominium lofts and redevelopment of land that had fallen into disuse have revitalized many communities, both large and small.

> ▸ **Fannie Mae**   Typically, dwellings best maintain their value when they are situated in neighborhoods that consist of other similar dwellings. Therefore, a single-family property in a neighborhood with apartments and commercial or industrial development may not have the stability required to sustain value over a long period of time. However, the negative impression of a property within a mixed-use neighborhood can be offset by factors that enhance the market value of the property through increased buyer demand. Typical enhancement factors include easy access to employment centers and a high level of community activity. Viable older neighborhoods frequently reflect a successful mix of commercial service uses such as grocery and other neighborhood stores or occasional multifamily properties.
>
> Enter the relative percentages of the *developed* [improved] land uses listed on the form, rather than simply referring to the zoning classifications. Undeveloped [unimproved] land, regardless of zoning, should be reported as vacant.

▸ **RHS** Enter percentage of predominant use within the neighborhood. All figures should total 100 percent.

One-Unit

Estimate and record the percentage of land in the subject neighborhood used for single-family homes, including condominiums and planned unit developments.

2–4 Unit

Estimate and record the percentage of land in the subject neighborhood used for two- to four-family housing.

Multi-Family

Estimate and record the percentage of land in the subject neighborhood used for properties that contain five or more units.

Commercial

Estimate and record the percentage of land in the subject neighborhood developed for businesses such as retail shops, office buildings, motels, hotels, theaters, restaurants, factories, warehouses, and other commercial uses.

Other

Note the extent of any land use that may be regarded as having a significant impact on local property values—for example, the presence of a public institution—and discuss the effect of that land use below. If a substantial portion of the neighborhood consists of vacant land—that is, undeveloped land that otherwise is available for development—that fact can also be noted here.

▸ **Fannie Mae** If there is a "significant" amount of vacant or undeveloped land in the neighborhood, comment on that fact in the Neighborhood Description part of this section.

Neighborhood Boundaries

Neighborhood boundaries (streets, natural boundaries such as rivers, etc.) should be indicated in a neighborhood map that is included with the appraisal report or identified in this space. Explain here any of the responses provided earlier in this section regarding the neighborhood and the characteristics of property use noted. If more space is needed, an addendum may be attached to the report.

▸ **Fannie Mae** If a computer software program is used to generate Form 1004, any of the areas of the form that call for narrative comments may be expanded as necessary to accommodate a particular appraisal assignment, provided all of the Sales Comparison Approach section appears on the same page. Note also that, if an expandable computer-generated format is used, all information must be provided in the same order used in the preprinted version of the form. Any change or alteration to the appraisal report form may result in a mortgage being ineligible for delivery to Fannie Mae.

Neighborhood Description

The desirability of the neighborhood, in terms of the amenities it offers residents, is very important. In short, is the neighborhood considered a good place to live? Support facilities such as schools, places of worship, transportation, and shopping should be located conveniently for the residents of the neighborhood but not so close as to constitute a nuisance.

One of the best protective measures against adverse influences is adequate zoning that is strictly enforced. Private deed restrictions requiring reasonable uniformity in the size and style of a house and its placement on the lot are effective controls if enforced by the community. Other features of a neighborhood that may contribute to its stability are good police and fire protection, opportunities for stable employment, and attractive home sites.

The following is a list of items that are important to buyers in the marketplace.

- *Employment stability.* Consider the number of job opportunities and the variety and types of businesses and industries available to those living in the subject neighborhood. An area generally has greater employment stability if it has a diversity of businesses and industries rather than a single major industry or industries geared to the same economic cycles.

- *Convenience to employment.* What distance and travel time are required for neighborhood residents to get to their jobs? Availability, cost, and convenience of public transportation should be considered as an alternative to private transportation.

- *Convenience to shopping.* What distance and travel time are required for residents to get to both major and minor shopping areas? Availability, cost, and convenience of public transportation should be considered as an alternative to private transportation.

- *Convenience to schools.* What distance and travel time are required for neighborhood residents to get to elementary and secondary schools? Quality of schools should be noted, because this feature can vary tremendously from one district to another and can have a significant impact on property values.

- *Adequacy of public transportation.* Determine the types, quality, cost, and convenience of public transportation servicing the subject neighborhood.

- *Recreation facilities.* Consider the number, types, and quality of recreational facilities available to neighborhood residents. These include movie theaters, stadiums, parks, tennis courts, golf courses, swimming pools, and health spas.

- *Adequacy of utilities.* Take into account the quality, reliability, and costs of utilities and other services available to the neighborhood. These include water, sewers, electricity, gas, telephone, and garbage collection.

- *Property compatibility.* Many houses suffer a loss in value because they do not conform to the neighborhood in which they are located. Too much conformity, on the other hand, where all houses look the same, will also diminish value. Houses within a neighborhood should have enough variation in style and design to make the overall effect pleasing to the eye. Typical factors to consider in this category include types of land uses prevalent in the neighborhood, lot sizes, and the degree of similarity among houses (style, age, size, quality, and price range).

■ *Protection from detrimental conditions.* Smoke, fog, noxious fumes, radon contamination, use of asbestos-containing materials and urea-formaldehyde insulation, and proximity to toxic waste dumps are just some of the environmental conditions that can threaten the health of neighborhood residents. The presence of such hazards also can have a significant negative effect on the value and marketability of property in the area.

▸ **Fannie Mae**   In July 1989, Fannie Mae provided lenders and appraisers with the following guideline regarding environmental hazards: "The typical residential appraiser is neither expected nor required to be an expert in the field of environmental hazards. However, the appraiser has a responsibility to note in the appraisal report any adverse conditions that were observed during the inspection of the subject property or information that he or she became aware of through normal research in performing an appraisal."

■ *Police and fire protection.* Determine whether the neighborhood has adequate police and fire protection. Check also whether fire protection is provided by a full-time or a volunteer department. Volunteers have demonstrated exceptional skill in fighting fires, but a paid fire department usually is better equipped and more responsive to alarms. Insurance companies usually set lower rates for fire insurance where paid fire departments are located.

■ *General appearance of properties.* The neighborhood's general appearance is important. Are yards well landscaped? Or filled with weeds? Are broken-down cars, bikes, or appliances present in the yards? These can signal sloppy homeowners and lack of community concern. If city property is being appraised, are there vacant lots? Boarded-up stores? If so, how long have they been that way? They may indicate a neighborhood suffering economic as well as physical deterioration.

Check the outside appearance of houses. What condition are they in? Are the houses generally in good shape or falling apart? Do many need painting? Answers to such questions should tell much about the quality of the neighborhood—whether it is one of the best in the area or suffering from neglect.

▸ **Fannie Mae**   General appearance of the properties in the neighborhood is a key factor. Consider the extent to which the properties are receiving proper maintenance. Signs of maintenance and care usually reflect a strong neighborhood with stable or increasing values.

■ *Appeal to market.* What is the overall attractiveness of the subject neighborhood? Typical characteristics to consider include natural scenic beauty, landscaping appeal, neighborhood design (the pattern of streets, parks and public areas, and the separation of commercial, industrial, multifamily, and single-family residential areas), architectural appearance of houses, and the presence or lack of environmental hazards.

No one neighborhood will be perfect, but there will be many whose faults can be overlooked because their positive qualities overcome their liabilities.

▸ **Fannie Mae** Consider how all aspects of the neighborhood will appeal to the typical purchaser in the market. An individual property by itself cannot overcome a generally prevailing reluctance of the market to invest in a neighborhood. On the other hand, a relatively weak property in a strong and viable neighborhood is likely to sustain its value, although it still must be carefully analyzed.

Market Conditions (including support for the above conclusions)

Describe any influences or conditions outside the subject property that may have a negative or positive effect on its value. For example, what is the current and anticipated supply and demand situation for housing in the market area? Are any special financing arrangements prevalent in the market area that would cause the transaction price of one property to differ from that of an identical property? The buyer of a comparable property may have assumed an existing mortgage at a favorable interest rate. Or a seller may have arranged a buydown, paying cash to the lender so that a mortgage could be offered at an interest rate lower than the prevailing market rate. In either case the buyer probably paid a higher price for the property to obtain below-market financing. On the other hand, interest rates at above-market levels often result in lower sales prices.

In this section the appraiser should provide supporting data for identifiable market trends affecting value. One indicator may be the length of time it takes to sell the average property. How has the number of properties on the market changed in recent months relative to the number of closed sales? Is the market inundated with properties for sale? Are financing concessions a factor in some sales? Are property sellers expected to assist buyers by carrying some of the financing?

What is the trend of sales prices? The appraiser should be alert to early evidence of declining values. Analysis of the asking prices of competitive properties currently for sale in the neighborhood may reveal that market expectations have been lowered by weak demand.

Although the latest revision of the URAR greatly increases the amount of room available on the form for the appraiser to explain market indicators and their likely effect on property value, additional commentary can be provided in an addendum, if necessary.

▸ **Fannie Mae** Include comments related to general market conditions in the subject market area in this space.

▸ **HUD/FHA** Explain financing concessions for the subject and the market area. Also explain whether the subject is consistent with or different from the market area in that regard.

▸ **VA** Fee appraisers must report here the existence or nonexistence of sales or financing incentives or concessions in the subject market area and make a statement regarding their effect, if any, on the sales prices of comparable homes. This must be done in each and every case, proposed or existing. The appraiser is not required to investigate incentives or concessions involving the subject property. Statements in this section must be consistent with those in the SALES COMPARISON APPROACH section on page 2 of the URAR.

APPRAISAL 1

Note: Race and the racial composition of the neighborhood are not appraisal factors.												
Neighborhood Characteristics				**One-Unit Housing Trends**				**One-Unit Housing**		**Present Land Use %**		
Location	Urban	X Suburban	Rural	Property Values	X Increasing	Stable	Declining	PRICE	AGE	One-Unit	100 %	
Built-Up	X Over 75%	25-75%	Under 25%	Demand/Supply	Shortage	X In Balance	Over Supply	$(000)	(yrs)	2-4 Unit	%	
Growth	Rapid	X Stable	Slow	Marketing Time	X Under 3 mths	3-6 mths	Over 6 mths	400	Low New	Multi-Family	%	
Neighborhood Boundaries	On North by Bee Ridge Rd, on East by Bee Ridge							550	High 15	Commercial	%	
extension, on South by Proctor Rd, on West by Sara Lane.								425	Pred. 8	Other	%	
Neighborhood Description	The subject neighborhood is 100% built-out, with mature landscaping. Values have increased											
annually due to proximity to downtown business district, schools and services, and highway access.												
Market Conditions (including support for the above conclusions)	Employment has risen steadily in metropolitan area due to business											
expansion and development. Area population has increased approximately 5% per year for the last five years, bolstering the												
housing market. Despite new-home development in the overall area, existing home sales have been strong.												

In Appraisal 1, the subject property is located in a desirable subdivision a few miles east of Sarasota, Florida. The 15-year-old neighborhood is 100 percent developed with single-family homes ranging in value from $400,000 to $550,000. Most are valued at $425,000. Houses range in age from new to 15 years, with a predominant age of 8 years.

Employment stability in the subject neighborhood historically has been better than in competing areas. Convenience to the downtown business district, shopping, and schools, as well as police and fire protection, is normal for the market area; however, highway access and the quality, reliability, and cost of utilities and other services available to the subject neighborhood are outstanding and superior to those found in competing neighborhoods.

The general appearance, compatibility, and market appeal of properties in the subject neighborhood are good compared with those of the competing area. A population increase of approximately 5% per year over the last five years has resulted in a steady demand for housing, with a continuing uptrend in values during the past several years. Most houses on the market are sold within three months.

Current interest rates on conventional 30-year, fixed-rate mortgage loans are under 6 percent. As a result, loan discounts, interest rate buydowns, and sales concessions are not prevalent in the current resale market.

EXERCISE: APPRAISAL 2

Note: Race and the racial composition of the neighborhood are not appraisal factors.									
Neighborhood Characteristics			**One-Unit Housing Trends**			**One-Unit Housing**		**Present Land Use %**	
Location ☐ Urban ☐ Suburban ☐ Rural			Property Values ☐ Increasing ☐ Stable ☐ Declining			PRICE AGE		One-Unit	%
Built-Up ☐ Over 75% ☐ 25–75% ☐ Under 25%			Demand/Supply ☐ Shortage ☐ In Balance ☐ Over Supply			$ (000) (yrs)		2-4 Unit	%
Growth ☐ Rapid ☐ Stable ☐ Slow			Marketing Time ☐ Under 3 mths ☐ 3–6 mths ☐ Over 6 mths			Low		Multi-Family	%
Neighborhood Boundaries						High		Commercial	%
						Pred.		Other	%
Neighborhood Description									
Market Conditions (including support for the above conclusions)									

Complete the blank URAR NEIGHBORHOOD section provided above for Appraisal 2, using the following information. When you have finished, check your work against the completed Appraisal 2 in the Answer Key.

The subject property is located in a suburban subdivision ten miles from the downtown shopping and business areas of a medium-sized city that is the state capital. The 29-year-old neighborhood is 100 percent developed with about 200 single-family homes currently ranging in value from $325,000 to $395,000, with a predominant value of $360,000. The majority of homes are about 20 years old, but they range in age from 8 to 29 years. There have been few houses for sale in the subdivision and demand is high, creating a seller's market. Most houses on the market are sold within 30 to 60 days and steady price increases are reported for the last 48 months.

Good public transportation is available to the subject neighborhood. There is a regional shopping mall about two miles away, with national chains, local businesses, a bowling center, restaurants, banking facilities, and movie theaters. Growth of state offices and local business has resulted in a strong, stable workforce.

Except for the general appearance of properties and market appeal, which are above average, all other subject neighborhood amenities are on a par with those in competing areas. The current housing market is active and reflects a strong local economy. Typical financing in the area is through conventional mortgages at interest rates of 6 percent or less for a 30-year, fixed-rate loan. No loan discounts, interest buydowns, or sales concessions were found for the subject or for comparable sales in this market; thus, financing adjustments are not required.

SECTION 4: SITE

Dimensions				Area		Shape		View		
Specific Zoning Classification					Zoning Description					
Zoning Compliance ☐ Legal ☐ Legal Nonconforming (Grandfathered Use) ☐ No Zoning ☐ Illegal (describe)										
Is the highest and best use of the subject property as improved (or as proposed per plans and specifications) the present use? ☐ Yes ☐ No If No, describe										
Utilities	**Public**	**Other (describe)**			**Public**	**Other (describe)**		**Off-site Improvements—Type**	**Public**	**Private**
Electricity	☐	☐		Water	☐	☐		Street	☐	☐
Gas	☐	☐		Sanitary Sewer	☐	☐		Alley	☐	☐
FEMA Special Flood Hazard Area ☐ Yes ☐ No FEMA Flood Zone						FEMA Map #		FEMA Map Date		
Are the utilities and off-site improvements typical for the market area? ☐ Yes ☐ No If No, describe										
Are there any adverse site conditions or external factors (easements, encroachments, environmental conditions, land uses, etc.)? ☐ Yes ☐ No If Yes, describe										

The appraiser must adequately describe the property that is the subject of the appraisal, starting with the subject site. To do so the appraiser must

- give the dimensions and topography of the site;
- specify zoning and indicate whether or not the site is in compliance;
- describe utilities available to the site; and
- note whether the property is in a flood hazard zone and whether there are any encumbrances on the property or other adverse influences.

Dimensions

Give the perimeter measurements, in feet, of the parcel being appraised.

▸ **HUD/FHA** List all dimensions of the site. If the site has an irregular shape, enter the boundary dimensions; for example, 85' × 150' × 195' × 250'.

▸ **RHS** Enter site dimensions. If the site is irregular, enter total square footage. If the site contains more than one acre, enter the number of acres. The site must not be large enough to subdivide into more than one site under existing local zoning ordinances.

Area

Enter the total square footage of land area included in the parcel. If the site is more than 1 acre, the area can be given in acres and fractions of an acre; for example, 6½ acres.

Note how the site compares in size to other properties in the neighborhood; for example, **TYPICAL** or **OVERSIZED.** Any difference that affects value should be explained.

▸ **Fannie Mae** For the property to qualify for maximum financing, the site's size should be conforming and acceptable in the market area.

▸ **HUD/FHA** Enter area in square feet or in acres. Describe the subject site in relation to other properties in the neighborhood; for example, **TYPICAL, SMALL,** or **LARGE.**

> ▸ **VA**   Although VA does not make farm or other business loans, the law allows veterans to use their Loan Guaranty benefit to purchase a farm on which there is a farm residence.

The appraisal of properties with acreage should not present difficulties if a sufficient number of similar properties in the area were recently sold primarily for residential use. For VA purposes, the valuation must not include livestock, crops, or farm equipment and supplies. Installed facilities (such as a well, septic tank, etc.) serving the dwelling will be considered part of the dwelling when, in the opinion of the appraiser, such items contribute to the desirability and residential aspects of the property. Buildings other than the dwelling will be valued on the basis of the use of the property for residential purposes only.

Shape

Enter the shape of the perimeter of the site; for example, **SQUARE** or **RECTANGULAR.** If the site's value is affected by its irregular or a typical shape, provide the reason(s) for the effect on value.

> ▸ **Fannie Mae**   For the property to qualify for maximum financing, the site's shape should be conforming and acceptable in the market area.

> ▸ **HUD/FHA**   Enter the site's configuration; for example, **TRIANGULAR, SQUARE,** or **RECTANGULAR.**

View

Describe the kind of views seen from the interior of the house. The topography of the land and design of the house will determine the views. A house with views that are unobstructed, either because there are no nearby structures or because the house is on a hill, will be valued more highly than houses that do not share these amenities. The value of the view will be the premium paid in the area for that kind of property. A house built around an atrium or with walled patios or garden areas may have only interior views. If comparable properties have similar views, there will be no detrimental effect on value.

> ▸ **Fannie Mae**   For the property to qualify for maximum financing, the site's amenities should be conforming and acceptable in the market area.

> ▸ **HUD/FHA**   Briefly describe the view from the property. Identify a view that has a significant positive or negative influence on value as being average, superior, or inferior to other local sites; for example, **MOUNTAINS—AVERAGE.**

Specific Zoning Classification

Enter the zoning code and category title designated by the local zoning authority to show the permitted property use(s). Most municipal and county zoning districts use letter and number codes as well as short identifying labels, such as **R-1 RESIDENTIAL/SINGLE-FAMILY.** If the area is not zoned, enter **N/A.** In areas that do not have zoning, limitations on property use similar to those imposed by zoning are brought about by the use of conditions, covenants, and restrictions (CC&Rs) in deeds. CC&Rs also are frequently used in subdivisions so that architectural and property maintenance standards are met to ensure property values. The existence of any such deed restrictions, and the property's conformity with them, should be noted. Note also that other kinds of zones frequently overlay property use zones. Some of these are mentioned later in this section

> ▸ **Fannie Mae**   Give the zoning code for the area in which the property is located and a brief explanation of what the code stands for; for example, **R-1 SINGLE-FAMILY.**

> ▸ **HUD/FHA**   Enter the zoning type by both the abbreviation and descriptive label, such as **R-1 RESIDENTIAL/SINGLE-FAMILY.** Use the designation **HISTORIC,** if applicable. Always determine whether current property use is in compliance with zoning regulations.

The HUD/FHA comment above mentions properties that are designated *historic*. If the subject property has been so designated, the appraiser should obtain documentation from the municipal, state, or federal agency granting the designation, and make that documentation part of the work file for the assignment. Doing so will protect the appraiser from a challenge that the property is not really historic. It will also support the real or perceived desirability of such property in the eyes of the consumer, thus supporting the opinion of value.

Zoning Description

The zoning classification should be explained, especially if not apparent from the zoning designation.

Zoning Compliance

The appraiser must determine whether the subject property represents a legally permitted use of its site in conformance with the applicable zoning regulations.

Legal
Check this box if the present use of the subject site is a legally permitted one.

Legal Nonconforming (Grandfathered Use)
Check this box if the present property use is not in conformance with the applicable zoning but has been legally permitted by a zoning variance or special use permit issued to the property owner. A property use also can be a legal nonconforming one if it is "grandfathered in" at the time of a change in zoning classification. For example, an older commercial area, because of its proximity to a growing metropolitan area, may be rezoned for residential use, yet the existing commercial structures will be allowed to remain. If this box is checked, explain the special circumstances involved.

> ▸ **Fannie Mae**   If the property improvements do not reflect a legal conforming use of the land, as permitted by the applicable zoning, the appraiser should so indicate. Fannie Mae *will not* purchase a mortgage secured by property that is not a legally permissible use of the land. On the other hand, Fannie Mae *will* purchase a mortgage secured by property that is a legal but nonconforming use of the land, so long as the impact on property value and marketability of the nonconforming use is reflected in the appraiser's estimate of value.

> ▸ **HUD/FHA**   A legal nonconforming use requires some explanation.

No Zoning

Check this box if the area in which the subject property is located does not have zoning. Be alert to the fact that areas that do not have zoning may make use of other methods of regulating land use, such as deed restrictions.

Illegal (describe)

Check this box if the property use is not in conformance with the zoning code and has not been legally sanctioned by a zoning variance, special use permit, or other means. Explain your response below or in the *ADDITIONAL COMMENTS* section on page 3 of the form. Always take into account the effect on value of an illegal or nonconforming use as well as a prospective change of use.

> ‣ **RHS** Borrowers and lenders are required to comply with any federal, state, or local laws or regulatory commission rules that are in existence and that affect the project including, but not limited to, land use zoning.

Is the highest and best use of the subject property as improved (or as proposed per plans and specifications) the present use?

Yes or No: If No, describe

The highest and best use of property is a legally permitted use that is physically possible, financially feasible, and economically desirable (the most profitable alternative). Indicate whether or not the present or proposed use of the property is its highest and best use. If the current use of the property is its highest and best use, no further information need be supplied. If the present use of the property is not its highest and best use, however, a brief statement of what the highest and best use would be must be provided in the next space.

A study of the highest and best use for commercially zoned property may be many pages long, analyzing and comparing potential property uses. For residential appraisals, considerations of property use usually take into account whether the present structures are typical of the neighborhood and whether market demand is such that the site is more valuable with the improvements than without them. As a practical matter, zoning and other constraints usually simplify analysis of highest and best use for residential property. Of greater concern is the residence in an area that has been zoned or rezoned for nonresidential use. If the structure fronts on a major roadway and is zoned commercial, its highest and best use may be a commercial use. The extent to which the area is already devoted to commercial use, the ease with which the existing improvements can be converted to a potential new use, and the demand for that kind of commercial space must all be considered in the determination.

> ‣ **Fannie Mae** The highest and best use of a site is that reasonable and probable use that supports the highest present value on the effective date of the appraisal. A highest and best use must meet four criteria:
>
> 1. The use must be legally permitted.
>
> 2. The use must be financially feasible.
>
> 3. The use must be physically possible.
>
> 4. The use must provide more profit than any other use of the site would generate.

The URAR highest and best use analysis is not the type of strict analysis that considers the subject site as if vacant. Consider the site *as improved,* unless it is financially feasible to renovate the existing dwelling or remove it and build a new one. If the appraiser's comparable sales analysis indicates that the property is reasonably typical of the area and compatible with market demand, the only determination to be made is whether the site is more valuable with the existing improvements or without them.

If the current improvements do not represent the highest and best use of the site, Fannie Mae will *not* purchase a mortgage secured by the subject property.

> ▸ **HUD/FHA**   Consider the highest and best use of the site *in relation to the neighborhood.* If the present use is not the site's highest and best use, indicate the use that would be the site's highest and best use. Explain your response below or in the ADDITIONAL COMMENTS section on page 3 of the form.

■ UTILITIES

To be considered suitable for building purposes, a site must have certain utilities available to it. Electricity can be supplied by a variety of sources, including a private generator. Gas is desirable in addition to electricity in most areas as a lower-cost or more efficient alternative to electricity for cooking, heating, and other household purposes. There must be a source of water. Sewage must be disposed of in a legally permitted, safe, and hygienic way. Areas of high-density development or particular geologic features, such as bedrock close to the surface that inhibits water absorption, usually have storm sewers to decrease the risk of flooding.

> ▸ **Fannie Mae**   To qualify for maximum financing, the site should have utilities that meet community standards and are accepted generally by area residents.

> ▸ **RHS**   Identify utilities available for use to the site.

■ PUBLIC

Check this box if the listed utility is available to the subject property from a public source.

> ▸ **HUD/FHA**   Public utilities are those provided by a government.

■ OTHER (DESCRIBE)

If the listed utility is available to the subject property from a source other than a public one, whether on or off the site, indicate its ownership and (if it is not on the subject site) its location. For example, if the only water supply is a private on-site water well, enter **PRIVATE WELL.**

> ▸ **HUD/FHA**   A utility may be provided by an individual and/or community system, rather than a government. If this is the case, indicate here how service is provided.

Electricity

Check the box if electricity is available to the subject property from a public source. Enter any private source, such as an on-site generator, if applicable.

> ‣ **HUD/FHA** Indicate whether electricity is underground.

Gas

Check the box if natural gas for cooking and/or heating is available to the subject property from a public source. Enter any private source, such as propane stored in an on-site tank.

Water

Check the box if water is available to the subject property from a public source. Enter any private source.

> ‣ **Fannie Mae** If public water facilities are not available, a community or private well must be available and utilized by the subject property. A private well, if any, must be located on the subject site. If a private community facility is used, the owners of the subject property must have the right to access the system's facilities, which must be viable on an ongoing basis. The appraiser must comment on any effect on market value created by environmental hazards or any other condition affecting well, septic, or public water facilities.

Sanitary Sewer

Check the box if a sanitary sewer is available to the subject property from a public source. Enter any nonpublic community or private septic system.

> ‣ **Fannie Mae** If public sewer facilities are not available, a community or private septic system must be available and utilized by the subject property. A private septic system, if any, must be located on the subject site. If a private community septic system is used, the owners of the subject property must have the right to access the system's facilities, which must be viable on an ongoing basis.

■ OFF-SITE IMPROVEMENTS—TYPE: PUBLIC OR PRIVATE

In this section you will indicate the kinds of improvements that have been made to make the site more suitable for development. Enter the construction material used in any of the listed improvements on or adjacent to the subject property. An improvement is considered *Public* if it is made and maintained at public expense. An improvement is considered *Private* if it is made or maintained at the expense of the property owner, either individually or as part of a homeowners' association.

> ‣ **Fannie Mae** To qualify for maximum financing, the site should have street improvements that conform to those of the market area.

> ‣ **HUD/FHA** Describe the improvement briefly and check the appropriate box. For example, for *Street* you might enter **ASPHALT** and check *Public*. *Public* refers to a government that can regulate use; it does not

refer to a homeowners' association. If private, indicate whether there is year-round maintenance of the improvement.

‣ **RHS** Indicate site improvements.

Street

Indicate the material used to pave the street on which the property is located and whether the street is public or private.

‣ **Fannie Mae** The property should front on a publicly dedicated and maintained street that meets community standards. If the street does not meet community standards, comment in this section on the impact on the property's marketability and value.

If the street is privately owned, whether by a community or one or more homeowners, a legally enforceable maintenance agreement should be in effect, and the street should meet community standards. If there is no agreement and/or the street does not meet community standards, comment on the resulting impact on the property's marketability and value.

Alley

If the property is bordered on any side by an alley, enter the type of paving material used. If there is no alley, enter **NONE.**

‣ **Fannie Mae** If other properties in the area typically have access to an alley, the subject should have access to an alley. If the subject does not conform to other properties in the area, comment on the effect on marketability and value of the absence of this feature.

FEMA Special Flood Hazard Area: Yes or No

The Federal Emergency Management Agency (FEMA) has identified flood hazard areas throughout the United States. Check the local Flood Insurance Rate Map (FIRM) to determine whether the subject property is located in a flood hazard area. If part of the site is located in a flood hazard area but the improvements are located outside the flood hazard area, explain that fact in this section, or in the ADDITIONAL COMMENTS section on page 3 of the form.

‣ **Fannie Mae** Check this response if the property is located in a FEMA flood hazard area. Flood insurance is required if the property improvements are located in a special flood hazard area (zones A, AO, AH, A1-30, A-99, V, or V1-30). If part of the property is located in a flood hazard area but the improvements are not, flood insurance is not required.

Flood hazard area maps can be obtained from FEMA at 1-800-638-6620 (continental U.S.), 1-800-492-6605 (Maryland), or 1-800-638-6831 (Alaska, Hawaii, Puerto Rico, and the Virgin Islands). Written requests (required for more than five maps) can be made to Federal Emergency Management Agency, Flood Map Distribution Center, 6930 (A-F) San Tomas Road, Baltimore, MD 21227-6227.

‣ **HUD/FHA** If any part of the subject property is within a Special Flood Hazard Area, check *Yes;* otherwise, check *No.*

▸ **RHS**   State directors will refrain from enabling encroachments on flood plains unless there are no practicable alternatives.

▸ **VA**   Property is not eligible for appraisal if the improvements are or will be located in a Special Flood Hazard Area (SFHA) and it is proposed/under/new construction with elevation of the lowest floor below the 100-year flood level, or flood insurance is not available, or in an area subject to regular flooding for whatever reason, whether or not it is in an SFHA.

FEMA Flood Zone: FEMA Map No. and FEMA Map Date

If any part of the subject site is located in a flood hazard area, indicate the map number on which the site can be found, and the date of the map.

▸ **Fannie Mae**   If the subject property is located in a flood hazard area, provide the map or community panel number and specific flood zone on the appraisal report.

▸ **HUD/FHA**   If the previous response was *Yes,* enter the FEMA map and zone number. Properties within zones A *and* V require flood insurance because these zones are designated by FEMA as Special Flood Hazard Areas. Properties within zones B or C do not require flood insurance because those are not Special Flood Hazard Areas.

▸ **VA**   If the property is located in a special flood hazard area, provide the map number and designated zone.

Are the utilities and off-site improvements typical for the market area? Yes or No; If No, describe

Does the subject property conform to what is expected of properties in this neighborhood? If not, describe any deviations.

Are there any adverse site conditions or external factors (easements, encroachments, environmental conditions, land uses, etc.)?

This is the space in which to explain any responses in this section. If more space is needed, use the ADDITIONAL COMMENTS section on page 3 of the form or attach an addendum.

The general contour of the land and the approximate degree of any incline or decline from street level should be noted; for example, **LEVEL** or **30% DOWN-HILL GRADE.** If the site's topography is such that it should be valued lower than other properties in the neighborhood (because of increased construction costs or decreased utility, for instance), explain the effect on value.

Note any easements that are visible or discovered by inspection of the property; for instance, a shared road or the presence of a utility pole. Common easements also include underground utility lines, such as those for electricity, telephone, and cable television transmission. Also note any easements that may not be visible but are listed in the preliminary title report.

As noted under Specific Zoning Classification and Zoning Description, a variety of zones frequently overlay property use zones. In California, for instance, property located within one-quarter of a mile of an active earthquake fault may fall within a special studies zone and require special approval before a building permit is issued. The fact that property is located within such a zone must be disclosed to a prospective buyer of the property by the agent representing the seller, or by the seller if there is no agent. The California Division of Mines and Geology has maps available showing the location of the special studies zones throughout the state. California also recognizes and has special permit requirements for property located within coastal zones, which generally include all property from the Pacific coast inland about 1,000 yards.

A frequently used property classification throughout the country is the historic district designation, which may affect the potential use of the property, particularly in terms of additions to or remodeling of the existing structure(s). Any designation that has the potential to affect property value should be mentioned and analyzed by the appraiser.

▶ **Fannie Mae**   For the property to qualify for maximum financing, the site's topography should be conforming and acceptable in the market area. Because amenities, easements, and encroachments may affect the property's marketability, you must comment on them if the site is not typical for the neighborhood.

▶ **HUD/FHA**   Indicate the site's topography, such as level, sloped, and so on. If there appears to be an easement, check to make sure.

▶ **RHS**   Enter comments as appropriate to the site. Indicate conditions observed. Location of projects shall, to the extent practicable, result in the preservation of important farmlands and forestlands, prime rangeland, and wetlands.

▶ **VA**   Property is not eligible for appraisal if the improvements are/will be located in

■ an airport Noise Zone 3 (explained below), if proposed or under construction;

■ a transmission line easement involving high-pressure gas or liquid petroleum or high voltage electricity, if any part of the residential structure is located within the easement;

■ an area susceptible to geological or soil instability (earthquakes, landslides, or other history of unstable soils), if proposed/under/new construction and the builder cannot provide evidence that either the site is not affected or the problem has been adequately addressed in the engineering design; or

■ a Coastal Barrier Resources System (CBRS) area, as delineated on a CBRS map. Affected areas include portions of the Great Lakes, Gulf coast, Puerto Rico, Virgin Islands, and the Atlantic coast. Appraisers who work in CBRS areas must obtain the appropriate maps from the U.S. Geological Survey. Prohibited areas on the maps are those inside the solid heavy black lines.

The appraisal report must identify any airport noise zone or safety-related zone in which the property is located. Noise zones are defined in decibels (db) in the table below.

Noise Zone	CNS (Composite Noise Rating)	NEF (Noise Exposure Forecast)	DNL (Day/Night Average Sound Level)
1	Under 100 db	Under 30 db	Under 65 db
2	100–115 db	30–40 db	65–75 db
3	Over 115 db	Over 40 db	Over 75 db

Clear zones are areas of highest accident risk located immediately beyond the ends of a runway.

Accident potential zones are beyond the clear zones but still have significant potential for accidents. Only military airports identify them.

No existing property will be rejected because of airport influence if that property is already the security for an outstanding VA loan.

Depending on the type of construction and the airport noise or safety-related zone involved, the following requirements also apply with regard to the appraisal and/or VA value notice:

Type of Construction	Noise Zone One	Noise Zone Two	Noise Zone Three	Clear Zone	Accident Potential Zone
Proposed	A	A, B, C, D	E	F	A, C, H, I
New/Existing	A	A, D	A, D	A, C, G	A, C, I

	Requirement
A	The fee appraiser's market data analysis must include a consideration of the effect on value, if any, of the property being located near an airport.
B	Sound attenuation features must be built into the dwelling to bring the interior DNL of the living unit to 45 decibels or less.
C	Available comparable sales must indicate market acceptance of the subdivision in which the property is located.
D	The veteran must sign a statement that indicates his/her awareness that the property being purchased is located in an area near an airport and that aircraft noise may affect livability, value, and marketability of the property.
E	Not acceptable as the security for a VA loan unless the project was accepted by VA before noise zone 3 contours were changed to include it. In that situation, the requirements for proposed construction in noise zone 2 must be met.
F	Not acceptable as the security for a VA loan.
G	The veteran must sign a statement that indicates his/her awareness that the property being purchased is located near the end of an airport runway and that this may have an affect upon livability, safety, value, and marketability of the property.
H	The project in which the properties are located must be consistent with the recommendations found in the airport's Air Installation Compatible Use Zone (AICUZ) report.
I	The veteran must sign a statement that indicates his/her awareness that the property being purchased is located in an accident potential zone and that this may have an affect upon livability, safety, value, and marketability of the property.

APPRAISAL 1

<table>
<tr><td colspan="2">Dimensions 68Fx160LSx75Rx139RS</td><td>Area 10726 +/- sq. ft.</td><td>Shape Irregular</td><td>View Residential</td></tr>
<tr><td colspan="5">Specific Zoning Classification RSF-1   Zoning Description Residential Single-Family</td></tr>
<tr><td colspan="5">Zoning Compliance [X] Legal   [ ] Legal Nonconforming (Grandfathered Use)   [ ] No Zoning   [ ] Illegal (describe)</td></tr>
<tr><td colspan="5">Is the highest and best use of the subject property as improved (or as proposed per plans and specifications) the present use? [X] Yes   [ ] No If No, describe</td></tr>
</table>

Utilities	Public	Other (describe)		Public	Other (describe)	Off-site Improvements--Type	Public	Private
Electricity	X		Water	X		Street Asphalt	X	
Gas			Sanitary Sewer	X		Alley None		

FEMA Special Flood Hazard Area [ ] Yes [X] No FEMA Flood Zone _____ FEMA Map No. 1251440170   FEMA Map Date 5/95

Are the utilities and off-site improvements typical for the market area? [X] Yes [ ] No. If No, describe

Are there any adverse site conditions or external factors (easements, encroachments, environmental conditions, land uses, etc.)? [ ] Yes [X] No If Yes, describe

In Appraisal 1, the subject site is 68' by 160' by 75' by 139', for a total square footage of 10,726. The property is classified **RSF-1,** *a residential use. The property as improved is in compliance with the zoning requirements and represents the highest and best use of the site.*

The property has electricity, water, and sanitary sewer, all on public lines. There is no gas line available, however. The street is asphalt, publicly maintained. There are no alleys in this subdivision.

The subject site is level and rectangular, though irregularly shaped. Views from the house are of interior patio and atrium areas. The property is located in FEMA zone C, as indicated on map 1251440170 of 5-95.

No adverse easements, encroachments, or environmental conditions are visible on the property or in the immediate vicinity. Only normal utility easements are apparent.

EXERCISE: APPRAISAL 2

Dimensions			Area	Shape		View		
Specific Zoning Classification			Zoning Description					
Zoning Compliance ☐ Legal ☐ Legal Nonconforming (Grandfathered Use) ☐ No Zoning ☐ Illegal (describe)								
Is the highest and best use of the subject property as improved (or as proposed per plans and specifications) the present use? ☐ Yes ☐ No If No, describe								

Utilities	Public	Other (describe)		Public	Other (describe)	Off-site Improvements—Type	Public	Private
Electricity	☐	☐	Water	☐	☐	Street	☐	☐
Gas	☐	☐	Sanitary Sewer	☐	☐	Alley	☐	☐
FEMA Special Flood Hazard Area ☐ Yes ☐ No FEMA Flood Zone				FEMA Map #		FEMA Map Date		
Are the utilities and off-site improvements typical for the market area? ☐ Yes ☐ No If No, describe								
Are there any adverse site conditions or external factors (easements, encroachments, environmental conditions, land uses, etc.)? ☐ Yes ☐ No If Yes, describe								

(left margin vertical label: SITE)

Complete the blank URAR SITE section provided above for Appraisal 2, using the following information. When you have finished, check your work against the completed Appraisal 2 in the Answer Key.

The subject property is a rectangle, 75 feet (street frontage) by 150 feet, typical of the area. The property is in compliance with its zoning classification of SF-1, Single-Family Residential, and represents and highest and best use of the site.

The property is not located in a FEMA flood hazard zone, as per FEMA map XX999. Electricity, gas, water, and sanitary sewer are available as public services and are typical for this area. The public street is asphalt paved and there is no alley.

The site is gently rolling, with the house built on the highest part of the lot. There is a view of the surrounding hills from the house, typical of this area. There are no apparent easements other than underground utility lines.

SECTION 5: IMPROVEMENTS

General Description	Foundation	Exterior Description materials/condition	Interior materials/condition
Units ☐ One ☐ One with Accessory Unit	☐ Concrete Slab ☐ Crawl Space	Foundation Walls	Floors
# of Stories	☐ Full Basement ☐ Partial Basement	Exterior Walls	Walls
Type ☐ Det. ☐ Att. ☐ S-Det./End Unit	Basement Area sq. ft.	Roof Surface	Trim/Finish
☐ Existing ☐ Proposed ☐ Under Const.	Basement Finish %	Gutters & Downspouts	Bath Floor
Design (Style)	☐ Outside Entry/Exit ☐ Sump Pump	Window Type	Bath Wainscot
Year Built	Evidence of ☐ Infestation	Storm Sash/Insulated	Car Storage ☐ None
Effective Age (Yrs)	☐ Dampness ☐ Settlement	Screens	☐ Driveway # of Cars
Attic ☐ None	Heating ☐ FWA ☐ HWBB ☐ Radiant	Amenities ☐ Woodstove(s) #	Driveway Surface
☐ Drop Stair ☐ Stairs	☐ Other Fuel	☐ Fireplace(s) # ☐ Fence	☐ Garage # of Cars
☐ Floor ☐ Scuttle	Cooling ☐ Central Air Conditioning	☐ Patio/Deck ☐ Porch	☐ Carport # of Cars
☐ Finished ☐ Heated	☐ Individual ☐ Other	☐ Pool ☐ Other	☐ Att. ☐ Det. ☐ Built-in
Appliances ☐Refrigerator ☐Range/Oven ☐Dishwasher ☐Disposal ☐Microwave ☐Washer/Dryer ☐Other (describe)			
Finished area **above** grade contains: Rooms Bedrooms Bath(s) Square Feet of Gross Living Area Above Grade			
Additional features (special energy efficient items, etc.)			
Describe the condition of the property (including needed repairs, deterioration, renovations, remodeling, etc.).			
Are there any physical deficiencies or adverse conditions that affect the livability, soundness, or structural integrity of the property? ☐ Yes ☐ No If Yes, describe			
Does the property generally conform to the neighborhood (functional utility, style, condition, use, construction, etc.)? ☐ Yes ☐ No If No, describe			

Quality of construction and materials, as well as design, condition, utility, and physical characteristics of improvements, combine to influence demand and therefore the marketability and value of a property. A detailed and accurate description of the subject structure is essential to any valuation assignment—especially in selecting "comps" (comparable properties) for the sales comparison approach and in calculating reproduction or replacement cost and depreciation for the cost approach. The appraiser must

- describe the style, age, and condition of existing or incomplete property improvements;
- describe the exterior features of improvements;
- list the type of foundation and any evidence of deterioration or infestation;
- itemize the basement finishing materials; and
- indicate the type of insulation and any special energy-efficient items used.

■ GENERAL DESCRIPTION

The style, size, and age of improvements are listed in this part.

Units: One or One with Accessory Unit

Place an X in the box to indicate a property with one living unit, or a property with one living unit and an accessory unit (separate living area, typically with its own entrance, bath, and cooking facilities). Both Fannie Mae and Freddie Mac generally allow use of the URAR for one-unit properties only. Fannie Mae does allow the URAR to be used for homes with "in-law" or small rental units, if the property is not in an area zoned for multifamily residences. (In such cases, zoning typically is R-1, with a variance for the rental unit.)

> ▸ **Fannie Mae** Fannie Mae does not specify minimum size or living area requirements for properties. However dwelling units of any type should contain sufficient living area to be acceptable to typical purchasers or tenants in the subject market area. There should be comparables of a size similar to the subject property to support the general acceptability of a particular property type.

> ▸ **VA** Any nonresidential use of the property must be subordinate to its residential use and character. If any portion of a property is designed or used for nonresidential purposes, that property is eligible only if the nonresidential use does not

> ■ impair the residential character of the property or

> ■ exceed 25 percent of the total floor area. In making this calculation, the total nonresidential area must include storage areas or similar spaces that are integral parts of the nonresidential portion.

> Each living unit must have the space necessary to assure suitable living, sleeping, cooking, and dining accommodations and sanitary facilities.

of Stories

Enter the number of above-grade floors of finished living area.

> ▸ **HUD/FHA** Enter the number of stories above grade. Do *not* include any basement areas.

Type: Det., Att., or S-Det./End Unit

Determine whether the subject dwelling is detached (free-standing), attached (shares two or more common walls with another structure), or semidetached (shares one wall with another structure, or is the end unit of a multi-unit building) and enter the appropriate abbreviation.

> ▸ **HUD/FHA** Enter **DET.** (detached), **S/D** (semidetached), or **R** (row).

Existing, Proposed, or Under Const.

Enter an X in the **EXISTING** box if you are appraising a fully built structure. Otherwise, indicate **PROPOSED** or **UNDER CONST.**

   Note: If you are appraising a proposed structure or one that is under construction, indicate the plans and specifications used in the appraisal in the ADDITIONAL COMMENTS section on page 3 of the form.

> ▸ **HUD/FHA** Enter **EXISTING, PROPOSED,** or **UNDER CONST.,** as appropriate. A proposed use or one that is under construction requires

plans and specs for the appraiser to review. If the construction is the re-habilitation of an existing structure, enter **REHAB.**

▸ **VA**   A home that has either been previously owner-occupied or had all onsite and offsite improvements fully completed for one year or more is eligible for a VA loan guaranty as existing construction.

Newly completed properties (completed less than one year and nev-er owner-occupied) are eligible as new construction if either

■ covered by a one-year VA builder's warranty,

■ enrolled in a HUD-accepted ten-year insured protection plan, or

■ built by a veteran, as the general contractor, for his or her own oc-cupancy.

For any property appraised as either "proposed or under construc-tion" or "new construction," the builder must have a valid builder iden-tification number prior to a VA notice of value being issued. To obtain and maintain a valid, VA-assigned builder ID, all of the following must be fully executed, up-to-date, and on file at the VA office of jurisdiction over the location of the property:

■ VA Form 26-421, Equal Employment Opportunity Certification.

■ VA Form 26-8791, VA Affirmative Marketing Certification.

■ The identifying information and certifications shown in the opening figure of this section, as worded and in the order shown, and either on the builder's letterhead or attached to a statement on the builder's letterhead that references it.

In areas where there is no qualified VA or HUD fee inspector, prop-erties cannot be appraised until they qualify as "new construction" or "existing construction."

Appraisal requests involving veterans who are acting as the general contractor in building a home for their own occupancy must include

■ any construction exhibits needed for appraisal purposes, and

■ the veteran's written agreement to pay for any special VA fee inspec-tions that may be needed to ensure that the work meets VA Minimum Property Requirements for existing (not proposed) construction.

Design (Style)

Enter the name of the architectural design or style of the subject dwelling using terminology common to the area. For example, the structure may be identified by one of the traditional style designations, such as Tudor, Spanish Colonial, Colonial American, Georgian, Victorian, or by house type, such as ranch, Cape Cod, two-story, split-level, and raised ranch.

▸ **HUD/FHA**   Briefly describe the building style using local custom termi-nology. Some examples are Cape Cod, bi-level, split-level, split-foyer, town house, and so on. Do *not* use a builder's model name.

Year Built

Enter the year in which original construction was completed on the subject dwelling.

▸ **Fannie Mae**   In general a property should be within the general age range of the neighborhood. This will be the usual case, simply because most neighborhoods are developed over a relatively short time span. A property outside the general age range will require special consideration.

Unless there is strong evidence of long-term neighborhood stability, a new dwelling in an old neighborhood will carry some marginal risk. Conversely, an old dwelling in a newly developed area is generally acceptable if renovation will result in its conforming with the neighborhood.

Older properties in neighborhoods where the improvements have been maintained in a way that sustains the properties' values are acceptable for maximum financing. Because of their location, these properties frequently will have enough advantages over newer properties in outlying areas to create equal or greater market demand. Certain older properties also may be in demand because of their unique architectural design or other factors.

▸ **HUD/FHA**   Enter actual age. Construction records (if available) may be helpful.

Effective Age (Yrs)

Enter the subject dwelling's effective age—its age in years indicated by the condition and utility of the structure. A building's effective age may or may not coincide with its chronological age. If a building has had better-than-average maintenance, is superior in quality and design, or there is a scarcity of such buildings in the market, its effective age may be less than its actual age. A 50-year-old house, for example, may have an effective age of only 25 years because of rehabilitation, modernization, or strong market demand. On the other hand, a poorly constructed house that has been inadequately maintained may have an effective age greater than its actual age.

▸ **Fannie Mae**   The relationship between the actual and effective ages of the property is a good indication of its condition. A property that has been well maintained generally will have an effective age somewhat lower than its actual age. On the other hand, properties that have an effective age higher than their actual age probably have not been well maintained or may have a particular physical problem. In such cases, in its review of the appraisal the lender must pay particular attention to the condition of the subject property.

Fannie Mae does not place a restriction on the age of eligible dwellings. Consequently mortgages on older dwellings that meet general requirements are acceptable. The improvements for all properties must be of the quality and condition that will meet local building codes and must be acceptable to typical purchasers in the subject market area.

▸ **HUD/FHA**   Enter effective age if appropriate. Estimation of effective age is a subjective judgment of the appraiser. It may be preferable to give a range of years.

A difference between actual and effective ages typically is caused by a level of maintenance or remodeling that may be below or above average. Significant differences between the actual and effective ages should be noted.

■ FOUNDATION

The type of foundation construction and any evidence of water settlement, or insect infestation damage are entered in this part.

Concrete Slab

Enter an X for this item if the house rests on a concrete slab foundation. Slab construction consists of a poured concrete foundation that rests on a footing and has a slab of concrete flooring, usually four inches thick.

Crawl Space

Enter an X for this item if the house has a crawl space. Many houses do not have basements but are built over an excavation that may or may not have a concrete floor, but that is less than the height of a living space. The space between the ground or concrete and the first floor of the house is the crawl space. The minimum depth of such space should be 24 inches under the floor joists to allow access to the underfloor by crawling (hence the name).

> ‣ **HUD/FHA**   If there is a partial crawl space, include the percentage of floor area covered.

Full Basement or Partial Basement

If the house has a basement, indicate whether it is full or partial. The number of new houses with basements has declined steadily, particularly in the warmer areas of the United States, though the basement is still desirable in colder climates to provide insulation, storm shelter, and additonal storage space.

　　Note: If more than one type of foundation is found in a single house, indicate both. For example, if the foundation is one-half basement and one-half crawl space, check both the Basement and Crawl Space boxes.

Basement Area: sq. ft.

Enter the gross basement area in square feet, if the subject has a basement.

> ‣ **HUD/FHA**   Enter the number of square feet.

Basement Finish: %

Calculate and enter the percentage of total basement area that has been finished—that is, converted into usable living space. Enter **0%** if the basement is totally unfinished.

> ‣ **HUD/FHA** Enter the percentage of basement square footage (the figure entered on the line above) that is finished.

Outside Entry/Exit

Enter **YES** if the basement has an outside entrance and indicate whether the entry is at ground level. Enter **NO** if no outside entry or access is available. Ground-level access to the basement usually makes it more valuable as living space. The blank space at the bottom of this part can be used for any additional information or explanation about the basement area.

▸ **HUD/FHA**   Enter **YES** or **NO.** If **YES,** indicate the type of entry.

Sump Pump

Enter **YES** if the house has a sump pump in the basement. If it does not, enter **NO.** A sump pump to drain any accumulation of water from the basement can be a critical feature in an area with a high water table or one that is otherwise prone to flooding.

▸ **HUD/FHA**   Enter **YES** or **NO.**

Evidence of Infestation, Dampness, or Settlement

Infestation

Mark X in the box only if there are signs of insect infestation. The earth is infested with termites and other insects that are very destructive to wood. Before the slab for the foundation is poured, the ground should be chemically treated to poison termites and thus prevent them from coming up through or around the foundation and into the wooden structure. Chemical treatment of lumber used for sills and beams and installation of metal termite shields also provide protection. If a home is infested, termite control and repair by the owner should be included in the terms of the purchase. In some areas, notably California, any corrective work must be completed before a conventional loan will be granted. Be sure to check out the local practice.

▸ **Fannie Mae**   If you indicate that there is evidence of dampness, wood-boring insects, or settlement, comment on the effect on the subject property's marketability and value in an addendum. The lender must either provide satisfactory evidence that the condition was corrected or submit a professionally prepared report indicating that, based on an inspection of the property, the condition does not pose any threat of structural damage to the improvements.

▸ **HUD/FHA**   Look for all types of insects and damage. If there is any question, require a termite inspection.

Dampness

Mark X in the box only if the basement shows signs of dampness.

Wet basements can cause extensive damage. Cement flaking from walls and dark stains on the ceiling and walls are common signs of leaks and seepage. Look also for mildew and dry rot in the basement ceiling beams and structure. Check the condition of the exterior foundation walls around the house. Are there cracks and signs of water penetration? A damp basement can have a significant effect on both marketability and value. Correcting a wet basement condition is often expensive and sometimes impossible if the house was not built properly.

A vapor barrier, one of the best features of today's well-built houses, protects basements from water damage. It is usually a thick polyethylene sheet laid on the earth underneath the house. In slab construction, the barrier is between the concrete floor and the layer of gravel spread over the ground. Although the barrier is completely hidden in slab or basement houses, it should be visible in crawl spaces. Clay drain tiles laid along the outer base of the foundation wall leading away from the house are another protection against basement water.

Note: If you check the box for Dampness, give your opinion of its effect on value in the Additional Comments section or in an addendum to the URAR. If the problem appears serious, you may need to consult a professional inspector or contractor.

Settlement

Check the box here if you see signs of settlement. If there appears to be a settlement problem, you should comment on its seriousness and probable effect on value; however, you are not expected to perform an engineer's function. A recommendation that the client consult a structural engineer to determine the extent of any settlement damage, whether the problem can be cured, and what the work will cost, may need to be made. If necessary, the appraisal report can be made subject to the client obtaining and reviewing a structural engineer's report. A basement is always the lowest level of a house and is usually left unfinished by the builder. If the basement has not been finished, the exposed foundation walls can tell a lot about the structural soundness of the house. For example, look for curves or bows in the walls. They might indicate excessive weight being applied in that area. Small hairline cracks in foundation walls, the result of years of settling and shrinking, ordinarily do not pose a structural threat. On the other hand, cracks that are wider at the top than the bottom, called V-cracks, are cause for alarm. V-cracks are signs that point to a settlement problem.

> ‣ **HUD/FHA**   Check the box if there is evidence of settlement. Check for cracks.

■ EXTERIOR DESCRIPTION: MATERIALS/CONDITION

Examine and describe the exterior of the subject dwelling. For each item in this block

- ■ identify the type of material used for each building component and
- ■ rate (good, average, fair, or poor) the quality of materials, workmanship, and condition of the materials in terms of the standard in the neighborhood.

Foundation Walls

Enter the type of material used for the foundation. Foundations are constructed of cut stone, stone and brick, concrete block, or poured concrete. Poured concrete is the most common foundation material because of its strength and resistance to moisture. Enter **GOOD, AVG, FAIR,** or **POOR.**

> ‣ **HUD/FHA**   Enter the type of construction, such as poured concrete, concrete block, or wood.

Exterior Walls

Enter the type of wall construction (such as wood-frame or masonry) and siding materials used to form the exterior walls of the house. Wood-frame construction is by far the type used most frequently in building single-family houses. Many different types of exterior siding are used as coverings over the house frame. Wood shingles, wood clapboard, aluminum, vinyl, brick veneer, and stucco are the most often seen. Sometimes wood panels, asbestos-cement shingles, and asphalt shingles are used on the exterior walls of homes. Siding materials are meant to make the walls weather tight and to create an attractive facade. Enter **GOOD, AVG, FAIR,** or **POOR.**

> ‣ **HUD/FHA**   Enter the type of construction material. Examples include aluminum, wood siding, brick veneer, porcelain, log, or stucco. If a combination of materials has been used, show the predominant material first.

Roof Surface

Enter the type of material used to cover the roof of the house. Common materials include asphalt shingles (with a base mat of cellulose or fiberglass), wood shingles and shakes, clay and concrete tile, slate, and metal. Enter **GOOD, AVG, FAIR,** or **POOR.**

> ‣ **HUD/FHA**   Enter the type of roof material, such as composition, wood, slate, or tile.

Gutters & Downspouts

Enter the type of material used for gutters along the roof edges and downspouts leading from the gutters to a drainage area. Aluminum and vinyl gutters are now the most common kind as they require virtually no maintenance. Galvanized metal gutters must be kept painted inside and out. Although seldom seen today, wood gutters were once the standard. Enter **GOOD, AVG, FAIR,** or **POOR.**

> ‣ **HUD/FHA**   Enter the type of gutters and downspouts, if any, such as galvanized, aluminum, wood, or plastic. If only part of the house has gutters and downspouts, state where they are located. If there are no gutters or downspouts, enter **NONE.**

Window Type

Enter the predominant window type found in the house and indicate the window frame material used (wood, aluminum, vinyl, and so on). Common window types are described in Figure 5.

> ‣ **HUD/FHA**   Describe the type of window, such as double-hung, casement, or sliding. Identify the construction type, such as aluminum, wood, or vinyl.

Storm Sash/Insulated

Storm sashes (also called storm windows) provide good insulation and can save on fuel costs. Indicate the material and condition. Enter **PARTIAL** if they are not available for some windows. Enter **GOOD, AVG, FAIR,** or **POOR.**

> ‣ **HUD/FHA**   Describe the combination or style of storm sash and screen. If the use is only partial, state the window locations where storm sashes and/or screens are used.

Screens

All windows that open should have screens. If there are screens for the windows, indicate the material and condition. Enter **PARTIAL** if they are not available for some windows, and enter **GOOD, AVG, FAIR,** or **POOR.**

FIGURE 5
Common Window Types

Double-hung

The double-hung window has both an upper and lower sash that slides vertically along separate tracks. This arrangement allows cool air to come in at the bottom and warm air to go out through the top.

Awning

An awning window is hinged at the top and swings open at the bottom, providing good ventilation and protection from the rain.

Horizontal Sliding

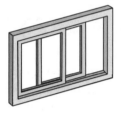

The horizontal sliding window moves back and forth on tracks. As with the double-hung type, only 50 percent of the window can be opened for fresh air.

Hopper

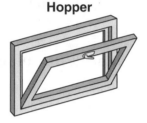

A hopper window is hinged at the bottom and opens into the room. It is best suited to a basement, where the hopper opens above head level and there is little danger of bumping into it.

Casement

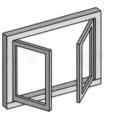

Casement windows are hinged at the side and open outward. One advantage of the casement window is that the entire window can be opened for ventilation.

Jalousie

Jalousie, or louver, windows consist of a series of overlapping horizontal glass louvers that pivot together in a common frame and are opened and closed with a lever or crank.

Fixed

A fixed window usually consists of a wood sash with a large single pane of insulated glass that cannot be opened for ventilation.

Source: William L. Ventolo, Jr., *The Complete Home Inspection Kit* (Chicago, Dearborn Financial Publishing, Inc., 1990), 67.

■ INTERIOR: MATERIALS/CONDITION

This part of the URAR is used to record information about the type, quality, and condition of interior surface materials used throughout the house. Interior finishes include all wall and floor coverings. For each item in this block

■ identify the type of material that covers each surface and

■ rate (good, average, fair, or poor) the quality of materials, workmanship, and condition of the finished surfaces in terms of the standard in the neighborhood.

For example, an entry of **WD/CPT/CT/AVG** means wood floors, carpeting, ceramic tile floors, and a rating of average. Ratings of **FAIR** and **POOR** must be explained in the Additional Comments section or in an addendum.

> ‣ **Fannie Mae**   A less-than-average rating indicates that the rated item is inferior to that of competing properties in the subject market area and will probably meet buyer resistance. A **FAIR** or **POOR** rating will make a property ineligible for maximum financing. Comment on the reasons for the rating and its effect on the subject's marketability and value.

> ‣ **VA**   Comment only on items rated **POOR.**

Floors

Enter the type of materials used for floors; enter **GOOD, AVG, FAIR,** or **POOR,** as appropriate.

Common floor coverings include wall-to-wall carpeting, vinyl tile, vinyl sheet goods (often called linoleum), and hard surfaces such as wood, slate, brick, marble, terrazzo, stone, and ceramic tile.

Walls

Enter the types of wall finish found throughout the interior of the house; enter **GOOD, AVG, FAIR,** or **POOR.** Most interior wall surfaces are covered with wallboard (also called plasterboard, sheetrock, or drywall), plaster, prefinished paneling, or solid wood paneling. Decorative finishes include paint, wallpaper, or wallcoverings such as vinyl, suede, silk, foil, burlap, and cork.

Trim/Finish

Enter the type of material used for trim; enter **GOOD, AVG, FAIR,** or **POOR.** Also called *molding,* trim usually describes the pieces used to finish walls around openings, at corners, and where two different materials meet. Most interior trim is made of Ponderosa pine or Idaho white pine. Trim for painting is milled from pine, gum, poplar, and similar woods; trim for staining comes from a decorative hardwood such as oak, walnut, chestnut, birch, or mahogany. Hardboard and vinyl moldings are the latest substitutes for wood.

Bath Floor

Enter the type of material used for bathroom floors; enter **GOOD, AVG, FAIR,** or **POOR.**

Ceramic tile and vinyl tile and sheeting continue to be the most popular bathroom floor coverings, but other materials such as carpeting, marble, hardwood, rubber, and asphalt tile also are used.

Bath Wainscot

Enter the type of material used for bathroom wainscoting; enter **GOOD, AVG, FAIR,** or **POOR.**

Wainscoting is the lower part of a wall that is finished differently from the wall above. Materials used on shower walls and around tubs and sinks include ceramic tile, plastic tile, fiberglass, and other synthetic water-resistant coverings.

Attic

Complete this section only if the subject house has an attic. If the house does not have an attic, mark X in the None box and leave the rest of the section blank. The attic is the area located between the rafters and the ceiling joists. If the subject has an attic, specify type of access, whether it has a floor, and whether it is heated or finished. Enter any additional features of the attic space that should be noted.

None

Enter X in this box if the house does not have an attic.

Drop Stair

Enter X in this box if access is gained by pulling down a folding ladder or stair-case hidden in the ceiling below the attic floor.

Stairs

Enter X in this box if there are permanent or fixed stairs leading to the attic.

Floor

Enter X in this box if the attic has a floor.

Scuttle

Enter X in this box if entry is through a covered opening in the ceiling.

Finished

Enter X in this box if the attic has finished floors, walls, and ceiling. If only part of the attic is finished, enter **PARTIAL.**

Heated

Enter X in this box if the attic is heated.

Note: Attic space that warrants above-grade living area consideration should be included in the Rooms section.

> ▸ **HUD/FHA**   Additional space such as an attic or room above the garage should be described in terms of how it actually can be used. The essential question is whether it can be included in the above-grade living area.

Heating

Heating systems fall into two basic categories, central heating, and space heating. They draw their heat from one of four sources: warm air, hot water, steam, or the sun. The systems are powered by gas, oil, electricity, or solid fuels such as coal and wood.

Central Heating Systems

There are three basic central heating systems: *warm-air, hot-water,* and *steam.*

In a warm-air system, a furnace heats air that is then distributed to the rooms in the house via ducts. The older gravity-type warm-air heating system operates on the principle that lighter warm air rises and heavier cold air sinks. The modern version, a forced warm-air system, operates on the same principle but adds a fan or blower to increase air movement. The blower forces the air through the ducts so that heat arrives more quickly in all areas of the house. Most homes today have blower-forced warm-air heating systems with continuous air circulation.

A hot-water system operates on the principle of circulation and recirculation of heated water. Water heated in the boiler is pumped through the pipes to the radiators, where heat is distributed into the rooms. As the water cools, it returns to the boiler to start the cycle over again.

Unlike a warm-air system that uses a furnace to heat air, a steam system uses a boiler to generate steam. Water in the boiler is heated until steam forms. The steam circulates through the pipes (without the aid of a pump) until it reaches the radiators in the rooms. Air in the radiators is expelled through air vents. As the steam cools, it turns back into water and returns to the boiler.

Although steam systems are no longer installed in new construction, they are still found in older homes.

Space Heating Systems

Space heaters are the simplest and least expensive of all heating devices. In this category are stoves, circulatory heaters, unit heaters, floor heaters, wall heaters, and resistance heaters. In northern climates, central heating systems are sometimes supplemented with space heaters in entryways, glassed-in porches, bathrooms, and unheated garages used as workshops.

Solar Heating

Most solar heating units suitable for residential use operate by gathering the heat from the sun's rays with one or more *solar collectors*. Water or air is forced through a series of pipes in the solar collector to be heated by the sun's rays. The hot air or water is then stored in a heavily insulated storage tank until it is needed to heat the house.

Solar heating systems do have drawbacks. They are more expensive than conventional heating systems, and if local utility costs are low enough, the addition of a solar system to an existing house may be impractical. The heat production of a solar system is limited by both storage capacity and the need for good (sunny) weather, which means that most such systems must have an independent heating unit for backup.

Heat Pump

A *heat pump* is an electrically powered unit that provides both heating in winter and cooling in summer. It is actually an air-conditioning system that is used in reverse during the winter.

The most commonly used residential-size heat pump takes heat from the outdoor air in winter (sometimes water is used) and pumps it indoors. In summer the cycle is reversed—warm air is taken out of the house.

Heat pumps are most efficient in mild climates where temperatures do not drop below 30°F for any length of time. In northern climates auxiliary heat boosters may be added to the indoor unit. Under normal weather conditions these heat boosters do not operate. When necessary, they turn on to make up the difference in temperature and reduce the strain on the heat pump.

As is true with any air-conditioning system, the heat pump's compressor/condenser is mounted outside the house, and the evaporator is inside.

FWA/HWBB/Radiant/Other

Indicate the type of heating system found in the house; for example, blower-forced warm-air, hot water baseboard, radiant heat under the flooring, or other.

Fuel

Indicate whether the heating system is powered by gas, oil, electricity, coal, wood, or solar energy.

> ▸ **VA**   Mechanical systems must
>
> - be safe to operate;
>
> - be protected from destructive elements;
>
> - have reasonable future utility, durability, and economy; and
>
> - have adequate capacity and quality.
>
>   Solar systems for domestic water heating and/or space heating must
>
> - meet standards in HUD Handbook 4930.2, Solar Heating and Domestic Hot Water Heating Systems, and
>
> - be backed up 100 percent with a conventional thermal energy subsystem or other backup system that will provide the same degree of reliability and performance as a conventional system.
>
>   **Note:** VA field stations may determine that climatic conditions are such that mechanical heating is not required.

Cooling

Central Air Conditioning

Enter an X here if the subject house has central air-conditioning. In areas of the country where summer temperatures warrant, new homes typically are centrally air-conditioned. In other areas, new homes may be prepared ("prepped") for air-conditioning by installing a compatible forced-air heating system.

Air-conditioning units are rated either in BTUs or in tons. Twelve thousand BTUs are the equivalent of a 1-ton capacity. In general a house normally requires 1 ton of cooling capacity for every 600 square feet of air-conditioned space. Thus an 1,800-square-foot house would require a 3-ton system.

Most central forced-air systems operate on gas or electricity, although some use oil for fuel. Some types have the heating and cooling apparatus in two separate units with the condenser/compressor located outside the house and the remaining parts (evaporator, coil, blower, and controls) located either in the attic or in the furnace area. Less-expensive central forced-air systems have the heating and cooling systems built into a single unit.

Most warm-air furnaces today are designed so that a cooling unit can be added at a later time. All types can use the same ducts, blowers, and filters whether they are heating or cooling the house.

Individual

In areas in which the number of hot, humid days doesn't warrant the cost of installing central air-conditioning, individual room air conditioners provide low-cost summer comfort. These units contain a compact compression cooling system. The condenser faces outdoors and removes the heat from the high-pressure hot gas. The evaporator faces the room, and a blower cools the room by drawing room air over the cold evaporator coils.

Remember: Tangible items not permanently attached to real estate, and thus not considered fixtures, are classified as *personal property* and usually are not included in an appraisal of the real property. A window air conditioner, for example, would ordinarily be considered personal property, but if a hole were cut in a wall expressly for the installation of the air conditioner, the unit would probably be considered part of the real estate.

Other

Enter X if some other form of cooling, such as the evaporative cooler ("swamp cooler") found in arid areas, is used in the subject property.

Amenities

Even among structures in the same neighborhood, put up by the same builder at about the same time, using similar materials and quality of construction, many additional features can add value to residential property. The features discussed below are included in the Amenities section. The form also leaves space for a special feature not included in this list to be added by the appraiser.

Woodstove(s)

Enter X in the box if the subject property has one or more woodstoves, and indicate the number. The woodstove should have an outside vent and should be placed on ceramic tile or other fireproof material.

> ▸ **VA**   Homes with a wood-burning stove as a primary heat source must also have a permanently installed conventional heating system that maintains a temperature of at least 50°F in areas with plumbing.

Fireplace(s)

Check the box if the subject property has a fireplace and indicate the number of fireplaces. Most fireplaces are constructed of brick or stone and have a single opening with a damper and hearth. This category does not include the type of freestanding unit that uses a gel-type fuel canister.

  Note: Fireplaces are assumed to be wood-burning unless otherwise stated.

Fence

Check the box if the subject property is enclosed by a fence and indicate the type of fencing material used. The desirability (and thus the value) of fencing varies greatly from one part of the country to another. In the East, solid wood board fences as high as six feet may be found only in the most densely populated urban areas, while such privacy fences are common in residential subdivisions in western and southwestern states. In the Midwest, open lawns predominate, although some homeowners choose to use chain link fences that are no higher than necessary to enclose children and pets.

Patio/Deck

An outdoor living area highlighted by a graded and paved surface can increase a home's desirability, even if only by visually expanding indoor living areas. Check the box if the property has a patio and indicate the surface material (usually concrete, brick, or flagstone) and size of the patio. Note any special feature, such as a barbecue pit, that is likely to add to property value.

  Even homes that lack enough flat yard space for a patio can usually benefit from a wood deck. Check the box if the subject has a wood deck. Note the material used (usually stained redwood, cedar, or pressure-treated pine, or a composite material) as well as the size of the deck area.

Porch

Check the box if the subject has a porch. If the porch is enclosed, that fact should be noted. Though once out of favor, the old-fashioned "sitting porch" is making a strong comeback, particularly with modern designs that echo elements of Victorian architecture. The country farmhouse with a wraparound porch furnished with well-cushioned wicker chairs offers an inviting place to relax. Porches are distinguished from decks by being roofed and, in some cases, enclosed with screening or windows. Because it has a roof, a porch is likely to be painted to match the rest of the house. An enclosed porch, in particular, can be a valuable extension of the indoor living area.

Pool

Check the box if the subject property has a swimming pool and indicate the size of the pool and whether it is above or below ground. In addition to its construction cost, a swimming pool requires regular maintenance that can be time consuming and/or expensive. The presence of a swimming pool thus may add to or detract from property value. In some areas of the Sun Belt states, a swimming pool may be a common amenity and its cost may contribute to property value. In other areas, particularly those with relatively modest housing, a swimming pool may be an extravagance that will not add its cost to total property value. For some prospective buyers, such as those with small children, the presence of a swimming pool may be considered enough of a property detriment to remove that property from consideration. For other prospective buyers, particularly in the luxury home market, a property may be considered incomplete if it does not have a swimming pool.

Other

Enter X here and indicate any special feature, such as a gazebo, that is likely to add to property value.

Car Storage

If the dwelling does not have a garage or carport, mark the None box and leave the rest of this section blank. If there is a garage or carport but it is below neighborhood standards in size or type, explain any resulting effect on value in the Comments section below this section or in an addendum.

None

If this box is marked, give your opinion of its effect on the marketability and value of the house.

Driveway

Enter X in this box if the property has a driveway.

of Cars

If the property has a driveway, indicate the number of cars that can be parked there at one time.

Driveway Surface

If the property has a driveway, enter the type of paving.

> ▸ **HUD/FHA**   Enter type of driveway paving, such as **CONCRETE, ASPHALT,** or **GRAVEL.**

Garage

Enter X in the box if the subject property has a garage.

of Cars

Enter the number of cars the garage can hold.

A garage may be designed to store more than just one or more cars. In many retirement or resort communities, for instance, an extra half-space allows a garage to accommodate a golf cart. In communities with waterfront access, the "boat-deep" garage that is ten feet (or more) longer than a garage designed only for automobiles may be used for boat and trailer storage. Some garages (attached or detached) have a space with the extra height required for a recreational vehicle (RV), with a correspondingly imposing garage door. Explain any unusual features in the Additional Comments section on page 3 of the URAR form.

Carport

Enter an X if the subject property has a carport.

of Cars

Enter the number of cars the carport can hold.

Att.

Enter X in the box if the garage is attached to (shares at least one common wall with) the house.

Det.

Enter X in the box if the garage shares no common wall with the house.

Built-in

Enter X in the box if the garage shares at least one common wall with the house and the second floor of the house extends above the garage.

Appliances

In this section of the URAR, you will identify those appliances or other items of equipment in the subject kitchen that are considered fixtures. A fixture is something that was once personal property but has since been installed or attached to the land or building in a permanent manner; that is, it cannot be removed easily or without damaging the building. Unless specifically excluded in the sales contract, a fixture is regarded by law as part of the real estate and must be included in the valuation process.

Mark X in the box beside each built-in appliance or other item of equipment that is considered a fixture. These must be included in your estimate of market value. If the subject kitchen does not have an appliance or other item of equipment listed, leave that box blank.

Note: Some lines in this section list two different items; for example, Fan/Hood. If the subject kitchen has one item but not the other, cross out the missing item and mark the box.

Refrigerator

Enter X in the box if present as a fixture.

Range/Oven

Enter X in the box if present as a fixture.

Dishwasher

Enter X in the box if present as a fixture.

Disposal

Enter X in the box if present as a fixture.

Microwave

Enter X in the box if present as a fixture.

Washer/Dryer

Enter X in the box if both items are present fixtures.

Other (describe)

If any other appliances are part of the property, such as a separate freezer, enter X in the box and identify the appliance(s).

Finished area above grade contains:

Indicate the finished area of the subject structure that is above grade—number of rooms, number of bedrooms, number of baths, and square feet of living area. Areas of the building that should be mentioned include the following.

- *Below grade:* Finished living area less than about four feet below exterior grade; for example, the below-grade-level finished space in a bi-level, split-level, trilevel, and so on. The value of below grade space, while lower than that of above grade space, would depend on its acceptability in the marketplace. Is such space typical of other properties in the neighborhood? If so, the most appropriate comparables would have the same type of space. Alternatively, the appraiser would use a price-per-square-foot for this space based on sales of similar properties.

- *Basement:* Generally considered fully below exterior grade and *not* counted as gross living area (GLA), even if finished. *Exception:* The lower level of a house built into a hillside or cliff, provided it has windows and a quality of finish equal to or better than the rest of the house.

- *Above grade:* All finished living area at or above exterior grade; for example, space in a ranch, 1½-story (Cape Cod), two story, and so on.

- *Attic:* An attic should be included in the GLA only if the following conditions are met:

  - The quality of finish is equal to other finished areas of the house;

  - The area is heated;

  - The ceiling is an average of seven feet or more in height (if there is a sloping ceiling over part or all of the space); and

  - The space contains windows that provide light and air equal to that available in the other finished areas of the house.

FIGURE 6
Minimum Room Sizes

Name of Space	Living Unit with 1 BR (sq. ft.)	Living Unit with 2 BR (sq. ft.)	Living Unit with 3 BR (sq. ft.)	Living Unit with 4 BR (sq. ft.)	Least Dimension
Living Room	160	160	170	170	11' 0''
Dining Room	80	80	95	110	8' 0''
BR (Primary)	120	120	120	120	9' 4''
BR (Secondary)	–	80	80	80	8' 4''
Total BR Area	120	200	280	360	

Rooms

Enter the total number of rooms above grade. Areas such as foyers, baths, unfinished attics, and laundry rooms are normally not included in this count. Figure 6 is from the *HUD Minimum Property Standards* for a single-family residence.

Bedrooms

Enter the total number of bedrooms above grade.

Bath(s)

Enter the total number of bathrooms above grade.

Square Feet of Gross Living Area Above Grade

Calculate and record the total square feet of living area above grade. Figure 7 describes how gross living area (GLA) is measured.

▸ **Fannie Mae**   Fannie Mae considers a level to be below grade if any portion of it is below grade, regardless of the quality of its finish or the window area of the room. Therefore a walk-out basement with finished rooms would *not* be included in the above-grade room count.

Nevertheless, rooms not included in the above-grade room count may add substantially to the value of the property, particularly if the quality of the finish is high. For that reason, report the basement or other partially below-grade areas separately and make appropriate adjustments for them on the Basement & Finished Rooms Below Grade line in the SALES COMPARISON APPROACH grid. To ensure consistency in the sales comparison analysis, compare above-grade areas to above-grade areas and below-grade areas to below-grade areas. However, if it becomes necessary to deviate from this approach because of the style of the subject property or of any comparables, explain the reason for the deviation and clearly describe the comparisons being made.

▸ **HUD/FHA**   Enter the total square footage *above* grade. In general a room totally underground is not as valuable as one above ground. Calculate the overall square footage of each level from the exterior dimensions of the structure.

The living area of a house is the area enclosed by the outside dimensions of the heated and air-conditioned portions of the house. This excludes basements (even if finished and heated), open porches, garages, unfinished attics, and so on.

When measuring a house in preparation for calculating living area, follow these steps:

1. Draw a sketch of the foundation.
2. Measure *all* outside walls.
3. If the house has an attached garage, treat the inside garage walls that are common to the house as outside walls of the house.
4. Measure the garage.
5. Round off all measuring to the nearest half-foot (for example, 32'4" becomes 32½') for ease of calculating.
6. Before leaving the house, check to see that net dimensions of opposite sides are equal. If they are not, remeasure.
7. Section off the sketch into rectangles.
8. Calculate the area of each rectangle.
9. Add up the areas, being careful to *subtract* the area of the garage, *if necessary*.
10. Before leaving the house, *always* recheck all dimensions.

Additional features (special energy efficient items, etc.)

Enter here any features of the subject property not previously described, such as a wet bar, skylight, hot tub, sauna, greenhouse, security device, and so on. This is also the space to note any property features, besides insulation, that contribute to the energy efficiency of the home. Such items include fans, fireplace inserts, low-emissivity (low-E) glass, active or passive solar-heating systems, and high-efficiency furnaces and water heaters.

▸ **Fannie Mae**   An energy-efficient property is one that uses cost-effective design, materials, equipment, and site orientation to conserve nonrenewable fuels. Special energy-saving items should be recognized in the appraisal process. The nature of these items and their contribution to value will vary throughout the country because of differing climatic conditions and utility costs.

You will also list energy-efficient items in the SALES COMPARISON APPROACH grid on page 2 of the URAR and note the overall contribution of these items to the market value of the subject property.

▸ **HUD/FHA**   Identify any special energy-efficient items such as extra insulation, attic vents, heat pump, or design of home (such as solar or earth sheltered).

Describe the condition of the property (including needed repairs, deterioration, renovations, remodeling, etc.)

Indicate the condition of improvements, including whether the subject structure suffers from any form of deterioration and what corrective action, if any, needs to be taken.

As they age, most structures suffer some value-reducing effects on their physical qualities, resulting from ordinary use, disintegration, and action of the elements. The degree to which a structure is subject to deterioration depends mainly on the quality of materials and workmanship that were put into it and the degree to which the structure has been maintained. Deterioration may be normal or minor in a well-constructed, well-maintained house. However, in a poorly constructed, poorly maintained house, deterioration will occur much more rapidly, often resulting in serious damage to walls, foundations, roof, or floor construction.

The effects of deterioration may be a leaky roof, internal water damage, corroded plumbing lines, cracked plaster, peeling paint, worn flooring, broken steps, and numerous other physical deficiencies that make the property less desirable to potential buyers.

Functional depreciation may stem from either a deficiency within the property (such as poor traffic patterns, inferior design, inefficient room layout, or outmoded style) or a superadequacy. A superadequacy is an overimprovement, such as excessive quality or size of building components and equipment in a moderately priced neighborhood.

External depreciation is a loss in value due to factors outside the property boundaries. Typical causes are

- population movements that either *reduce* the total number of people available to buy property or *replace* higher-economic-level buyers with those on a lower economic level;

- growth of industrial and commercial areas that, in the absence of adequate zoning, encroach on residential areas;

- proximity to airports with their noise and danger potential;

- nuisances and hazards such as excessive noise, smoke, and traffic;

- excessive real estate taxes and assessments; and

- deterioration in quality and accessibility of schools, shopping, and community facilities.

Note: Comments should be consistent with the information on depreciation given in the COST APPROACH section on page 3 of the URAR.

▸ **Fannie Mae** Report the condition of the improvements in factual, specific terms. Any condition that may affect the value or marketability of the subject property must be reported to ensure that the property is described adequately. Address any needed repairs or any physical, functional, or external inadequacies. Report the detrimental condition of improvements even if that condition is also typical for competing properties. For instance, if a property is characterized by deferred maintenance or a lack of updating, you should note that fact even if the same condition applies to competing properties in the neighborhood.

▸ **VA** Property in a badly deteriorated condition is not eligible for appraisal unless VA agrees there is a reasonable likelihood that it can be repaired to meet VA Minimum Property Requirements (MPRs) prior to loan closing.

Are there any physical deficiencies or adverse conditions that affect the livability, soundness, or structural integrity of the property? Yes or No; If Yes, describe

This new addition to the URAR is intended to clarify the role of the appraiser in disclosing any adverse environmental conditions on the subject property or in the vicinity that were revealed during the course of the appraiser's work.

Note that, although the appraiser must reveal any adverse environmental conditions that were uncovered, the Statement of Assumptions and Limiting Conditions, which appears on page 4 of the URAR form, makes clear that the appraiser's responsibility extends only to those conditions actually observed by the appraiser or of which the appraiser has become aware during the course of the appraisal. The appraiser is not required to make a search for the presence of specific conditions and is not required to guarantee the absence of conditions other than those noted.

Nevertheless, the Uniform Standards of Professional Appraisal Practice, in the Competency Provision that appears in Section 1, require that the appraiser have the knowledge and experience necessary to complete the appraisal assignment competently, or disclose any lack of knowledge and/or experience to the client before accepting the assignment, take all steps necessary or appropriate to complete the assignment competently, and in the appraisal report, describe the lack of knowledge and/or experience and the steps taken to complete the appraisal assignment competently. The appraiser is presumed to have a certain degree of familiarity with the area in which the subject property is located. As stated in the Comment that follows the Competency Provision to USPAP Section 1, if lacking this knowledge, the appraiser must take whatever steps are necessary to "understand the nuances of the local market and the supply and demand factors relating to the specific property type and the location involved."

To the extent that adverse environmental conditions affecting market value, such as the presence of hazardous wastes or toxic substances, would be suspected and recognized by someone familiar with the area, they should be identified in the appraisal report and their effect on value explained.

> ▸ **Fannie Mae**   The appraiser must report what he or she has become aware of through the inspection of the property and the normal research involved in performing the appraisal.

> ▸ **VA**   If there are local building authority requirements due to building code enforcement or urban renewal, either

>> ■ provide evidence with the appraisal request that those requirement(s) are satisfied, or

>> ■ the notice of value will be conditioned to require such evidence.

Does the property generally conform to the neighborhood (functional utility, style, condition, use, construction, etc.)? Yes or No; If No, describe.

Enter an X in the Yes or No box to indicate whether or not the subject property is typical of other properties in the neighborhood. This is critical if comparable properties are to be found for the Sales Comparison Approach. Explain any differences between the subject property and typical properties in the neighborhood.

APPRAISAL 1

IMPROVEMENTS	General Description			Foundation		Exterior Description	materials/condition	Interior	materials/condition
	Units	X	One	One with Accessory Unit	X	Concrete Slab	Crawl Space	Foundation Walls	Concrete/good	Floors	Hdwd/cpt/good
	# of Stories					Full Basement	Partial Basement	Exterior Walls	Cedar/stucco/good	Walls	Drywall/good
	Type	X	Det.	Att.	S-Det/End Unit	Basement Area	sq. ft.	Roof Surface	Asphalt shingle/good	Trim/Finish	Wood/good
	X	Existing	Proposed	Under Const.	Basement Finish	%	Gutters & Downspouts	Aluminum/good	Bath Floor	Cer/good
	Design (Style)	Ranch/Typical			Outside Entry/Exit	Sump Pump	Window Type	Single-hung/good	Bath Wainscot	Cer/good
	Year Built	1994			Evidence of	Infestation	Storm Sash/Insulated		Car Storage	None
	Effective Age (Yrs)	5-7			Dampness	Settlement	Screens	Yes/good	Driveway	# of Cars

	Attic		X	None		Heating	X	FWA		HWBB		Radiant		Amenities			WoodStove(s)#	Driveway Surface	Asphalt
		Drop Stair			Stairs		Other		Fuel				X	Fireplace(s) # 1	X	Fence		X	Garage	# of Cars	2
		Floor			Scuttle		Cooling	X	Central Air Conditioning		X	Patio/Deck	X	Porch		Carport	# of Cars
		Finished			Heated		Individual		Other		X	Pool		Other		X	Att.	Det.	Built-in

Appliances | X | Refrigerator | X | Range/Oven | X | Dishwasher | X | Disposal | | Microwave | X | Washer/Dryer | X | Other (describe) | Dryer

Finished area **above** grade contains: 7 Rooms 3 Bedrooms 2.00 Bath(s) 2,120 Square Feet of Gross Living Area Above Grade

Additional features (special energy efficient items, etc.) Ceiling fans in every room; roof vent; high-efficiency heating and cooling system

Describe the condition of the property (including needed repairs, deterioration, renovations, remodeling, etc.). Improvements overall are up-to-date and in good condition, typical of this neighborhood; depreciation is thus no more than approximately 10% of reproduction cost; no immediate repairs to major systems or structure are indicated.

Are there any physical deficiencies or adverse conditions that affect the livability, soundness, or structural integrity of the property? ☐ Yes ☐ No If Yes, describe
A routine inspection was made and no hazardous substances or detrimental environmental conditions were found on or near the subject property.

Does the property generally conform to the neighborhood (functional utility, style, condition, use, construction, etc.)? X Yes ☐ No If No, describe

---

In Appraisal 1, the subject property is an 11-year-old, single-family ranch with an effective age estimated at five to seven years.

The house has a concrete slab foundation with no apparent settlement or infestation problems. The roof is covered by heavyweight, top-grade asphalt shingles. Maintenance-free aluminum gutters are pitched toward the downspouts so that rainwater can drain away properly. The exterior siding is a combination of cedar and stucco. Window frames are made of aluminum; all windows have screens. All building components are in good condition.

The subject property contains a foyer, three bedrooms, two baths, kitchen, living room, dining room, laundry room, and glassed-in porch area with carpet, ceiling fans, and its own heating and air-conditioning system. Gross area, based on outside dimensions, is 2,645 square feet—including a 21' × 25' attached garage that is approached over a paved asphalt driveway. There is no attic. The house has an energy-efficient central forced-air heating and cooling system fueled by electricity. The system is in good shape with adequate output.

Additional data on interior and exterior improvements include the following:

- *Hardwood floors in kitchen, dining room, foyer, and hallways—good condition*
- *Ceramic tile floor and wainscoting in bathrooms—average condition*
- *Finished oak flooring covered with wall-to-wall carpeting in other rooms—good condition*
- *Ponderosa pine trim throughout—good condition*
- *Stone wood-burning fireplace in family room*
- *Wall covering of drywall, taped, and painted or papered—good condition*

■ *Kitchen built-ins—oven and range, refrigerator, garbage disposal, and washer and dryer*

■ *Other appliances—refrigerator*

■ *Enclosed porch of 458 square feet at the rear of the house*

■ *In-ground swimming pool, 15' by 30', enclosed in a bronze A-frame cage*

■ *Patio of approximately 500 square feet around the swimming pool*

■ *Wood fencing enclosing the rear yard*

E X E R C I S E :   A P P R A I S A L   2

General Description	Foundation	Exterior Description materials/condition	Interior materials/condition
Units ☐ One ☐ One with Accessory Unit	☐ Concrete Slab ☐ Crawl Space	Foundation Walls	Floors
# of Stories	☐ Full Basement ☐ Partial Basement	Exterior Walls	Walls
Type ☐ Det. ☐ Att. ☐ S-Det./End Unit	Basement Area sq. ft.	Roof Surface	Trim/Finish
☐ Existing ☐ Proposed ☐ Under Const.	Basement Finish %	Gutters & Downspouts	Bath Floor
Design (Style)	☐ Outside Entry/Exit ☐ Sump Pump	Window Type	Bath Wainscot
Year Built	Evidence of ☐ Infestation	Storm Sash/Insulated	Car Storage ☐ None
Effective Age (Yrs)	☐ Dampness ☐ Settlement	Screens	☐ Driveway # of Cars
Attic ☐ None	Heating ☐ FWA ☐ HWBB ☐ Radiant	Amenities ☐ Woodstove(s) #	Driveway Surface
☐ Drop Stair ☐ Stairs	☐ Other Fuel	☐ Fireplace(s) # ☐ Fence	☐ Garage # of Cars
☐ Floor ☐ Scuttle	Cooling ☐ Central Air Conditioning	☐ Patio/Deck ☐ Porch	☐ Carport # of Cars
☐ Finished ☐ Heated	☐ Individual ☐ Other	☐ Pool ☐ Other	☐ Att. ☐ Det. ☐ Built-in
Appliances ☐Refrigerator ☐Range/Oven ☐Dishwasher ☐Disposal ☐Microwave ☐Washer/Dryer ☐Other (describe)			
Finished area **above** grade contains: Rooms Bedrooms Bath(s) Square Feet of Gross Living Area Above Grade			
Additional features (special energy efficient items, etc.)			
Describe the condition of the property (including needed repairs, deterioration, renovations, remodeling, etc.).			
Are there any physical deficiencies or adverse conditions that affect the livability, soundness, or structural integrity of the property? ☐ Yes ☐ No If Yes, describe			
Does the property generally conform to the neighborhood (functional utility, style, condition, use, construction, etc.)? ☐ Yes ☐ No If No, describe			

Complete the blank URAR IMPROVEMENTS section provided above for Appraisal 2, using the following information. When you have finished, check your work against the completed Appraisal 2 in the Answer Key.

The subject property is an 18-year-old one-story detached ranch-style house of 1,980 square feet, with a full basement that is approximately 75 percent finished and has a sump pump.

The wood-frame house, which was built on-site, has vinyl siding with brick veneer trim and a mineral fiber shingle roof. Gutters and downspouts are made of aluminum. The wood-framed double-hung windows have thermopane glass and aluminum combination storms and screens.

There are no signs of dampness or smells of mildew in the basement, which is entered from the kitchen. There is no evidence of settlement in the walls or floor. The ceilings and floors in the rest of the house seem plumb, square, and level.

The finished basement area, which is used as a recreation room, has an acoustic tile ceiling, wood-paneled walls, and vinyl tile flooring over a plywood subfloor. There are no visible signs of termites or other wood-boring insects. In fact, a recent professional termite inspection proved negative.

The house contains the following above-grade rooms: foyer, living room, dining room, kitchen, family room, four bedrooms, and two baths (each with toilet, sink, and tub/shower); total gross living area above grade is 1,980 square feet.

The subject property has wall-to-wall carpeting throughout the above-grade living area, except for ceramic tile flooring in the kitchen and baths. All wall surfaces are painted drywall, with painted pine trim. All interior doors are six-panel wood, painted. There is a masonry fireplace in the family room. All interior surfaces are in good condition.

The heating and cooling systems are gas-fired forced-air with central air-conditioning. They are in good condition and are adequate for a home of this size. According to the homeowner they are five years old.

The kitchen has built-in oven and range top, microwave oven with fan over the range top, dishwasher, and garbage disposal. The refrigerator is the personal property of the owners and is not included in the sale. Kitchen cabinets are standard-grade oak, with a stained and varnished finish. There is no attic.

Exterior amenities include a wood deck of 300 square feet at the rear of the house. The subject property also has a two-car detached garage with an electric double garage door opener and separate side entrance over a concrete driveway. The wood-frame structure is typical of the neighborhood and is in good condition.

Overall, the construction quality of the home's interior is good, as is its condition. Because the subject is part of a subdivision built primarily by the same builder, room sizes and layout vary little throughout the neighborhood. Closets and other storage spaces are typically adequate. The home is also typical of the neighborhood in having no special energy-efficient items and has never been remodeled.

SECTION 6: SALES COMPARISON APPROACH

There are	comparable properties currently offered for sale in the subject neighborhood ranging in price from $				to $		
There are	comparable sales in the subject neighborhood within the past twelve months ranging in sale price from $				to $		

FEATURE	SUBJECT	COMPARABLE SALE # 1		COMPARABLE SALE # 2		COMPARABLE SALE # 3	
Address							
Proximity to Subject							
Sale Price	$		$		$		$
Sale Price/Gross Liv. Area	$ sq. ft.	$ sq. ft.		$ sq. ft.		$ sq. ft.	
Data Source(s)							
Verification Source(s)							
VALUE ADJUSTMENTS	DESCRIPTION	DESCRIPTION	+(-) $ Adjustment	DESCRIPTION	+(-) $ Adjustment	DESCRIPTION	+(-) $ Adjustment
Sale or Financing Concessions							
Date of Sale/Time							
Location							
Leasehold/Fee Simple							
Site							
View							
Design (Style)							
Quality of Construction							
Actual Age							
Condition							
Above Grade	Total Bdrms. Baths	Total Bdrms. Baths		Total Bdrms. Baths		Total Bdrms. Baths	
Room Count							
Gross Living Area	sq. ft.	sq. ft.		sq. ft.		sq. ft.	
Basement & Finished Rooms Below Grade							
Functional Utility							
Heating/Cooling							
Energy Efficient Items							
Garage/Carport							
Porch/Patio/Deck							
Net Adjustment (Total)		☐ + ☐ - $		☐ + ☐ - $		☐ + ☐ - $	
Adjusted Sale Price of Comparables		Net Adj. % / Gross Adj. % $		Net Adj. % / Gross Adj. % $		Net Adj. % / Gross Adj. % $	

I ☐ did ☐ did not research the sale or transfer history of the subject property and comparable sales. If not, explain

My research ☐ did ☐ did not reveal any prior sales or transfers of the subject property for the three years prior to the effective date of this appraisal.

Data source(s)

My research ☐ did ☐ did not reveal any prior sales or transfers of the comparable sales for the year prior to the date of sale of the comparable sale.

Data source(s)

Report the results of the research and analysis of the prior sale or transfer history of the subject property and comparable sales (report additional prior sales on page 3).

ITEM	SUBJECT	COMPARABLE SALE # 1	COMPARABLE SALE # 2	COMPARABLE SALE # 3
Date of Prior Sale/Transfer				
Price of Prior Sale/Transfer				
Data Source(s)				
Effective Date of Data Source(s)				

Analysis of prior sale or transfer history of the subject property and comparable sales

Summary of Sales Comparison Approach

Indicated Value by Sales Comparison Approach $

After all the factual information about the subject property has been gathered and recorded, the next step is to develop an opinion of its market value. Page 2 of the URAR form starts with the sales comparison approach.

The sales comparison approach is the most widely used appraisal method for valuing residential properties. In this approach, an opinion of value is developed by comparing the subject property to recently sold, similar, nearby properties. The basic premise of the sales comparison approach is that the value of the subject is directly related to the sale prices of the comparables. The mathematical formula for the sales comparison approach is

$$\text{Sales Price of Comparable Property} \pm \text{Adjustments} = \text{Indicated Value of Subject Property}$$

The SALES COMPARISON APPROACH section of the URAR form lists most of the significant property variables that may require price adjustments. To arrive at a value opinion using this approach, the appraiser must

- describe the subject property and comparables,
- adjust the sales price of each comparable to account for property differences,
- analyze the impact of any prior recent sale or pending sale, option, or listing of the subject property and comparables, and
- determine the indicated value that best reflects the market value of the subject property.

COMPARABLE PROPERTIES

The appraiser's ability to obtain good comparables is limited by the level of recent sales activity in the subject's neighborhood.

At the top of the SALES COMPARISON APPROACH section you are asked to enter the following information:

- The number and price range of comparable property *listings* in the subject neighborhood
- The number and price range of comparable *sales* in the subject neighborhood within the past 12 months

THE ADJUSTMENT PROCESS

In an ideal market for applying the sales comparison approach, a large number of recent sales would be available between buyers and sellers who are knowledgeable and familiar with the local market, the sold properties would be substantially similar to the subject property, and financing would be consistent with current terms and conditions. In reality two properties are seldom, if ever, exactly alike. Each comparable must therefore be compared to the subject and the sale price of the comparable adjusted to account for any dissimilar features.

Adjustments are made to the sale price of a comparable property by adding the value of features present in the subject but not in the comparable, and subtracting the value of features present in the comparable but not in the subject. The adjusted sale prices of the comparables represent the probable value range of the subject property. From this range a single market value opinion can be selected that most accurately reflects the unique nature of the subject property. The objective of the adjustment process, then, is to estimate the price at which the comparable property would have sold if its significant characteristics were the same as those of the subject property.

The most difficult step in using the sales comparison approach is determining the dollar amount of each adjustment. The accuracy of an appraisal using this approach depends on the use of reliable adjustment values. Ideally, if properties could be found that were exactly alike except for one variable, the adjustment value of that variable would be the difference in selling prices of the two properties.

> *Example:* House A is very similar to house B, except that house A has central air-conditioning and house B does not. House A sold for $258,500; house B sold for $253,000. Because central air-conditioning is the only significant difference between the two properties, its market value is the difference between the selling price of $258,500 and the selling price of $253,000. Thus the value of central air-conditioning *in this market and as of the time of these sales* is $5,500.

This reasoning is called matched pair, or paired sales, analysis. However, an adjustment supported by just one matched pair, as in the example, may be unreliable. In actual practice, the appraiser should analyze as many properties as needed to isolate each significant variable and to substantiate the accuracy of an adjustment value. Most neighborhoods have very similar properties, so usually this is not as difficult as it may first appear.

■ ADVANTAGES AND LIMITATIONS

The most obvious advantage of the sales comparison approach is its simplicity. It is not complex either as a concept or as a mechanical technique. Furthermore, its simplicity and directness appeal to both clients and the courts. When there are sufficient, recent, and reliable market transactions, the sales comparison approach is probably the most logical and objective approach to value. The chief limitation of the sales comparison approach is that it depends on a substantial volume of reliable information for its validity. When the number of market transactions is insufficient, the reliability of the approach is seriously reduced. Adjustments may be lengthy and complex in some cases, with relatively little available basis for evaluating differences. Finally, it is sometimes difficult to determine whether a transaction is a bona fide, arm's-length sale or whether the sale price was distorted by a hidden motive.

■ COMPLETING THE ADJUSTMENT GRID

Although adjustments may be made for some differences between the subject property and the comparables, most of the factors listed should be similar.

- Style of house
- Age
- Number of rooms
- Number of bedrooms

- Number of bathrooms
- Size of lot
- Size of dwelling
- Terms of sale
- Type of construction
- General condition

If possible the comparable properties should be from the same neighborhood as the subject property. If you use comparable sales outside the neighborhood, an explanation should be included in an addendum attached to the report.

Even though the URAR requires data on only three comparable sales, you should have investigated many more properties before determining the three most appropriate for the appraisal. The number of sales needed for an accurate estimate of market value cannot be easily specified, but the fewer the sales, the more carefully they need to be investigated. The amount of data considered by you to support conclusions may be much more extensive than the specific data shown in the appraisal report. For example, an analysis of the sales properties not used directly in the report may be helpful in establishing neighborhood values, price trends, and time adjustments.

> ▸ **Fannie Mae**   The sales comparison approach to value, traditionally referred to as the *market data approach,* is an analysis of comparable sales, contract offerings, and current listings of properties that are the most comparable to the subject property. However, Fannie Mae requires the appraiser to report recent past sales and current pending transactions on only the subject property and comparable sales included in the appraisal report. Each comparable sale must be verified, analyzed, and adjusted for differences between the comparable property and the subject property.
>
> Analyze each comparable property used in the sales comparison approach for differences and similarities between it and the property being appraised. Make appropriate adjustments for location; terms and conditions of sale; date of sale; and physical characteristics of the properties.
>
> Comparable property sales figures must be adjusted *to* the subject property—except for sales and financing concessions, which are adjusted to the market at the time of sale. The subject property is the standard against which the comparable sales are evaluated and adjusted. Thus if an item in the comparable property is superior to that in the subject property, a minus (–) adjustment is required to bring the value of that item *down* to the value of that feature in the subject property. Conversely, if an item in the comparable property is inferior to that in the subject property, a plus (+) adjustment is required to bring the value of that item *up* to the value of that feature in the subject property. If an item in a comparable property is equal to that in the subject property, no adjustment is required.
>
> The proper selection of comparable properties minimizes both the need for, and the size of, any dollar adjustments. Occasionally there may be no similar or truly comparable sales for a particular property, because of the uniqueness of the property or other conditions. In such cases you must use your knowledge and judgment to select comparable sales that represent the best indicators of value for the subject property and to

make adjustments to reflect the actions of typical purchasers in the market. Dollar adjustments should reflect the market's reaction to the difference in the properties, not necessarily the cost of the difference. Swimming pools, electronic air filters, intercom systems, elaborately finished basements, carpets, and other special features generally do not increase value by the full amount of their cost.

▸ **HUD/FHA**   Always select the comparables that have the fewest dissimilarities for the URAR report. It is important to note that the accuracy of the sales comparison approach is dependent on the appraiser's use of reliable adjustment values.

■ THE SALES COMPARISON APPROACH GRID

There are five column headings on the Sales Comparison Approach grid: Feature, Subject, Comparable Sale #1, Comparable Sale #2, and Comparable Sale #3.

Feature

The important factors that affect property value are listed here.

Subject

In this column, enter the required information for the subject property. The easiest way to complete the sales comparison section is to enter all details of the subject property, then do the same for each comparable in turn.

Comparable sale #1

Enter the required information for the first comparable selected.

Comparable sale #2

Enter the required information for the second comparable selected.

Comparable sale #3

Enter the required information for the third comparable selected.

Address

Enter the street address or rural route number. Enough information must be provided to locate the property. Be sure the subject's address is the same as the address entered in the SUBJECT section on page 1 of the form.

▸ **HUD/FHA**   Enter the address that can be used to locate each property. If necessary, include the name of the community. For rural properties, list the location by road name and nearest intersection and indicate on which side of the road the property is located.

Proximity to Subject

Enter the approximate distance—in terms of blocks, fractions of a mile, and miles—and the direction of each comparable property from the subject; for example, ¼ **MILE NE.**

You should comment on any comparable property located a substantial distance away from the subject property.

> ▸ **Fannie Mae**   Be specific when describing the comparable's proximity to the subject property; for example, **TWO BLOCKS SOUTH.** Whenever possible, use comparable sales from the same neighborhood as the subject, because those sales should reflect the same positive and negative locational characteristics. The use of comparables that are located in competing neighborhoods is acceptable as long as the appraiser adequately documents his or her analysis and explains why these comparables were used.

> ▸ **VA**   Distance and direction should be given when describing a comparable sale's proximity to the subject; for example, **THREE BLOCKS EAST** or **FIVE MILES NORTHWEST.** A suitable reference map would also be acceptable.

Sale Price

Enter the reported sale price of each comparable property. If there is no current pending sale price for the subject, leave that space blank.

> ▸ **Fannie Mae**   The sale price of each comparable sale should be within the general range of the opinion of market value for the subject property. A $100,000 comparable sale for a $75,000 subject property would raise questions about the validity of the comparable.

> ▸ **HUD/FHA**   Enter the total price paid by the buyer, including extras.

Sale Price/Gross Liv. Area

Enter the price per square foot of gross living area for the subject and comparables. Divide the sale price of the property by the number of square feet of gross living area in the dwelling. For example, if the sale price is $250,000 and the gross living area is 2,000 square feet, then the Sale Price/Gross Liv. Area is $125 per square foot. Gross living area for the subject dwelling can be found in three different sections of the URAR form: Improvements on page 1, the Cost Approach on page 3, and the Sales Comparison Approach discussed here.

Note: The price per square foot of living area computed here is *not* the same as the price per square foot used to estimate reproduction cost on page 3 of the URAR form. In the sales comparison approach, the price per square foot is used simply as a way to compare the relative sales prices of the subject and comparables and is not intended to be an accurate reflection of the reproduction or replacement cost of their improvements.

> ▸ **HUD/FHA**   Enter the price per square foot based on the number of square feet of living area *above grade.*

> ▸ **VA**   Compute the price per square foot of gross living area *only* if it is considered a valid method of comparison.

■ SOURCES AND VERIFICATION OF MARKET DATA

There are many sources of market data, ranging from public records at the county assessor's office to private organizations such as multiple listing services (MLS). Each source may be useful for different types of information. You can confirm the reliability of the information you collect by cross-checking the data with another source.

Data Source(s)

Enter the source of the market data used, such as personal inspection, parties to the transaction (buyer, seller, and their agents), lender, public records, multiple listing service, or some similar response.

Verification Source(s)

Enter the source from which you verified the accuracy of the data collected. Basic sources may include public records, the appraiser's own files, multiple listing services, REALTORS®, and lenders.

▸ **Fannie Mae**　Because an appraiser's opinion of market value is no better than the reliability of the comparable data used, you must exercise due diligence to ensure the reliability of comparable sales data. The quality of the data available for single-family residential properties varies from source to source and from one locality to another. In view of this, a single data source may be adequate if the source provides quality sales data that is confirmed or verified by closed or settled transactions. If your basic data source does not confirm or verify the sales data, however, you will need to use additional sources.

When comparable sales data are provided by a party having a financial interest in either the sale or financing of the subject property, you must reverify the data with a party who does not have a financial interest in the subject transaction.

▸ **HUD/FHA**　Enter the name of the source or location where price and property information was obtained, such as tax stamps, MLS, and so on. Also show the type of financing, such as **CONV., FHA,** or **VA.**

▸ **VA**　In verifying sales, you can use a single source if you have written confirmation of the sale—such as a sheet from a multiple listing service. If you don't have written confirmation, you must use additional sources to obtain verification.

■ VALUE ADJUSTMENTS

Up to this point you have recorded only descriptive or factual data about the subject and comparables. The remaining items in the property variables list may require plus or minus adjustments. In most home appraisals, good comparables usually are available, thus requiring few adjustments. Remember, however, that all adjustments must be supported by documented market evidence. In most cases market-based price adjustments can be developed through matched pairs (or paired sales) analysis.

> **HUD/FHA** Location, Site, View, Design and Appeal, Quality of Construction, Age, Condition, and Functional Utility (Column 1) are all subjective value factors that require subjective adjustments. Make sure that your adjustments are reasonable—that is, not excessive. Overvaluation of property very often can be traced to an excessive adjustment somewhere in this section.

■ DESCRIPTION

Enter all of the required information on the listed property or transaction characteristics for the subject property, then the comparables.

■ + (–) $ ADJUSTMENT

Enter a dollar value for any listed feature that differs significantly between the subject and a comparable. Comparable sales data should be adjusted *to* the subject property. The subject property is the standard against which the comparable sales are evaluated and adjusted. Thus, the dollar value will be a plus adjustment to the sale price of the comparable if the feature makes the subject more valuable than the comparable. The dollar value will be a minus adjustment to the sale price of the comparable if the feature makes the subject less valuable than the comparable.

Sale or Financing Concessions

This is the first *value adjustment* to consider. Describe any special sale or financing arrangement that may have affected the sale price of a comparable property, such as a mortgage assumption, buydown, installment sales contract, or wraparound loan. Then enter the estimated value of the adjustment, if any, and provide an explanation in the ADDITIONAL COMMENTS section on page 3 or in an addendum attached to the report form.

If a gifted down payment program, such as AmeriDream, Heart, or Nehemiah, has been used to help finance a purchase, that fact should be noted, as well as its likely impact on the purchase price. A seller making a gift of part or all of the down payment is likely to resist lowering the initial asking price for the property and may in fact set a higher than usual asking price to accommodate the anticipated gift.

The appraiser should also be on the alert for any situation in which the MLS listing price for a property is increased after the property has gone under contract in order to make the contract price appear to be no more than the listing price. Such fraudulent conduct by a listing agent can distort the data used by the appraiser.

> **Fannie Mae** The dollar amount of sales or financing concessions paid by the seller must be reported for the comparables if the information is reasonably available. Generally, sales or financing data for comparable sales—such as the mortgage amount, loan type, interest rate, term, and any fees or concessions the seller paid—are available. Be sure to obtain this information from an individual who was a party to the comparable transaction (the broker, buyer, or seller) or from a data source you con-

sider reliable. Fannie Mae recognizes that there may be some situations in which sales or financing information is not available because of legal restrictions or other disclosure-related problems. In such cases you must explain why the information is not available; however, Fannie Mae will not accept an explanation indicating that you did not make an effort to verify the information. In all other cases you must provide the sales and financing concession information that was available (and verified) for the comparables. If the appraisal report form does not provide enough space to discuss this information, make adjustments for the concessions on the form and explain them in the ADDITIONAL COMMENTS section or in an addendum to the appraisal report.

Examples of sales or financing concessions include interest rate buy-downs or other below-market-rate financing, loan discount points, loan origination fees, closing costs customarily paid by the buyer, payment of condominium or PUD association fees, refunds of (or credit for) the borrower's expenses, absorption of monthly payments, assignment of rent payments, and the inclusion of nonrealty items in the transaction. The amount of the negative adjustment to be made to each comparable with sales or financing concessions is equal to any increase in the purchase price of the comparable that the appraiser determines to be attributable to the concessions.

The need to make negative adjustments and the amount of the adjustments to the comparables for sales and financing concessions are not based on how typical the concessions might be for a segment of the market area—large sales concessions can be relatively typical in a particular segment of the market and still result in sales prices that reflect more than the value of the real estate. Adjustments based on mechanical, dollar-for-dollar deductions that are equal to the cost of the concessions to the seller (as a strict cash equivalency approach would dictate) are not appropriate. Fannie Mae recognizes that the effect of the sales concessions on sales prices can vary with the amount of the concessions and differences in various markets. The adjustments must reflect the difference between what the comparables actually sold for with the sales concessions and what they would have sold for without the concessions so that the dollar amount of the adjustments will approximate the market's reaction to the concessions.

Positive adjustments for sales or financing concessions are not acceptable. For example, if local tradition or law results in virtually all of the property sellers in the market area paying a 1 percent loan origination fee for the purchaser, and a property seller in that market did not pay any loan fees or concessions for the purchaser, the sale would be considered a cash equivalent sale in that market. Note comparable sales that sold for all cash or with cash equivalent financing and use them as comparables if they are the best indicators of value for the subject property. Such sales also can be useful in determining those costs normally paid by sellers as the result of tradition or law in the market area.

▸ **HUD/FHA** Enter any necessary adjustments for sales or financing concessions here. Adjust each comparable in accordance with the instructions in mortgage letter 86-15. Explain the adjustment in *Summary of Sales Comparison Approach* and, if necessary, use an addendum.

> **VA**   You *must* consider and report the effect of any sales or financing incentives that were involved in the comparable sales transactions. Fee appraisers should consult local release 86-18 (DVB Circular 26-86-9, par. 4f) stating the VA's policy regarding seller incentives.

Date of Sale/Time

Enter the closing date of each comparable sale and, if needed, an adjustment for time. In an active market, comparable properties that sold within the past four to six months should be readily available. Most underwriters require the appraiser to explain the use of any comparable sale that occurred more than six months before the date of appraisal. In a slow market, however, it may be necessary to use comparable sales from as long as a year ago. In that event, market conditions may have changed, thus creating the need for a time adjustment. If other types of properties have increased in value over the same period, a general rise in prices may be indicated. If the market has shown little price fluctuation over that period, no adjustment may be necessary.

A downward adjustment may be indicated if prices have tended to fall over the period since the sale of the comparable—a situation that was common throughout the country in the early 1990s. Currently, the United States is experiencing the highest rate of homeownership in its history, along with a record increase in price appreciation and property values. You must determine whether the comparable property that sold a year ago is part of the general trend (upward, stable, or downward) and, if necessary, adjust the sale price of the comparable accordingly.

> **Fannie Mae**   Provide the date of the sales contract and the settlement or closing date for each comparable sale. Unless you believe the exact date is critical to understanding the adjustments, only the month and year of the sale need be reported. If you do not report both the contract date and settlement or closing date, identify the reported sale date as either the "contract date" or the "settlement or closing date." If you report only the contract date, state whether the contract resulted in a settlement or a closing.
>
> Time adjustments must be representative of the market and should be supported by the comparable sales whenever possible. The adjustments must reflect the time that elapsed between the contract date (or the date of the "meeting of the minds") for the comparable sale and the effective date of the appraisal for the subject property.
>
> In general, use comparable sales that have been settled or closed within the past 12 months. However, you may use older comparable sales as additional supporting data, if you believe that is appropriate. You must comment on the reasons for using any comparable sales that are more than six months old.
>
> In addition, you may use the subject property as a fourth comparable sale or as supporting data if the property previously was sold (and closed or settled). If you believe that it is appropriate, you also may use contract offerings and current listings as supporting data.

> **HUD/FHA**   Enter the month and year of closing. A specific date is not necessary unless it is meaningful, e.g., occurring in a rapidly changing market.

Use older sales only if more recent ones are not available. If older sales are used as comparables, explain their use in the Comments on Sales Comparison part of this section of the URAR.

▸ **VA**   Explain the use of comparable sales over 12 months old. In rapidly changing markets, it is possible that even more recent sales—6 to 12 months old—could be considered outdated. This situation would also require an explanation.

Location

Two comparisons are required in this entry, followed by the adjustment value (plus or minus) for any significant locational difference between the subject and comparable.

1. Rate the overall location of the subject within the neighborhood or market area. Enter **GOOD, AVG, FAIR,** or **POOR** as appropriate. Some lenders also require reference to an actual map page and grid number.

2. Rate the location of each comparable against the subject. Enter **SUPERIOR, EQUAL,** or **INFERIOR** as appropriate. Again, reference to an actual map page and grid number may be required.

   ▸ **Fannie Mae**   For properties in established subdivisions or for units in established condominium or PUD projects (those that have resale activity), you should use comparable sales from within the subject property's subdivision or project if any are available. Resale activity from within the subdivision or project should be the best indicator of value for properties in that subdivision or project. If you use sales of comparable properties located outside of the subject neighborhood, you must include an explanation with the analysis.

   For properties in new subdivisions or for units in new (or recently converted) condominium or PUD projects, you must compare the subject property to other properties in its general market area as well as to properties within the subject subdivision or project. This comparison should help demonstrate market acceptance of new developments and the properties within them. Generally you should select one comparable sale from the subject subdivision or project, one comparable sale from outside the subject subdivision or project and one comparable sale from inside *or* outside the subject subdivision or project, provided you consider it to be a good indicator of value for the subject property. In selecting the comparables, keep in mind that sales or resales from within the subject subdivision or project are preferable to sales from outside the subdivision or project *as long as the developer or builder of the subject property is not involved in the transactions.*

   ▸ **HUD/FHA**   Enter **GOOD, AVG,** or **FAIR** for each comparable as compared to the subject property, using the same standard as that used for the subject.

   ▸ **VA**   The use of comparable sales located outside the subject's market area must be explained.

Leasehold/Fee Simple

All comparable property sales chosen should reflect the same type of property interest as that of the subject being appraised. This information is first indicated for the subject property in the SUBJECT section on page 1 of the URAR. In most cases the property interest appraised will be a fee simple interest. If the property interest appraised is a leasehold interest, special considerations come into play. Then, as required by Standards Rule 1-4 of the Uniform Standards of Professional Appraisal Practice, you must consider and analyze the effect on value, if any, of the terms and conditions of the lease(s).

Site

Give the size of each site in square feet; your figure for the subject should agree with the entry in the SITE section on page 1. Rate each site as **GOOD, AVG, FAIR,** or **POOR,** as appropriate. Site adjustments may reflect differences in size, shape, topography, landscaping, drainage, streets, sidewalks, or other features.

> ▸ **HUD/FHA**   Enter the size of the lot. If the property's size is typical for the area, small differences in lot sizes usually do not call for an adjustment.

View

Give a brief description of the view and rate it as **GOOD, AVG, FAIR,** or **POOR;** for example, **WATER/GOOD** or **NBHD/AVG.** In areas of relatively flat terrain, view adjustments are uncommon; however, adjustments for houses with water or mountain views may be very substantial.

> ▸ **HUD/FHA**   Explain the view, if appropriate. Adjustments may come from a view rated **SUPERIOR** or **INFERIOR** to that of the subject property.

Design (Style)

First identify the architectural design or style of the subject and comparables (ranch, Cape Cod, two-story, and so on). Then rate the subject as **GOOD, AVG, FAIR,** or **POOR.** Rate each comparable against the subject by entering **SUPERIOR, EQUAL,** or **INFERIOR** after your description of the comparable's architectural design or style. Finally, enter the value of any required adjustment. This category refers to exterior design, interior qualities, special features, and any other characteristics that would make a property appealing to the typical buyer and affect its livability, marketability, and value. The style of a house probably should follow the rule of conformity; that is, the design should be compatible with that of others in the neighborhood.

> ▸ **HUD/FHA**   Describe the style according to local custom and indicate the property's appeal by **G, A, F,** or **P.**

Quality of Construction

Rate the construction quality of the subject and comparables as **GOOD, AVG, FAIR,** or **POOR** and enter appropriate adjustments. Remember that this entry covers all aspects of construction, from foundation to finish work. The quality of workmanship and quality and durability of materials used in the construction of the structure must be considered. If adjustments are to be made for differences in materials, these should be identified by the appraiser. An excessively high adjustment for quality should be well documented and appropriately explained.

▶ **HUD/FHA**   Enter **GOOD, AVERAGE,** or **FAIR** and the construction type, such as aluminum siding, wood siding, brick, and so on.

Actual Age

Enter the actual age (or the actual year of construction) of the subject dwelling and comparables and, if necessary, make adjustments indicated by the market. If good comparables are available, the ages of the subject and comparables will be very close, and no adjustment will be necessary.

Note: In some appraisals, *effective* age may be used as the basis for comparison. In that event, strike out *actual age* and write in *effective age*. Any reference to effective age will require a comment as to why it was used.

▶ **HUD/FHA**   If both actual and effective age are used, enter and note both, such as **A-25, E-20.** A difference between actual and effective age typically is caused by modernization or significant maintenance, or the lack of either. Any difference is the basis for a plus or minus adjustment.

Condition

Rate the overall condition of the subject and comparables as **GOOD, AVG, FAIR,** or **POOR.** An adjustment is indicated if the comparable is in better or worse condition than the subject.

Note: Be careful not to "double adjust" for age and condition, because both variables require judgments on elements of deterioration.

▶ **HUD/FHA**   Enter **GOOD, AVERAGE, FAIR,** or **POOR** when compared to the subject.

Above Grade Room Count/Gross Living Area

Enter the number of finished above-grade rooms, the number of bedrooms and baths, and the total above-grade square-foot living area for the subject and comparables. The living area and room count for the subject must correspond to the information entered in the IMPROVEMENTS section on page 1 of the form. If an adjustment is necessary, it is usually to reflect differences in the number of baths or minor differences in square footage. Large variances between the subject property and a comparable property should be carefully analyzed to determine whether the comparable should be kept or thrown out.

▶ **Fannie Mae**   Include only finished above-grade areas in calculation of gross living area. Report the basement and other partially below-grade areas separately and adjust for them accordingly. Room count and gross living area should be similar for the subject property and all comparables; for example, a four-bedroom comparable generally is not acceptable to support the value of a two-bedroom subject property. Address large differences between the subject property and the comparable sales, because they raise doubts about the validity of the comparables as good indicators of value.

▶ **HUD/FHA**   Enter room count, being consistent with page 1 of the report. There are three common adjustments:

1. an adjustment for "expendable space," such as a bath, with a deficiency in the number of baths adjusted first,

2. a separate adjustment for a difference in square feet, and

3. an adjustment for room count.

These can be entered separately or combined, but all adjustment values should be extracted from the market.

Typically an appraiser will *not* make an adjustment for a difference in square footage as well as an adjustment for a difference in room count; for example, a very large home may have a small room count. Any property requiring an adjustment for both square footage *and* room count should be explained.

Basement & Finished Rooms Below Grade

If a house has a basement, enter **FULL** or **PARTIAL,** as appropriate, and indicate the number of square feet it contains. A percentage indicating basement space could be given instead; for example, **100%** or **50%.** If the house has no basement or finished rooms below grade, enter **NONE** or **0%.** Indicate whether there are any finished rooms below grade (including the basement). If there are, identify the room types; for example, **REC ROOM, DEN, BDRM,** and so on. Make appropriate adjustments to reflect differences between comparables and subject property. As in all adjustments, value is dictated by the market and not by construction cost.

▶ **HUD/FHA**   Enter the type of improvements in the basement, such as **BEDROOM, REC ROOM, LAUNDRY,** and so on. Explain any special features. Show the number of square feet of *finished* below-grade area.

Functional Utility

Rate the subject and comparables as **GOOD, AVG, FAIR,** or **POOR.** Adjust for differences. Functional utility refers to a dwelling's overall compatibility with its intended use and environment, as defined by market standards. This category includes design features (such as layout, room size, storage area, security, and privacy) that are in line with current trends in the market area. A layout has functional inutility if it has poor traffic patterns. For example, people should not have to walk through bedrooms to get to other parts of the house. As another example, bathrooms should be accessed directly or through a hall and not through a second bedroom. Marketability is the ultimate test of functional utility. When judging the functional utility of homes, the appraiser must interpret the reaction of typical buyers in the subject market area.

▶ **Fannie Mae**   Sometimes improvements can be overimprovement for the neighborhood but still be within the neighborhood price range. An example would be a property with an in-ground swimming pool, a large addition, or an oversized garage in a market that does not demand these kinds of improvements. Comment on such overimprovements and indicate their contributory value in the Sales Comparison Approach adjustment grid.

Because an overimproved property may not be acceptable to the typical purchaser, the lender's underwriter must review appraisals of this type of property carefully to ensure that the appraiser has reflected only the contributory value of the overimprovement in the analysis.

▸ **HUD/FHA**   Enter **EQUAL, SUPERIOR,** or **INFERIOR** as a total of the items rated, compared to the subject. Make liberal use of the ADDITIONAL COMMENTS section and explain special features.

Typically this is the category in which to deduct for functional obsolescence observed in the subject property and recorded on page 1 but not found in the comparables. The value of any necessary adjustments should be extracted from the market. For example, a negative adjustment for functional obsolescence would be made for a poor floor design that includes two bedrooms located so that entrance to one is possible only by passing through the other. In such a case the bedroom without separate access would not be counted as a bedroom.

Heating/Cooling

Identify the types of heating and cooling systems present in the subject house and comparable houses. Adjustments should be based on such things as type of system, presence or absence of air-conditioning, and condition and effectiveness of the equipment. Adjustments should be derived from market data, not cost data.

▸ **HUD/FHA**   If appropriate, enter an adjustment for heating and cooling systems; adjustment values should be based on local market expectations.

Energy Efficient Items

Identify all energy efficient items contained in the homes. Price adjustments for energy conservation features should reflect how much more the market will pay for the property because of their existence. Such items include fans, fireplace inserts, low-emissivity (low-E) glass, active or passive solar-heating systems, and high-efficiency furnaces and water heaters. Your entry for the subject property should reflect the information provided in the IMPROVEMENTS section at the bottom of page 1.

▸ **Fannie Mae**   Fannie Mae recommends that lenders give special underwriting consideration to buyers of properties with energy-efficient improvements. In such cases higher monthly housing expenses and debt payment ratios may be justified because of the potential savings in energy costs. The nature of these items and their contribution to value will vary throughout the country because of differing climatic conditions and utility costs.

▸ **HUD/FHA**   Enter an adjustment for any energy-efficient items, such as storm windows or doors, solar installations, and so on, as appropriate.

Garage/Carport

Indicate whether the subject and comparables have garages or carports and the number of cars they hold. If a property does not have a garage or carport, enter **NONE.**

Adjustments should be based on the typical value buyers place on garages or carports, not on cost data.

▸ **HUD/FHA** Enter any required adjustment for car storage. Adjustments should be calculated in accordance with market acceptance of carport versus garage, as well as the impact of size on market value.

Porch/Patio/Deck

Porches, patios, decks, fireplace(s), and any other special feature of the basic structure should be noted here. Indicate also the presence of a fence, swimming pool, spa, greenhouse, or any other structure not considered part of the primary house. Blank lines provide additional space for entries. Adjustments for such features should reflect local market expectations and buyer requirements.

▸ **Fannie Mae** Dollar adjustments should reflect the market's reaction to the differences between properties, not necessarily the cost of the difference in actual dollars. Items such as electronic air filters, intercom systems, elaborately finished basements, carpets, swimming pools, and other special features do not affect value to the extent of their cost.

▸ **HUD/FHA** Enter any necessary adjustments for special features, such as a fireplace, based on local market expectations. For example, a property with a swimming pool in an area where a swimming pool is an expected feature might bring a dollar premium, compared with a comparable property without a pool. On the other hand, an improvement such as a swimming pool in a low-income area might bring a negative adjustment because of increased maintenance expenses.

Additional Comments (Page 3)

This is a catchall space in which you can adjust for differences between the subject and comparables for items such as modernization and remodeling or other features not categorized elsewhere in the SALES COMPARISON APPROACH section.

▸ **HUD/FHA** Enter adjustments for any features not covered elsewhere.

Net Adjustment (Total)

Total the dollar amounts of the positive (+) and negative (−) adjustments for each comparable to find the net adjustment and enter that amount, checking the + or − box as appropriate.

The proper selection of comparable properties minimizes both the need for and the size of adjustments. Very substantial adjustments suggest that the properties are not comparable. The software used by the appraiser will most likely keep a running total of gross adjustments as they are entered, so that the appraiser will be aware when they exceed the recommended guidelines.

▸ **Fannie Mae** Fannie Mae has established guidelines for the net and gross percentage adjustments that underwriters may rely on as a general indicator of whether a property should be used as a comparable sale. Generally the total dollar amount of the net adjustments for each comparable sale should not exceed 15 percent of the comparable's sales price.

If the adjustments exceed 15 percent, you must comment on the reasons for not using a more similar comparable.

Further, the dollar amount of the *gross* adjustment for each comparable sale should not exceed 25 percent of the comparable's sales price. The amount of the gross adjustment is determined by adding all individual adjustments without regard to the plus or minus signs. If the adjustments exceed 25 percent, you must comment on the reasons for not using a more similar comparable. You should explain individual adjustments that are excessively high, and they should be reviewed carefully by the lender's underwriter. In some circumstances the use of comparables with higher-than-normal adjustments may be warranted, but you must satisfactorily justify your use of them.

You must research the market and select the most comparable sales available for the subject property. Then adjust those sales to reflect the market's reaction to the differences (except for sales and financing concessions) between the comparable sales and the subject property, without regard for the percentage or amount of the dollar adjustments. If your adjustments do not fall within Fannie Mae's net and gross percentage adjustment guidelines but you believe the comparable sales used to be the best available, as well as the best indicators of value for the subject property, you simply have to provide an appropriate explanation.

If the extent of your adjustments to the comparable sales is great enough to indicate that the property may not conform to the general market area, the lender's underwriter must give special consideration to the case. An atypical property might require more conservative mortgage terms because it might not appeal to a typical purchaser in the market area.

▸ **HUD/FHA**   Check either the (+) or (–) box to indicate whether the total net adjustment will increase or decrease the sales price.

If any adjustment is excessive, the comparables should be reviewed to determine whether the best ones were selected. Any adjustment that appears excessive should be explained.

▸ **VA**   The VA has no requirements for maximum gross or net adjustments. But the selection of any comparable sale with large overall adjustments must be explained.

Adjusted Sale Price of Comparables

The net adjustment is added to or subtracted from the sale price of the comparable property to obtain an adjusted sale price. This is the appraiser's opinion of what the comparable property would have sold for had it possessed all the significant characteristics of the subject property.

As mentioned earlier, Fannie Mae has established guidelines for the net and gross percentage adjustments that review appraisers or loan underwriters may rely on as a general indicator of whether a property should be used as a comparable sale. Generally, the total dollar amount of the *net* adjustment should not exceed 15 percent. The dollar amount for the *gross* adjustment should not exceed 25 percent. The amount of the gross adjustment is computed by adding all adjustments without regard to the plus or minus signs.

Record the *net* and *gross* percentage adjustments in the space provided (which may be entered automatically by the software used):

Net Adjustment %
Divide total net dollar adjustment by comparable property's sale price.

Gross Adjustment %
Divide total dollar adjustment by comparable property's sale price.

> ▸ **HUD/FHA**   Total all adjustments and add to or subtract from the sales price of each comparable.
>
> Keep track of the magnitude of the adjustments by comparing each one to the sales price of the comparable property. In general, the total dollar amount of the net adjustments for each comparable sale should not exceed 15 percent of the comparable's sale price. The dollar amount of the gross adjustment for each comparable sale should not exceed 25 percent of the comparable's sale price.

▪ TRANSFER HISTORY OF SUBJECT PROPERTY AND COMPARABLE SALES

This next section of the form is provided for the appraiser to report prior sales or transfers of the subject property and comparables.

I did or did not research the sale or transfer history of the subject property and comparable sales. If not, explain.

Check the appropriate box. If you checked the "did not" box, explain why you did not research prior sales or transfers. Use the blank lines below for your comments.

My research did or did not reveal any prior sales or transfers of the subject property for the three years prior to the effective date of this appraisal.

Check the appropriate box.

Data source(s)

Enter the source or sources of the data you collected.

My research did or did not reveal any prior sales or transfers of the comparable sales for the year prior to the date of the sale of the comparable sale.

Check the appropriate box.

Data source(s)

Enter the source or sources of the data you collected.

Report the results of the research and analysis of the prior sale or transfer history of the subject property and comparable sales (report additional prior sales on page 3).

In the block below, provide information on any prior sale or transfer of the subject or comparable properties. Record additional prior sales or transfers on the blank lines at the top of page 3 or in an addendum attached to the form.

> ▸ **Fannie Mae**   The data source for the prior sales of the subject and the comparables does not have to be the same as the data and/or verification source that was reported at the top of the adjustment grid.

Analysis of prior sale or transfer history of the subject property and comparable sales

Summarize your conclusions on the sale and/or transfer history of the subject property and comparable sales used in the appraisal.

Standards Rule 1-5 of USPAP requires the appraiser to analyze all agreements of sale, options, or listings of the subject property current as of the effective date of the appraisal. In addition, Standards Rule 1-5 requires the appraiser to analyze all sales of the subject property that have occurred within three years.

> ▸ **Fannie Mae**   Use this space for your analysis of any prior sales of the subject property and comparables.

Summary of Sales Comparison Approach

Use this space to

- explain the reconciliation process that supports your choice of the adjusted sale price that most accurately reflects the market value of the subject property,
- expand on any significant adjustments developed, or
- record additional comments concerning the sales comparison approach.

If more space is needed, additional remarks can be made on the blank lines at the top of page 3 or in an addendum attached to the form.

> ▸ **Fannie Mae** Your comments should reflect your reconciliation of the adjusted (or indicated) values for the comparable sales and identify the comparable(s) you gave the most weight in arriving at the indicated value for the subject property. If you have provided adequate supporting information, the underwriter should understand how you arrived at your conclusion and agree with it.
>
> ▸ **VA**   Provide an adequate, supportable explanation of any adjustments made to the comparables, either in the Summary of Sales Comparison Approach block or in an addendum.

Indicated Value by Sales Comparison Approach $

Enter the dollar amount of your opinion of market value by the sales comparison approach. The adjusted values of the comparable properties probably will not be identical. It is your task to choose the adjusted value that best reflects the characteristics of the subject property. There is no formula for reconciling the indicated values. The reconciliation process involves application of careful analysis and judgment for which no mathematical or mechanical formula can be substituted.

▸ **Fannie Mae**   The lender's underwriter should make a thorough review of the Sales Comparison Approach adjustment grid. The sales comparison analysis provides many places in which an error can be made in the use of dollar adjustments. A spot check must always be made of the adjustment calculations and the use of plus (+) and minus (-) signs. Errors in arithmetic can have a significant effect on the value conclusion, making it necessary for the lender to contact the appraiser.

APPRAISAL   1

In Appraisal 1, the subject property is located at 456 Cherry Hill Road in Sarasota, Florida. The house is a three-bedroom, two-bath ranch with a total of seven rooms above grade, excluding the foyer, baths, attic, and laundry area. The lender has indicated that there is no sales contract pending.

Three properties have been selected as comparables. According to public records, all are current sales with conventional mortgage financing with no sale or financing concessions:

- *Sale 1 is located at 403 Bent Tree Lane—1/4 mile NW of the subject property. It sold one month ago for $445,000.*
- *Sale 2 is located at 475 Cherry Hill Road, just up the street from the subject property. It sold two months ago for $424,250.*
- *Sale 3 is located at 191 Forest Trail—approximately one mile NE of the subject property. It sold five months ago for $430,000.*

Based on matched pairs analysis, the appraiser has assigned the adjustment values shown in the table to account for significant differences between the subject property and the three comparables.

	Subject	*Comp 1*	*Comp 2*	*Comp 3*
Location	GOOD	GOOD	GOOD	AVG/INF/BUSY STREET/$5,000
Site	13,907 SF/GD	14,200 SF/GD	11,370/AVG/$5,000	14,000 SF/GD
Roofing Material	ASPHALT	ASPHALT	SUP/TILE/$2,000	ASPHALT
Age	11	11	10	5/$3,000
Gross Living Area	2,119 SF	2,115 SF	1,895 SF/$4,500	1,717 SF/$8,100
Garage	YES/2-CAR	YES/2-CAR	YES/2-CAR	YES/2-CAR
Enclosed Porch	YES	YES	SMALLER/$5,000	SMALLER/$5,000
Fireplace	YES/1	NO/$1,500	NO/$1,500	YES/1
Caged Pool	YES	SMALLER/$4,000	SIMILAR	SIMILAR

There are	comparable properties in the subject neighborhood ranging in price from $				to $		
There are	comparable sales in the subject neighborhood within the past twelve months ranging in sale price from $				to $		

FEATURE	SUBJECT	COMPARABLE SALE # 1		COMPARABLE SALE # 2		COMPARABLE SALE # 3	
Address	456 Cherry Hill Road	403 Bent Tree Lane		475 Cherry Hill Road		191 Forest Trail	
	Sarasota	Sarasota		Sarasota		Sarasota	
Proximity to Subject		1/4 mile N/W		Same block		1 mile N/E	
Sale Price	$ 454,500	$	445,000	$	424,250	$	430,000
Sale Price/Gross Liv. Area	$ 214.39 sq. ft.	$ 210.40 sq. ft.		$ 223.76 sq. ft.		$ 250.29 sq. ft.	
Data Source(s)		Sales Agent		Sales Agent		Sales Agent	
Verification Source(s)		Public Records		Public Records		Public Records	
VALUE ADJUSTMENTS	DESCRIPTION	DESCRIPTION	+(-)$ Adjustment	DESCRIPTION	+(-)$ Adjustment	DESCRIPTION	+(-)$ Adjustment
Sale or Financing		Conv. mort.		Conv. mort.		Conv. mort.	
Concessions		No concess.		No concess.		No concess.	
Date of Sale/Time		8-10-05		7-15-05		4-8-05	
Location	Suburban	Sub/equal		Sub/equal		Busy street	+8,000
Leasehold/Fee Simple	Fee Simple	Fee Simple		Fee Simple		Fee simple	
Site	10726 sf/Gd	11,200 sf/Gd		8,250 sf/Avg	+5,000	10,000 sf/Gd	
View	Residential/Gd	Residential/Gd		Residential/Gd		Residential/Gd	
Design (Style)	Ranch/Typical	Ranch/Equal		Ranch/Equal		Ranch/Equal	
Quality of Construction	Good	Good		Good		Good	
Actual Age	11	11		10		5	-5,000
Condition	Good	Good		Good		Good	
Above Grade	Total / Bdrms. / Baths	Total / Bdrms. / Baths		Total / Bdrms. / Baths		Total / Bdrms. / Baths	
Room Count	7 / 3 / 2.00	7 / 3 / 2		7 / 3 / 2.5	-4,000	7 / 3 / 2	
Gross Living Area	2,120 sq. ft.	2,115 sq. ft.		1,896 sq. ft.	+5,500	1,718 sq. ft.	+8,500
Basement & Finished							
Rooms Below Grade	None	None		None		None	
Functional Utility	Good	Good		Good		Good	
Heating/Cooling	FWA/CAC	FWA/CAC		FWA/CAC		FWA/CAC	
Energy Efficient Items	H/C Syst/Fans	H/C Syst/Fans		H/C Syst/Fans		H/C Syst/Fans	
Garage/Carport	Gar 2 attached	Gar 2 attached		Gar 2 attached		Gar 2 attached	
Porch/Patio/Deck	Enclosed porch	Encl porch		Encl p/smaller	+4,500	Encl p/smaller	+4,500
Fireplace	Stone 1	Stone 1		None	+8,500	Stone 1	
Pool	Caged	Caged/smaller	+5,500	Caged/similar		Caged/similar	
Fence	Wood	Wood		Wood		Wood	
Net Adjustment (Total)		X + / -	$ 5,500	X + / -	$ 19,500	X + / -	$ 16,000
Adjusted Sale Price		Net Adj. 1.20 %		Net Adj. 4.60 %		Net Adj. 3.70 %	
of Comparables		Gross Adj. 1.20 %	$ 450,500	Gross Adj. 6.50 %	$ 443,750	Gross Adj. 6.00 %	$ 446,000

I [X] did [ ] did not research the sale or transfer history of the subject property and comparable sales. If not, explain

My research [ ] did [X] did not reveal any prior sales or transfers of the subject property for the three years prior to the effective date of this appraisal.
Data Source(s)   County Assessor's Office
My research [ ] did [X] did not reveal any prior sales or transfers of the comparable sales for the prior year to the date of sale of the comparalbe sale.
Data Source(s)   County Assessor's Office
Report the results of the research and analysis of the prior sale or transfer history of the subject property and comparable sales (report additional prior sales on page 3).

ITEM	SUBJECT	COMPARABLE SALE # 1	COMPARABLE SALE # 2	COMPARABLE SALE # 3
Date of Prior Sale/Transfer				
Price of Prior Sale/Transfer				
Data Source(s)				
Effective Date of Data Source(s)				

Analysis of prior sale or transfer history of the subject property and comparable sales

Summary of Sales Comparison Approach   All three comparable sales are located within the same neighborhood. Comparable 1 was given the most weight in the final analysis because it required the fewest adjustments and is most similar to the subject overall. All reported sales of comparable properties occurred within one to three months of listing; sale prices were within 98% of listing prices.

Indicated Value by Sales Comparison Approach $ 450,500

There have been no sales of the subject or comparables, other than those reported here, within the last three years.

EXERCISE: APPRAISAL 2

FEATURE	SUBJECT	COMPARABLE SALE # 1		COMPARABLE SALE # 2		COMPARABLE SALE # 3	

There are ____ comparable properties currently offered for sale in the subject neighborhood ranging in price from $ ____ to $ ____

There are ____ comparable sales in the subject neighborhood within the past twelve months ranging in sale price from $ ____ to $ ____

FEATURE	SUBJECT	COMPARABLE SALE # 1	COMPARABLE SALE # 2	COMPARABLE SALE # 3
Address				
Proximity to Subject				
Sale Price	$	$	$	$
Sale Price/Gross Liv. Area	$ sq. ft.	$ sq. ft.	$ sq. ft.	$ sq. ft.
Data Source(s)				
Verification Source(s)				

VALUE ADJUSTMENTS	DESCRIPTION	DESCRIPTION	+(-) $ Adjustment	DESCRIPTION	+(-) $ Adjustment	DESCRIPTION	+(-) $ Adjustment
Sale or Financing Concessions							
Date of Sale/Time							
Location							
Leasehold/Fee Simple							
Site							
View							
Design (Style)							
Quality of Construction							
Actual Age							
Condition							
Above Grade Room Count	Total Bdrms. Baths	Total Bdrms. Baths		Total Bdrms. Baths		Total Bdrms. Baths	
Gross Living Area	sq. ft.	sq. ft.		sq. ft.		sq. ft.	
Basement & Finished Rooms Below Grade							
Functional Utility							
Heating/Cooling							
Energy Efficient Items							
Garage/Carport							
Porch/Patio/Deck							
Net Adjustment (Total)		□ + □ - $		□ + □ - $		□ + □ - $	
Adjusted Sale Price of Comparables	$	Net Adj. % Gross Adj. % $		Net Adj. % Gross Adj. % $		Net Adj. % Gross Adj. % $	

I □ did □ did not research the sale or transfer history of the subject property and comparable sales. If not, explain

My research □ did □ did not reveal any prior sales or transfers of the subject property for the three years prior to the effective date of this appraisal.
Data source(s)
My research □ did □ did not reveal any prior sales or transfers of the comparable sales for the year prior to the date of sale of the comparable sale.
Data source(s)
Report the results of the research and analysis of the prior sale or transfer history of the subject property and comparable sales (report additional prior sales on page 3).

ITEM	SUBJECT	COMPARABLE SALE # 1	COMPARABLE SALE # 2	COMPARABLE SALE # 3
Date of Prior Sale/Transfer				
Price of Prior Sale/Transfer				
Data Source(s)				
Effective Date of Data Source(s)				

Analysis of prior sale or transfer history of the subject property and comparable sales

Summary of Sales Comparison Approach

Indicated Value by Sales Comparison Approach $

Complete the blank URAR SALES COMPARISON APPROACH section provided above for Appraisal 2, using the following information. When you have finished, you can check your work against the completed Appraisal 2 in the Answer Key.

The description of the subject property was verified by the appraiser through personal in-spection. It is a single-family ranch-style residence containing eight rooms, four bedrooms, and two baths; gross living area is 1,980 square feet. The property is located at 1053 Locust Lane, a typical residential street for this neighborhood, which is considered good for the area. The house is 18 years old, with an effective age of 12 years; remaining economic life is estimated to be 48 years.

The subject lot is a rectangle, 75' x 150'; site and view are average for this market area. The improvements conform in design and appeal to the market area. Construction is good quality, as is condition of exterior and interior. There is a partial finished basement—ap-proximately 1,490 square feet. The functional utility of the home is good. The heating and cooling systems are gas-fired forced air with central air-conditioning. There is a two-car detached garage. There are no special energy-efficient items. The home has a wood deck in back and a masonry fireplace in the family room. The financing is a conventional mort-gage, typical of the area.

Adjustment values based on local market data are: condition (Comp 1), $17,000; extra 130 square feet of living space (Comp 2), $12,000; fireplace, $3,000; wood deck, $3,500; full finished basement (Comp 4), $6,000; updated kitchen (comp 4), $5,000 ; lot size, $20,000 (comp 4); living area size (comp 4), $20,000 .

Comparable sales data compiled from the multiple listing service, which have been veri-fied by brokers involved in the transaction, are shown below. All of these sales involved a fee simple interest. Other than the recent sales reported here, there have been no sales of the subject or comparable properties within the last three years.

	Comp 1	Comp 2	Comp 3	Comp 4
Address	310 Minagua St.	1091 Locust Lane	453 Chelsea Ct.	565 Lord Ave.
Proximity to Subject	½ mi. NW	Same Block	¾ mi. NE	2 mi. S
Sale Price	$340,000	$349,000	$362,000	$410,000
Financing	Conv. Mortgage	Conv. Mortgage	Conv. Mortgage	Conv. Mortgage
Date of Sale	3 Mos. Ago	4 Mos. Ago	3 Mos. Ago	7 Mos. Ago
Location	Suburban/Gd.	Suburban/Gd.	Suburban/Gd.	Suburban/Gd.
Site	11,000 sq. ft.	10,880 sq. ft	10,500 sq. ft	15,000 sq. ft
View	Hills/Good	Hills/Good	Hills/Good	Hills/Good
Design (Style)	Ranch	Ranch	Ranch	Ranch
Construction	Good	Good	Good	Good
Age	20 yrs.	18 yrs.	19 yrs.	17 yrs.
Condition	Fair	Good	Good	Good
No. of Rms./ Bedrms./Baths	8/4/2	7/3/2	8/4/2	8/4/2
Sq. Ft. of Living Space	2,000	1,850	1,980	2,500
Basement/Finished	2,000/1,600	1,850/1,400	1,980/1,490	2,500
Functional Utility	Good	Good	Good	Good
Heating/Cooling	FA/Cent.	FA/Cent.	FA/Cent.	FA/Cent.
Energy-Efficient Items	None	None	None	None
Garage	2-Car Det.	2-Car Det.	2-Car Det.	2-Car Det.
Deck	None	Wood Deck/360 sq. ft.	Wood Deck/300 sq. ft.	None
Fireplace(s)	Masonry/1	None	None	Masonry/1
Other Interior Improvements	None	None	None	Mod. Kit.

SECTION 7: RECONCILIATION

R E C O N C I L I A T I O N	Indicated Value by: Sales Comparison Approach $ Cost Approach (if developed) $ Income Approach (if developed) $

This appraisal is made ☐ "as is", ☐ subject to completion per plans and specifications on the basis of a hypothetical condition that the improvements have been completed, ☐ subject to the following repairs or alterations on the basis of a hypothetical condition that the repairs or alterations have been completed, or ☐ subject to the following required inspection based on the extraordinary assumption that the condition or deficiency does not require alteration or repair:

Based on a complete visual inspection of the interior and exterior areas of the subject property, defined scope of work, statement of assumptions and limiting conditions, and appraiser's certification, my (our) opinion of the market value, as defined, of the real property that is the subject of this report is
$, as of   , which is the date of inspection and the effective date of this appraisal.

In the RECONCILIATION section on page 2 of the URAR form, the appraiser brings all elements of the appraisal together to present and comment on the final conclusion of the market value of the subject property. The order in which the appraisal approaches are presented on the form may seem inconsistent, since the cost and income approaches do not appear until page 3. Because of the importance of the sales comparison approach in appraising homes, Fannie Mae no longer requires that the cost and income approaches be used. For other purposes, however, the appraiser (in consultation with the client) may use all three approaches. The discussion below assumes that all three approaches have been used.

The separate value opinions reached by the different appraisal approaches rarely will be identical. Through the process of reconciliation the appraiser compares and analyzes the opinions derived from the approaches used (sales comparison, cost, and/or income). By considering the appropriateness of each approach for the property appraised, the value opinion that most accurately represents the market value of the subject can be determined.

The process of reconciliation is not a simple averaging of figures. One approach may have more validity for certain properties at certain times. Another approach may have little utility for the type of property being appraised. For instance, because most single-family residences are not purchased for their income-producing capability, the value reached by applying the income approach in the appraisal of a single-family residence is rarely a significant determinant of market value. Overall, the approach likely to receive the most weight in appraising a single-family residence is the sales comparison approach. The sales comparison approach tells the appraiser what buyers in the marketplace have been willing to pay for properties similar to the subject property.

Of course, accurate data must be collected concerning market forces in the area and neighborhood, and there must be a sufficient number of recent comparable property sales. Even when using the sales comparison approach to appraise a single-family residence, however, the appraiser must remember that past performance is never a guarantee of future performance and must always be alert to changing market conditions. Layoffs by a major employer, for instance, could signal decreased demand for housing as well as an increased supply of homes on the market. Either result could have a devastating effect on sale prices. In recent years, more than one area of the country has seen a boom turn to a bust with frightening speed. Rising expectations can blind homebuyers and investors to the harsh realities of the marketplace. An appraiser always must be aware of the potential for the real estate market to turn down as well as up. In the process of reconciliation the appraiser will

- note and explain any work to be performed as a condition of the appraised valuation;

- reconcile the value opinions resulting from the appraisal approaches used to reach a final opinion of market value and explain the conclusion;

- state the purpose of the appraisal;

- provide the definition of market value used;

- identify the intended use and users of the report;

- review the entire appraisal, making sure the amount of data collected is adequate; the analytical techniques, assumptions, and logic applied are sound; and the mathematical computations are accurate;

- state the terms under which the appraisal is performed and the limitations on its use; and

- certify by signature that the appropriate property inspections have been made by the appraiser personally and that the appraisal is based on the appraiser's knowledge and belief that the facts and data used in the appraisal are true and correct.

Indicated Value by:

First enter your opinion of value derived for the sales comparison approach, the cost approach, and the income approach. Then on the blank lines below, explain how you reconciled each approach to value in arriving at a final opinion of market value.

- ▸ **Fannie Mae**   The reconciliation process that leads to the estimate of market value is an ongoing process throughout the appraiser's analysis. In the final reconciliation you must reconcile the reasonableness and reliability of each approach to value and the reasonableness and validity of the indicated values and the available data, and then you must select and report the approach(es) that were given the most weight. The final reconciliation must never be an averaging technique. If you have provided a comprehensive and logical analysis of the neighborhood and property, the lender's underwriter should be able to reach a sound conclusion on the adequacy of the property as security for the mortgage.

- ▸ **HUD/FHA**   This section should contain the appraiser's reasoning for arriving at the final value.

- ▸ **RHS**   Briefly explain the basis for the final reconciliation, including the type and availability of data.

- ▸ **VA** The appraiser should rely on the value developed by the sales comparison approach—except in very unusual circumstances.

This appraisal is made . . .

Check the appropriate box to indicate whether the final value opinion is based on the present condition of the property "as is," or if not, how the condition of the property is expected to change. Building or remodeling work may be under way, as may repairs necessitated by termite damage or other property inspection reports. If the appraisal is based on any work that is not yet completed, the value opinion must be made subject to the work described.

> ▸ **Fannie Mae**   Appraisals developed for Fannie Mae are made under one of the following conditions: "As is," "Subject to completion," or "subject to alterations or repairs," as described below.

As is

Most appraisal assignments will be based on the "as is" condition of the subject property. For existing homes, an appraisal may be "as is" even if minor conditions exist that do not affect the livability of the property.

> ▸ **VA**   The fee appraiser must check "as is" if the property meets minimum property requirements (MPRs) with no repairs needed.

Subject to completion

For new or proposed construction, an appraisal may be based on plans and specifications or on an existing model home. The lender must obtain a certification of completion before delivering the mortgage to Fannie Mae. In some cases, the completion of items that do not affect the ability to obtain an occupancy permit can be postponed (for example, landscaping or a driveway). The mortgage may be delivered to Fannie Mae if it warrants that the improvements will be completed within 180 days after the date of the mortgage. The appraisal report must show both the cost of completing the postponed items and the "as completed" opinion of value of the property after completion.

Subject to alterations or repairs

When you determine there are incomplete items or conditions that affect the livability of the property or physical deficiencies that could affect the soundness or structural integrity of the improvements, you must appraise the property subject to completion of these specific alterations or repairs.

> ▸ **HUD/FHA**   FHA appraisals are done "As Repaired," or as stated on the URAR, "subject to the repairs, alterations, inspections, or conditions . . . ." This means the indicated value is reported as if all the repair items were completed.
>
> ▸ **RHS**   Check the appropriate box.
>
> ▸ **VA**   The fee appraiser must check "Subject to the following repairs . . ." if repairs are needed to make the property meet MPRs. In that situation, the appraiser must also provide an itemized list of recommended repairs or other action necessary to make the property meet MPRs.

Based on a complete visual inspection of the interior and exterior areas of the subject property, defined scope of work, statement of assumptions and limiting conditions, and appraiser's certification . . .

Enter your final value conclusion and the effective date of the appraisal. If the purpose of the appraisal is to determine current market value, this is typically the date of the property inspection.

Terms Under Which an Appraisal Is Conducted

To estimate property value accurately, you must define the conditions under which the appraisals were made. As an appraiser, you also want to place limits on the representations you make with regard to the appraisal or its use.

In developing a real property appraisal, the appraiser must state the terms under which the appraisal is conducted (see Figure 8, pages 4, 5, and 6 of the URAR form). The appraiser must

- identify the *scope of work* necessary to complete the assignment;
- identify the *intended use* of the appraiser's opinions and conclusions;
- identify the client and other *intended users;*
- define *market value;*
- list the *assumptions and limiting conditions* of the appraisal; and
- list the *certifications that show the appraiser's neutrality, responsibility and compliance with the Uniform Standards of Professional Appraisal Practice.*

  ‣ **Fannie Mae**   The appraiser may expand the scope of work to include any additional research or analysis necessary, based on the complexity of the appraisal assignment. The appraiser is not permitted to make changes to the intended use, intended user, definition of market value, or assumptions and limiting conditions. Fannie Mae will allow additional certifications (not limitations) to be added on a separate page if such certifications are required by state law, or if they cover such matters as the appraiser's continuing education or membership in an appraisal organization(s).

Scope of Work

At a minimum, the appraiser must

- perform a complete visual inspection of the interior and exterior areas of the subject property;
- inspect the neighborhood;
- inspect each of the comparable sales from at least the street;
- research, verify, and analyze data from reliable public and/or private sources; and
- report his or her analysis, opinions, and conclusions in this appraisal report.

Intended Use

Usually, the intended use of this appraisal report is for the lender/client to evaluate the property for a mortgage finance transaction.

Intended User

The lender/client normally is the intended user of the appraisal report.

Definition of Market Value

Most residential appraisals are conducted to determine the subject property's market value. Market value is the most probable price the property is likely to

FIGURE 8

Definitions, Statement of Assumptions and Limiting Conditions, and Appraiser's Certification

Uniform Residential Appraisal Report   File

This report form is designed to report an appraisal of a one-unit property or a one-unit property with an accessory unit; including a unit in a planned unit development (PUD). This report form is not designed to report an appraisal of a manufactured home or a unit in a condominium or cooperative project.

This appraisal report is subject to the following scope of work, intended use, intended user, definition of market value, statement of assumptions and limiting conditions, and certifications. Modifications, additions, or deletions to the intended use, intended user, definition of market value, or assumptions and limiting conditions are not permitted. The appraiser may expand the scope of work to include any additional research or analysis necessary based on the complexity of this appraisal assignment. Modifications or deletions to the certifications are also not permitted. However, additional certifications that do not constitute material alterations to this appraisal report, such as those required by law or those related to the appraiser's continuing education or membership in an appraisal organization, are permitted.

SCOPE OF WORK: The scope of work for this appraisal is defined by the complexity of this appraisal assignment and the reporting requirements of this appraisal report form, including the following definition of market value, statement of assumptions and limiting conditions, and certifications. The appraiser must, at a minimum: (1) perform a complete visual inspection of the interior and exterior areas of the subject property, (2) inspect the neighborhood, (3) inspect each of the comparable sales from at least the street, (4) research, verify, and analyze data from reliable public and/or private sources, and (5) report his or her analysis, opinions, and conclusions in this appraisal report.

INTENDED USE: The intended use of this appraisal report is for the lender/client to evaluate the property that is the subject of this appraisal for a mortgage finance transaction.

INTENDED USER: The intended user of this appraisal report is the lender/client.

DEFINITION OF MARKET VALUE: The most probable price which a property should bring in a competitive and open market under all conditions requisite to a fair sale, the buyer and seller, each acting prudently, knowledgeably and assuming the price is not affected by undue stimulus. Implicit in this definition is the consummation of a sale as of a specified date and the passing of title from seller to buyer under conditions whereby: (1) buyer and seller are typically motivated; (2) both parties are well informed or well advised, and each acting in what he or she considers his or her own best interest; (3) a reasonable time is allowed for exposure in the open market; (4) payment is made in terms of cash in U. S. dollars or in terms of financial arrangements comparable thereto; and (5) the price represents the normal consideration for the property sold unaffected by special or creative financing or sales concessions* granted by anyone associated with the sale.

*Adjustments to the comparables must be made for special or creative financing or sales concessions. No adjustments are necessary for those costs which are normally paid by sellers as a result of tradition or law in a market area; these costs are readily identifiable since the seller pays these costs in virtually all sales transactions. Special or creative financing adjustments can be made to the comparable property by comparisons to financing terms offered by a third party institutional lender that is not already involved in the property or transaction. Any adjustment should not be calculated on a mechanical dollar for dollar cost of the financing or concession but the dollar amount of any adjustment should approximate the market's reaction to the financing or concessions based on the appraiser's judgment.

STATEMENT OF ASSUMPTIONS AND LIMITING CONDITIONS: The appraiser's certification in this report is subject to the following assumptions and limiting conditions:

1. The appraiser will not be responsible for matters of a legal nature that affect either the property being appraised or the title to it, except for information that he or she became aware of during the research involved in performing this appraisal. The appraiser assumes that the title is good and marketable and will not render any opinions about the title.

2. The appraiser has provided a sketch in this appraisal report to show the approximate dimensions of the improvements. The sketch is included only to assist the reader in visualizing the property and understanding the appraiser's determination of its size.

3. The appraiser has examined the available flood maps that are provided by the Federal Emergency Management Agency (or other data sources) and has noted in this appraisal report whether any portion of the subject site is located in an identified Special Flood Hazard Area. Because the appraiser is not a surveyor, he or she makes no guarantees, express or implied, regarding this determination.

4. The appraiser will not give testimony or appear in court because he or she made an appraisal of the property in question, unless specific arrangements to do so have been made beforehand, or as otherwise required by law.

5. The appraiser has noted in this appraisal report any adverse conditions (such as needed repairs, deterioration, the presence of hazardous wastes, toxic substances, etc.) observed during the inspection of the subject property or that he or she became aware of during the research involved in performing this appraisal. Unless otherwise stated in this appraisal report, the appraiser has no knowledge of any hidden or unapparent physical deficiencies or adverse conditions of the property (such as, but not limited to, needed repairs, deterioration, the presence of hazardous wastes, toxic substances, adverse environmental conditions, etc.) that would make the property less valuable, and has assumed that there are no such conditions and makes no guarantees or warranties, express or implied. The appraiser will not be responsible for any such conditions that do exist or for any engineering or testing that might be required to discover whether such conditions exist. Because the appraiser is not an expert in the field of environmental hazards, this appraisal report must not be considered as an environmental assessment of the property.

6. The appraiser has based his or her appraisal report and valuation conclusion for an appraisal that is subject to satisfactory completion, repairs, or alterations on the assumption that the completion, repairs, or alterations of the subject property will be performed in a professional manner.

FIGURE 8

Definitions, Statement of Assumptions and Limiting Conditions, and Appraiser's Certification (continued)

Uniform Residential Appraisal Report   File

APPRAISER'S CERTIFICATION: The Appraiser certifies and agrees that:

1. I have, at a minimum, developed and reported this appraisal in accordance with the scope of work requirements stated in this appraisal report.

2. I performed a complete visual inspection of the interior and exterior areas of the subject property. I reported the condition of the improvements in factual, specific terms. I identified and reported the physical deficiencies that could affect the livability, soundness, or structural integrity of the property.

3. I performed this appraisal in accordance with the requirements of the Uniform Standards of Professional Appraisal Practice that were adopted and promulgated by the Appraisal Standards Board of The Appraisal Foundation and that were in place at the time this appraisal report was prepared.

4. I developed my opinion of the market value of the real property that is the subject of this report based on the sales comparison approach to value. I have adequate comparable market data to develop a reliable sales comparison approach for this appraisal assignment. I further certify that I considered the cost and income approaches to value but did not develop them, unless otherwise indicated in this report.

5. I researched, verified, analyzed, and reported on any current agreement for sale for the subject property, any offering for sale of the subject property in the twelve months prior to the effective date of this appraisal, and the prior sales of the subject property for a minimum of three years prior to the effective date of this appraisal, unless otherwise indicated in this report.

6. I researched, verified, analyzed, and reported on the prior sales of the comparable sales for a minimum of one year prior to the date of sale of the comparable sale, unless otherwise indicated in this report.

7. I selected and used comparable sales that are locationally, physically, and functionally the most similar to the subject property.

8. I have not used comparable sales that were the result of combining a land sale with the contract purchase price of a home that has been built or will be built on the land.

9. I have reported adjustments to the comparable sales that reflect the market's reaction to the differences between the subject property and the comparable sales.

10. I verified, from a disinterested source, all information in this report that was provided by parties who have a financial interest in the sale or financing of the subject property.

11. I have knowledge and experience in appraising this type of property in this market area.

12. I am aware of, and have access to, the necessary and appropriate public and private data sources, such as multiple listing services, tax assessment records, public land records and other such data sources for the area in which the property is located.

13. I obtained the information, estimates, and opinions furnished by other parties and expressed in this appraisal report from reliable sources that I believe to be true and correct.

14. I have taken into consideration the factors that have an impact on value with respect to the subject neighborhood, subject property, and the proximity of the subject property to adverse influences in the development of my opinion of market value. I have noted in this appraisal report any adverse conditions (such as, but not limited to, needed repairs, deterioration, the presence of hazardous wastes, toxic substances, adverse environmental conditions, etc.) observed during the inspection of the subject property or that I became aware of during the research involved in performing this appraisal. I have considered these adverse conditions in my analysis of the property value, and have reported on the effect of the conditions on the value and marketability of the subject property.

15. I have not knowingly withheld any significant information from this appraisal report and, to the best of my knowledge, all statements and information in this appraisal report are true and correct.

16. I stated in this appraisal report my own personal, unbiased, and professional analysis, opinions, and conclusions, which are subject only to the assumptions and limiting conditions in this appraisal report.

17. I have no present or prospective interest in the property that is the subject of this report, and I have no present or prospective personal interest or bias with respect to the participants in the transaction. I did not base, either partially or completely, my analysis and/or opinion of market value in this appraisal report on the race, color, religion, sex, age, marital status, handicap, familial status, or national origin of either the prospective owners or occupants of the subject property or of the present owners or occupants of the properties in the vicinity of the subject property or on any other basis prohibited by law.

18. My employment and/or compensation for performing this appraisal or any future or anticipated appraisals was not conditioned on any agreement or understanding, written or otherwise, that I would report (or present analysis supporting) a predetermined specific value, a predetermined minimum value, a range or direction in value, a value that favors the cause of any party, or the attainment of a specific result or occurrence of a specific subsequent event (such as approval of a pending mortgage loan application).

19. I personally prepared all conclusions and opinions about the real estate that were set forth in this appraisal report. If I relied on significant real property appraisal assistance from any individual or individuals in the performance of this appraisal or the preparation of this appraisal report, I have named such individual(s) and disclosed the specific tasks performed in this appraisal report. I certify that any individual so named is qualified to perform the tasks. I have not authorized anyone to make a change to any item in this appraisal report; therefore, any change made to this appraisal is unauthorized and I will take no responsibility for it.

20. I identified the lender/client in this appraisal report who is the individual, organization, or agent for the organization that ordered and will receive this appraisal report.

Freddie Mac Form 70 March 2005   Page 5 of 6   Fannie Mae Form 1004 March 2005

FIGURE 8
Definitions, Statement of Assumptions and Limiting Conditions, and Appraiser's Certification (continued)

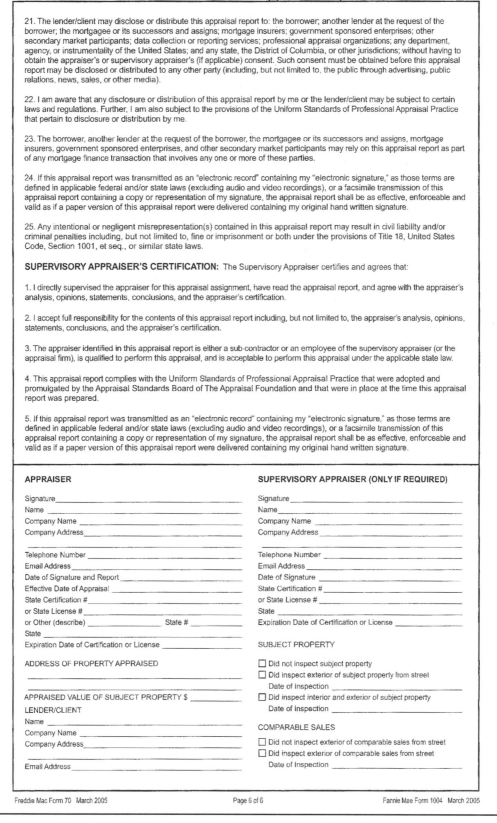

Uniform Residential Appraisal Report   File #

21. The lender/client may disclose or distribute this appraisal report to: the borrower; another lender at the request of the borrower; the mortgagee or its successors and assigns; mortgage insurers; government sponsored enterprises; other secondary market participants; data collection or reporting services; professional appraisal organizations; any department, agency, or instrumentality of the United States; and any state, the District of Columbia, or other jurisdictions; without having to obtain the appraiser's or supervisory appraiser's (if applicable) consent. Such consent must be obtained before this appraisal report may be disclosed or distributed to any other party (including, but not limited to, the public through advertising, public relations, news, sales, or other media).

22. I am aware that any disclosure or distribution of this appraisal report by me or the lender/client may be subject to certain laws and regulations. Further, I am also subject to the provisions of the Uniform Standards of Professional Appraisal Practice that pertain to disclosure or distribution by me.

23. The borrower, another lender at the request of the borrower, the mortgagee or its successors and assigns, mortgage insurers, government sponsored enterprises, and other secondary market participants may rely on this appraisal report as part of any mortgage finance transaction that involves any one or more of these parties.

24. If this appraisal report was transmitted as an "electronic record" containing my "electronic signature," as those terms are defined in applicable federal and/or state laws (excluding audio and video recordings), or a facsimile transmission of this appraisal report containing a copy or representation of my signature, the appraisal report shall be as effective, enforceable and valid as if a paper version of this appraisal report were delivered containing my original hand written signature.

25. Any intentional or negligent misrepresentation(s) contained in this appraisal report may result in civil liability and/or criminal penalties including, but not limited to, fine or imprisonment or both under the provisions of Title 18, United States Code, Section 1001, et seq., or similar state laws.

SUPERVISORY APPRAISER'S CERTIFICATION: The Supervisory Appraiser certifies and agrees that:

1. I directly supervised the appraiser for this appraisal assignment, have read the appraisal report, and agree with the appraiser's analysis, opinions, statements, conclusions, and the appraiser's certification.

2. I accept full responsibility for the contents of this appraisal report including, but not limited to, the appraiser's analysis, opinions, statements, conclusions, and the appraiser's certification.

3. The appraiser identified in this appraisal report is either a sub-contractor or an employee of the supervisory appraiser (or the appraisal firm), is qualified to perform this appraisal, and is acceptable to perform this appraisal under the applicable state law.

4. This appraisal report complies with the Uniform Standards of Professional Appraisal Practice that were adopted and promulgated by the Appraisal Standards Board of The Appraisal Foundation and that were in place at the time this appraisal report was prepared.

5. If this appraisal report was transmitted as an "electronic record" containing my "electronic signature," as those terms are defined in applicable federal and/or state laws (excluding audio and video recordings), or a facsimile transmission of this appraisal report containing a copy or representation of my signature, the appraisal report shall be as effective, enforceable and valid as if a paper version of this appraisal report were delivered containing my original hand written signature.

APPRAISER

Signature_____
Name _____
Company Name _____
Company Address_____

_____

Telephone Number _____
Email Address _____
Date of Signature and Report _____
Effective Date of Appraisal _____
State Certification #_____
or State License #_____
or Other (describe) _____ State # _____
State _____
Expiration Date of Certification or License _____

ADDRESS OF PROPERTY APPRAISED

_____
_____

APPRAISED VALUE OF SUBJECT PROPERTY $ _____

LENDER/CLIENT
Name _____
Company Name _____
Company Address_____

_____

Email Address _____

SUPERVISORY APPRAISER (ONLY IF REQUIRED)

Signature _____
Name_____
Company Name _____
Company Address _____

_____

Telephone Number _____
Email Address _____
Date of Signature _____
State Certification # _____
or State License # _____
State _____
Expiration Date of Certification or License _____

SUBJECT PROPERTY

☐ Did not inspect subject property
☐ Did inspect exterior of subject property from street
    Date of Inspection _____
☐ Did inspect interior and exterior of subject property
    Date of Inspection _____

COMPARABLE SALES

☐ Did not inspect exterior of comparable sales from street
☐ Did inspect exterior of comparable sales from street
    Date of Inspection _____

Freddie Mac Form 70 March 2005   Page 6 of 6   Fannie Mae Form 1004 March 2005

bring in a competitive and open market under all conditions requisite to a fair sale, the buyer and seller each acting prudently and knowledgeably, and assuming the price is not affected by undue stimulus. Market value is not the highest price possible under the most favorable circumstances.

▸ **Fannie Mae**   Fannie Mae will not purchase a mortgage loan unless the underlying property appraisal is based on the most recent version of Form 1004, as revised in March 2005 (current as of publication of this book).

Fannie Mae's definition of *market value* takes into account the effect on value of special or creative financing or sales concessions, such as seller contributions, interest rate buydowns, and so on. Market value is reduced by whatever adjustments are necessary to adequately reflect such concessions. No adjustment is made for ". . . those costs which are normally paid by sellers as a result of tradition or law in a market area; these costs are readily identifiable since the seller pays these costs in virtually all sales transactions . . . ." The term *sellers* refers to all sellers in the market area, whether builders, developers, or individuals in the re-sale market. A practice of one seller, or even a group of sellers, that is not followed by other sellers would qualify as "special." For example, if a seller is paying part of the purchaser's closing costs (or an interest rate buydown or in some other way is helping to provide below-market financing for the buyer), but virtually no other sellers in the market are doing the same, an adjustment must be made by the appraiser. This is true even if another *group* of sellers, such as builders, is also offering concessionary financing.

The sale price of a comparable property that has special or creative financing or sales concessions can be adjusted by comparing it to properties that had third-party institutional lenders (conventional financing), as long as the lender is not involved in the appraisal's subject property or transaction. "The appraiser should use his or her judgment in establishing the dollar amount for any adjustment to assure that it approximates the market's reaction to the financing or concession at the time of the sale."

▸ **HUD/FHA**   Fee appraisers are required to base their value estimate on the Department of Veterans Affairs' regulatory definition of *reasonable value* (38 CFR 36.4301), which the VA considers synonymous with *market value*. Reasonable value is "that figure which represents the amount a reputable and qualified appraiser, unaffected by personal interest, bias, or prejudice, would recommend to a prospective purchaser as a property price or cost in the light of prevailing conditions." This definition is considered consistent with that used by Fannie Mae, Freddie Mac, and the Appraisal Institute. "It is the VA fee appraiser's responsibility to develop a market value for the subject property which is consistent with the current standard definition of market value and the VA regulatory definition of reasonable value."

▸ **USPAP**   Market value is the most probable price a property should bring in a competitive and open market under all conditions requisite to a fair sale, with buyer and seller each acting prudently and knowledgeably, and assuming the price is not affected by undue stimulus. Implicit in this definition is the consummation of a sale as of a specified date and passing of title from seller to buyer under conditions whereby

- buyer and seller are typically motivated;

- both parties are well informed or well advised, and each is acting in what he or she considers his or her own best interest;

- a reasonable time is allowed for exposure in the open market;

- payment is made in terms of cash in U.S. dollars or in terms of financial arrangements comparable to cash; and

- the price represents the normal consideration for the property sold, unaffected by special or creative financing or sales concessions granted by anyone associated with the sale.

Statement of Assumptions and Limiting Conditions (Figure 8, URAR page 4)

The Statement of Assumptions and Limiting Conditions is included in the report to protect the appraiser as well as to inform and protect the client and other users of the report.

Take the time now to read through the assumptions and limiting conditions listed on page 4 of the form.

Appraiser's Certification (Figure 8, URAR pages 5 and 6)

As an appraiser, you certify that the appraisal report contains your personal, unbiased, professional analyses, opinions, and conclusions, subject only to the assumptions and limiting conditions specified on page 4 of the URAR form.

Read through the list of certifications on pages 5 and 6 of the form.

Supervisory Appraiser's Certification (Figure 8, URAR page 6)

As a supervisory appraiser, you certify that you directly supervised the appraiser who prepared the appraisal report, agree with the statements and conclusions of the appraiser, and that the report complies with the Uniform Standards of Professional Appraisal Practice.

Appraiser

This space is for the appraiser who performed the appraisal, carrying out the necessary property inspection, collecting and examining the necessary data, and reconciling the derived value opinions to reach a final conclusion of value for the subject property.

The appraiser must sign the report under this heading and complete the appropriate information in that block.

> ‣ **HUD/FHA** The appraiser signs his or her name and prints the name below the signature with the assigned CHUMS identification number. The report is dated as of the day the property is inspected.

> ‣ **RHS** Appraiser signs.

Address of Property Appraised

Enter the full street address of the subject property and other information listed in that block.

Supervisory Appraiser (only if required)

This space is used to record information about the supervisory appraiser, if there is one. The supervisory appraiser certifies that he or she has directly supervised the preparation of the appraisal report and has reviewed it, agrees with its statements and conclusions, and takes full responsibility for it.

In this space,

- enter the signature of the appraiser who has supervised the preparation of the appraisal report and other personal information listed in this category, and

- check the appropriate boxes under Subject Property and Comparable Sales, indicating whether these properties were personally inspected by the supervisory appraiser.

  ‣ **HUD/FHA** If the report is approved, the supervisory appraiser signs, enters the CHUMS identification number and date of review, and then completes the Data Entry Sheet.

  ‣ **RHS** Supervisory appraiser signs as appropriate.

Review Appraiser

An appraiser who performs a *review* function must prepare a separate review report and attach it to the appraisal report.

Standard Exhibits

For most appraisals, you need to include the following exhibits with the URAR form:

- street map that shows the subject property and comparable sales;

- exterior building sketch that shows the dimensions of the subject property improvements along with calculations showing how gross living area was determined;

- photographs that show the front, back, and street scene of the subject property;

- photographs that show the front of each comparable sale, identified by location; and

- any other information you think is necessary to support your opinion of the subject property's market value.

■ FORM 2055

Because of the demands of the marketplace, Fannie Mae has developed streamlined property valuation and reporting options for lenders. One such option is the *Exterior-Only Inspection Residential Appraisal Report* (Form 2055, Figure 9) to be used in conjunction with Fannie Mae's Desktop Underwriter computer program (DU).

Like the URAR, Form 2055 relies totally on the sales comparison approach, the most reliable indicator of market value for residential properties. The cost and income approaches are not required by Fannie Mae. Thus Fannie Mae classifies the results as a limited appraisal and summary report, in accordance with USPAP.

FIGURE 9
Form 2055

Exterior-Only Inspection Residential Appraisal Report   File

The purpose of this summary appraisal report is to provide the lender/client with an accurate, and adequately supported, opinion of the market value of the subject property.

SUBJECT

| Property Address | | City | | State | Zip Code |

Borrower ___ Owner of Public Record ___ County

Legal Description

Assessor's Parcel # ___ Tax Year ___ R.E. Taxes $

Neighborhood Name ___ Map Reference ___ Census Tract

Occupant ☐ Owner ☐ Tenant ☐ Vacant   Special Assessments $ ___ ☐ PUD HOA $ ___ ☐ per year ☐ per month

Property Rights Appraised ☐ Fee Simple ☐ Leasehold ☐ Other (describe)

Assignment Type ☐ Purchase Transaction ☐ Refinance Transaction ☐ Other (describe)

Lender/Client ___ Address

Is the subject property currently offered for sale or has it been offered for sale in the twelve months prior to the effective date of this appraisal? ☐ Yes ☐ No

Report data source(s) used, offering price(s), and date(s).

CONTRACT

I ☐ did ☐ did not analyze the contract for sale for the subject purchase transaction. Explain the results of the analysis of the contract for sale or why the analysis was not performed.

Contract Price $ ___ Date of Contract ___ Is the property seller the owner of public record? ☐ Yes ☐ No Data Source(s)

Is there any financial assistance (loan charges, sale concessions, gift or downpayment assistance, etc.) to be paid by any party on behalf of the borrower? ☐ Yes ☐ No
If Yes, report the total dollar amount and describe the items to be paid.

NEIGHBORHOOD

Note: Race and the racial composition of the neighborhood are not appraisal factors.

Neighborhood Characteristics			One-Unit Housing Trends			One-Unit Housing		Present Land Use %	
Location ☐ Urban ☐ Suburban ☐ Rural			Property Values ☐ Increasing ☐ Stable ☐ Declining			PRICE	AGE	One-Unit	%
Built-Up ☐ Over 75% ☐ 25–75% ☐ Under 25%			Demand/Supply ☐ Shortage ☐ In Balance ☐ Over Supply			$ (000)	(yrs)	2-4 Unit	%
Growth ☐ Rapid ☐ Stable ☐ Slow			Marketing Time ☐ Under 3 mths ☐ 3–6 mths ☐ Over 6 mths			Low		Multi-Family	%
Neighborhood Boundaries						High		Commercial	%
						Pred.		Other	%

Neighborhood Description

Market Conditions (including support for the above conclusions)

SITE

| Dimensions | | Area | Shape | | View | |

Specific Zoning Classification ___ Zoning Description

Zoning Compliance ☐ Legal ☐ Legal Nonconforming (Grandfathered Use) ☐ No Zoning ☐ Illegal (describe)

Is the highest and best use of the subject property as improved (or as proposed per plans and specifications) the present use? ☐ Yes ☐ No If No, describe

Utilities	Public	Other (describe)		Public	Other (describe)	Off-site Improvements—Type	Public	Private
Electricity	☐	☐	Water	☐	☐	Street	☐	☐
Gas	☐	☐	Sanitary Sewer	☐	☐	Alley	☐	☐

FEMA Special Flood Hazard Area ☐ Yes ☐ No FEMA Flood Zone ___ FEMA Map # ___ FEMA Map Date

Are the utilities and off-site improvements typical for the market area? ☐ Yes ☐ No If No, describe

Are there any adverse site conditions or external factors (easements, encroachments, environmental conditions, land uses, etc.)? ☐ Yes ☐ No If Yes, describe

IMPROVEMENTS

Source(s) Used for Physical Characteristics of Property ☐ Appraisal Files ☐ MLS ☐ Assessment and Tax Records ☐ Prior Inspection ☐ Property Owner
☐ Other (describe) ___ Data Source(s) for Gross Living Area

General Description	General Description	Heating / Cooling	Amenities	Car Storage
Units ☐ One ☐ One with Accessory Unit	☐ Concrete Slab ☐ Crawl Space	☐ FWA ☐ HWBB	☐ Fireplace(s) #	☐ None
# of Stories	☐ Full Basement ☐ Finished	☐ Radiant	☐ Woodstove(s) #	☐ Driveway # of Cars
Type ☐ Det. ☐ Att. ☐ S-Det./End Unit	☐ Partial Basement ☐ Finished	☐ Other	☐ Patio/Deck	Driveway Surface
☐ Existing ☐ Proposed ☐ Under Const.	Exterior Walls	Fuel	☐ Porch	☐ Garage # of Cars
Design (Style)	Roof Surface	☐ Central Air Conditioning	☐ Pool	☐ Carport # of Cars
Year Built	Gutters & Downspouts	☐ Individual	☐ Fence	☐ Attached ☐ Detached
Effective Age (Yrs)	Window Type	☐ Other	☐ Other	☐ Built-in

Appliances ☐ Refrigerator ☐ Range/Oven ☐ Dishwasher ☐ Disposal ☐ Microwave ☐ Washer/Dryer ☐ Other (describe)

Finished area **above grade** contains: ___ Rooms ___ Bedrooms ___ Bath(s) ___ Square Feet of Gross Living Area Above Grade

Additional features (special energy efficient items, etc.)

Describe the condition of the property and data source(s) (including apparent needed repairs, deterioration, renovations, remodeling, etc.).

Are there any apparent physical deficiencies or adverse conditions that affect the livability, soundness, or structural integrity of the property? ☐ Yes ☐ No
If Yes, describe

Does the property generally conform to the neighborhood (functional utility, style, condition, use, construction, etc.)? ☐ Yes ☐ No If No, describe

Freddie Mac Form 2055 March 2005 ___ Page 1 of 6 ___ Fannie Mae Form 2055 March 2005

F I G U R E 9
Form 2055 (continued)

Exterior-Only Inspection Residential Appraisal Report   File

There are	comparable properties currently offered for sale in the subject neighborhood ranging in price from $		to $	
There are	comparable sales in the subject neighborhood within the past twelve months ranging in sale price from $		to $	

FEATURE	SUBJECT	COMPARABLE SALE # 1		COMPARABLE SALE # 2		COMPARABLE SALE # 3	
Address							
Proximity to Subject							
Sale Price	$	$		$		$	
Sale Price/Gross Liv. Area	$ sq. ft.	$ sq. ft.		$ sq. ft.		$ sq. ft.	
Data Source(s)							
Verification Source(s)							
VALUE ADJUSTMENTS	DESCRIPTION	DESCRIPTION	+(-) $ Adjustment	DESCRIPTION	+(-) $ Adjustment	DESCRIPTION	+(-) $ Adjustment
Sale or Financing Concessions							
Date of Sale/Time							
Location							
Leasehold/Fee Simple							
Site							
View							
Design (Style)							
Quality of Construction							
Actual Age							
Condition							
Above Grade	Total Bdrms. Baths	Total Bdrms. Baths		Total Bdrms. Baths		Total Bdrms. Baths	
Room Count							
Gross Living Area	sq. ft.	sq. ft.		sq. ft.		sq. ft.	
Basement & Finished Rooms Below Grade							
Functional Utility							
Heating/Cooling							
Energy Efficient Items							
Garage/Carport							
Porch/Patio/Deck							
Net Adjustment (Total)		☐ + ☐ -	$	☐ + ☐ -	$	☐ + ☐ -	$
Adjusted Sale Price of Comparables		Net Adj. % Gross Adj. %	$	Net Adj. % Gross Adj. %	$	Net Adj. % Gross Adj. %	$

I ☐ did ☐ did not research the sale or transfer history of the subject property and comparable sales. If not, explain

My research ☐ did ☐ did not reveal any prior sales or transfers of the subject property for the three years prior to the effective date of this appraisal.

Data source(s)

My research ☐ did ☐ did not reveal any prior sales or transfers of the comparable sales for the year prior to the date of sale of the comparable sale.

Data source(s)

Report the results of the research and analysis of the prior sale or transfer history of the subject property and comparable sales (report additional prior sales on page 3).

ITEM	SUBJECT	COMPARABLE SALE # 1	COMPARABLE SALE # 2	COMPARABLE SALE # 3
Date of Prior Sale/Transfer				
Price of Prior Sale/Transfer				
Data Source(s)				
Effective Date of Data Source(s)				

Analysis of prior sale or transfer history of the subject property and comparable sales

Summary of Sales Comparison Approach

Indicated Value by Sales Comparison Approach $

Indicated Value by: Sales Comparison Approach $ Cost Approach (if developed) $ Income Approach (if developed) $

This appraisal is made ☐ "as is", ☐ subject to completion per plans and specifications on the basis of a hypothetical condition that the improvements have been completed, ☐ subject to the following repairs or alterations on the basis of a hypothetical condition that the repairs or alterations have been completed, or ☐ subject to the following required inspection based on the extraordinary assumption that the condition or deficiency does not require alteration or repair:

Based on a visual inspection of the exterior areas of the subject property from at least the street, defined scope of work, statement of assumptions and limiting conditions, and appraiser's certification, my (our) opinion of the market value, as defined, of the real property that is the subject of this report is $, as of   , which is the date of the inspection and the effective date of this appraisal.

FIGURE 9
Form 2055 (continued)

Exterior-Only Inspection Residential Appraisal Report   File

ADDITIONAL COMMENTS

COST APPROACH TO VALUE (not required by Fannie Mae)

Provide adequate information for the lender/client to replicate the below cost figures and calculations.

Support for the opinion of site value (summary of comparable land sales or other methods for estimating site value)

ESTIMATED ☐ REPRODUCTION OR ☐ REPLACEMENT COST NEW	OPINION OF SITE VALUE..................................... = $	
Source of cost data	Dwelling Sq. Ft. @ $ ....=$	
Quality rating from cost service Effective date of cost data	Sq. Ft. @ $ ....=$	
Comments on Cost Approach (gross living area calculations, depreciation, etc.)		
	Garage/Carport Sq. Ft. @ $ ....=$	
	Total Estimate of Cost-New ....= $	
	Less Physical Functional External	
	Depreciation =$( )	
	Depreciated Cost of Improvements......................=$	
	"As-is" Value of Site Improvements.......................=$	
Estimated Remaining Economic Life (HUD and VA only) Years	Indicated Value By Cost Approach......................=$	

INCOME APPROACH TO VALUE (not required by Fannie Mae)

Estimated Monthly Market Rent $ X Gross Rent Multiplier   = $ Indicated Value by Income Approach

Summary of Income Approach (including support for market rent and GRM)

PROJECT INFORMATION FOR PUDs (if applicable)

Is the developer/builder in control of the Homeowners' Association (HOA)? ☐ Yes ☐ No   Unit type(s) ☐ Detached ☐ Attached

Provide the following information for PUDs ONLY if the developer/builder is in control of the HOA and the subject property is an attached dwelling unit.

Legal name of project

Total number of phases   Total number of units   Total number of units sold

Total number of units rented   Total number of units for sale   Data source(s)

Was the project created by the conversion of an existing building(s) into a PUD? ☐ Yes ☐ No If Yes, date of conversion

Does the project contain any multi-dwelling units? ☐ Yes ☐ No Data source(s)

Are the units, common elements, and recreation facilities complete? ☐ Yes ☐ No If No, describe the status of completion.

Are the common elements leased to or by the Homeowners' Association? ☐ Yes ☐ No If Yes, describe the rental terms and options.

Describe common elements and recreational facilities

FIGURE 9
Form 2055 (continued)

Exterior-Only Inspection Residential Appraisal Report   File

This report form is designed to report an appraisal of a one-unit property or a one-unit property with an accessory unit; including a unit in a planned unit development (PUD). This report form is not designed to report an appraisal of a manufactured home or a unit in a condominium or cooperative project.

This appraisal report is subject to the following scope of work, intended use, intended user, definition of market value, statement of assumptions and limiting conditions, and certifications. Modifications, additions, or deletions to the intended use, intended user, definition of market value, or assumptions and limiting conditions are not permitted. The appraiser may expand the scope of work to include any additional research or analysis necessary based on the complexity of this appraisal assignment. Modifications or deletions to the certifications are also not permitted. However, additional certifications that do not constitute material alterations to this appraisal report, such as those required by law or those related to the appraiser's continuing education or membership in an appraisal organization, are permitted.

SCOPE OF WORK: The scope of work for this appraisal is defined by the complexity of this appraisal assignment and the reporting requirements of this appraisal report form, including the following definition of market value, statement of assumptions and limiting conditions, and certifications. The appraiser must, at a minimum: (1) perform a visual inspection of the exterior areas of the subject property from at least the street, (2) inspect the neighborhood, (3) inspect each of the comparable sales from at least the street, (4) research, verify, and analyze data from reliable public and/or private sources, and (5) report his or her analysis, opinions, and conclusions in this appraisal report.

The appraiser must be able to obtain adequate information about the physical characteristics (including, but not limited to, condition, room count, gross living area, etc.) of the subject property from the exterior-only inspection and reliable public and/or private sources to perform this appraisal. The appraiser should use the same type of data sources that he or she uses for comparable sales such as, but not limited to, multiple listing services, tax and assessment records, prior inspections, appraisal files, information provided by the property owner, etc.

INTENDED USE: The intended use of this appraisal report is for the lender/client to evaluate the property that is the subject of this appraisal for a mortgage finance transaction.

INTENDED USER: The intended user of this appraisal report is the lender/client.

DEFINITION MARKET VALUE: The most probable price which a property should bring in a competitive and open market under all conditions requisite to a fair sale, the buyer and seller, each acting prudently, knowledgeably and assuming the price is not affected by undue stimulus. Implicit in this definition is the consummation of a sale as of a specified date and the passing of title from seller to buyer under conditions whereby: (1) buyer and seller are typically motivated; (2) both parties are well informed or well advised, and each acting in what he or she considers his or her own best interest; (3) a reasonable time is allowed for exposure in the open market; (4) payment is made in terms of cash in U. S. dollars or in terms of financial arrangements comparable thereto; and (5) the price represents the normal consideration for the property sold unaffected by special or creative financing or sales concessions* granted by anyone associated with the sale.

*Adjustments to the comparables must be made for special or creative financing or sales concessions. No adjustments are necessary for those costs which are normally paid by sellers as a result of tradition or law in a market area; these costs are readily identifiable since the seller pays these costs in virtually all sales transactions. Special or creative financing adjustments can be made to the comparable property by comparisons to financing terms offered by a third party institutional lender that is not already involved in the property or transaction. Any adjustment should not be calculated on a mechanical dollar for dollar cost of the financing or concession but the dollar amount of any adjustment should approximate the market's reaction to the financing or concessions based on the appraiser's judgment.

STATEMENT OF ASSUMPTIONS AND LIMITING CONDITIONS: The appraiser's certification in this report is subject to the following assumptions and limiting conditions:

1. The appraiser will not be responsible for matters of a legal nature that affect either the property being appraised or the title to it, except for information that he or she became aware of during the research involved in performing this appraisal. The appraiser assumes that the title is good and marketable and will not render any opinions about the title.

2. The appraiser has examined the available flood maps that are provided by the Federal Emergency Management Agency (or other data sources) and has noted in this appraisal report whether any portion of the subject site is located in an identified Special Flood Hazard Area. Because the appraiser is not a surveyor, he or she makes no guarantees, express or implied, regarding this determination.

3. The appraiser will not give testimony or appear in court because he or she made an appraisal of the property in question, unless specific arrangements to do so have been made beforehand, or as otherwise required by law.

4. The appraiser has noted in this appraisal report any adverse conditions (such as needed repairs, deterioration, the presence of hazardous wastes, toxic substances, etc.) observed during the inspection of the subject property or that he or she became aware of during the research involved in performing this appraisal. Unless otherwise stated in this appraisal report, the appraiser has no knowledge of any hidden or unapparent physical deficiencies or adverse conditions of the property (such as, but not limited to, needed repairs, deterioration, the presence of hazardous wastes, toxic substances, adverse environmental conditions, etc.) that would make the property less valuable, and has assumed that there are no such conditions and makes no guarantees or warranties, express or implied. The appraiser will not be responsible for any such conditions that do exist or for any engineering or testing that might be required to discover whether such conditions exist. Because the appraiser is not an expert in the field of environmental hazards, this appraisal report must not be considered as an environmental assessment of the property.

5. The appraiser has based his or her appraisal report and valuation conclusion for an appraisal that is subject to satisfactory completion, repairs, or alterations on the assumption that the completion, repairs, or alterations of the subject property will be performed in a professional manner.

FIGURE 9
Form 2055 (continued)

Exterior-Only Inspection Residential Appraisal Report   File

APPRAISER'S CERTIFICATION: The Appraiser certifies and agrees that:

1. I have, at a minimum, developed and reported this appraisal in accordance with the scope of work requirements stated in this appraisal report.

2. I performed a visual inspection of the exterior areas of the subject property from at least the street. I reported the condition of the improvements in factual, specific terms. I identified and reported the physical deficiencies that could affect the livability, soundness, or structural integrity of the property.

3. I performed this appraisal in accordance with the requirements of the Uniform Standards of Professional Appraisal Practice that were adopted and promulgated by the Appraisal Standards Board of The Appraisal Foundation and that were in place at the time this appraisal report was prepared.

4. I developed my opinion of the market value of the real property that is the subject of this report based on the sales comparison approach to value. I have adequate comparable market data to develop a reliable sales comparison approach for this appraisal assignment. I further certify that I considered the cost and income approaches to value but did not develop them, unless otherwise indicated in this report.

5. I researched, verified, analyzed, and reported on any current agreement for sale for the subject property, any offering for sale of the subject property in the twelve months prior to the effective date of this appraisal, and the prior sales of the subject property for a minimum of three years prior to the effective date of this appraisal, unless otherwise indicated in this report.

6. I researched, verified, analyzed, and reported on the prior sales of the comparable sales for a minimum of one year prior to the date of sale of the comparable sale, unless otherwise indicated in this report.

7. I selected and used comparable sales that are locationally, physically, and functionally the most similar to the subject property.

8. I have not used comparable sales that were the result of combining a land sale with the contract purchase price of a home that has been built or will be built on the land.

9. I have reported adjustments to the comparable sales that reflect the market's reaction to the differences between the subject property and the comparable sales.

10. I verified, from a disinterested source, all information in this report that was provided by parties who have a financial interest in the sale or financing of the subject property.

11. I have knowledge and experience in appraising this type of property in this market area.

12. I am aware of, and have access to, the necessary and appropriate public and private data sources, such as multiple listing services, tax assessment records, public land records and other such data sources for the area in which the property is located.

13. I obtained the information, estimates, and opinions furnished by other parties and expressed in this appraisal report from reliable sources that I believe to be true and correct.

14. I have taken into consideration the factors that have an impact on value with respect to the subject neighborhood, subject property, and the proximity of the subject property to adverse influences in the development of my opinion of market value. I have noted in this appraisal report any adverse conditions (such as, but not limited to, needed repairs, deterioration, the presence of hazardous wastes, toxic substances, adverse environmental conditions, etc.) observed during the inspection of the subject property or that I became aware of during the research involved in performing this appraisal. I have considered these adverse conditions in my analysis of the property value, and have reported on the effect of the conditions on the value and marketability of the subject property.

15. I have not knowingly withheld any significant information from this appraisal report and, to the best of my knowledge, all statements and information in this appraisal report are true and correct.

16. I stated in this appraisal report my own personal, unbiased, and professional analysis, opinions, and conclusions, which are subject only to the assumptions and limiting conditions in this appraisal report.

17. I have no present or prospective interest in the property that is the subject of this report, and I have no present or prospective personal interest or bias with respect to the participants in the transaction. I did not base, either partially or completely, my analysis and/or opinion of market value in this appraisal report on the race, color, religion, sex, age, marital status, handicap, familial status, or national origin of either the prospective owners or occupants of the subject property or of the present owners or occupants of the properties in the vicinity of the subject property or on any other basis prohibited by law.

18. My employment and/or compensation for performing this appraisal or any future or anticipated appraisals was not conditioned on any agreement or understanding, written or otherwise, that I would report (or present analysis supporting) a predetermined specific value, a predetermined minimum value, a range or direction in value, a value that favors the cause of any party, or the attainment of a specific result or occurrence of a specific subsequent event (such as approval of a pending mortgage loan application).

19. I personally prepared all conclusions and opinions about the real estate that were set forth in this appraisal report. If I relied on significant real property appraisal assistance from any individual or individuals in the performance of this appraisal or the preparation of this appraisal report, I have named such individual(s) and disclosed the specific tasks performed in this appraisal report. I certify that any individual so named is qualified to perform the tasks. I have not authorized anyone to make a change to any item in this appraisal report; therefore, any change made to this appraisal is unauthorized and I will take no responsibility for it.

Freddie Mae Form 2055   March 2005 | Page 5 of 6 | Fannie Mae Form 2055   March 2005

FIGURE 9
Form 2055 (continued)

Exterior-Only Inspection Residential Appraisal Report   File

20. I identified the lender/client in this appraisal report who is the individual, organization, or agent for the organization that ordered and will receive this appraisal report.

21. The lender/client may disclose or distribute this appraisal report to: the borrower; another lender at the request of the borrower; the mortgagee or its successors and assigns; mortgage insurers; government sponsored enterprises; other secondary market participants; data collection or reporting services; professional appraisal organizations; any department, agency, or instrumentality of the United States; and any state, the District of Columbia, or other jurisdictions; without having to obtain the appraiser's or supervisory appraiser's (if applicable) consent. Such consent must be obtained before this appraisal report may be disclosed or distributed to any other party (including, but not limited to, the public through advertising, public relations, news, sales, or other media).

22. I am aware that any disclosure or distribution of this appraisal report by me or the lender/client may be subject to certain laws and regulations. Further, I am also subject to the provisions of the Uniform Standards of Professional Appraisal Practice that pertain to disclosure or distribution by me.

23. The borrower, another lender at the request of the borrower, the mortgagee or its successors and assigns, mortgage insurers, government sponsored enterprises, and other secondary market participants may rely on this appraisal report as part of any mortgage finance transaction that involves any one or more of these parties.

24. If this appraisal report was transmitted as an "electronic record" containing my "electronic signature," as those terms are defined in applicable federal and/or state laws (excluding audio and video recordings), or a facsimile transmission of this appraisal report containing a copy or representation of my signature, the appraisal report shall be as effective, enforceable and valid as if a paper version of this appraisal report were delivered containing my original hand written signature.

25. Any intentional or negligent misrepresentation(s) contained in this appraisal report may result in civil liability and/or criminal penalties including, but not limited to, fine or imprisonment or both under the provisions of Title 18, United States Code, Section 1001, et seq., or similar state laws.

SUPERVISORY APPRAISER'S CERTIFICATION: The Supervisory Appraiser certifies and agrees that:

1. I directly supervised the appraiser for this appraisal assignment, have read the appraisal report, and agree with the appraiser's analysis, opinions, statements, conclusions, and the appraiser's certification.

2. I accept full responsibility for the contents of this appraisal report including, but not limited to, the appraiser's analysis, opinions, statements, and conclusions, and the appraiser's certification.

3. The appraiser identified in this appraisal report is either a sub-contractor or an employee of the supervisory appraiser (or the appraisal firm), is qualified to perform this appraisal, and is acceptable to perform this appraisal under the applicable state law.

4. This appraisal report complies with the Uniform Standards of Professional Appraisal Practice that were adopted and promulgated by the Appraisal Standards Board of The Appraisal Foundation and that were in place at the time this appraisal report was prepared.

5. If this appraisal report was transmitted as an "electronic record" containing my "electronic signature," as those terms are defined in applicable federal and/or state laws (excluding audio and video recordings), or a facsimile transmission of this appraisal report containing a copy or representation of my signature, the appraisal report shall be as effective, enforceable and valid as if a paper version of this appraisal report were delivered containing my original hand written signature.

APPRAISER	SUPERVISORY APPRAISER (ONLY IF REQUIRED)
Signature _____	Signature _____
Name _____	Name _____
Company Name _____	Company Name _____
Company Address _____	Company Address _____
Telephone Number _____	Telephone Number _____
Email Address _____	Email Address _____
Date of Signature and Report_____	Date of Signature_____
Effective Date of Appraisal _____	State Certification # _____
State Certification # _____	or State License # _____
or State License #_____	State_____
or Other (describe) _____ State #_____	Expiration Date of Certification or License _____
State _____	
Expiration Date of Certification or License _____	SUBJECT PROPERTY
ADDRESS OF PROPERTY APPRAISED	☐ Did not inspect exterior of subject property
_____	☐ Did inspect exterior of subject property from street
_____	Date of Inspection _____
APPRAISED VALUE OF SUBJECT PROPERTY $_____	
LENDER/CLIENT	COMPARABLE SALES
Name _____	☐ Did not inspect exterior of comparable sales from street
Company Name _____	☐ Did inspect exterior of comparable sales from street
Company Address _____	Date of Inspection _____
Email Address_____	

Form 2055 allows a drive-by inspection option based on a risk assessment of the loan. The DU system works best when there is a large quantity of current and accurate data, when properties in the area are highly similar, and when a property's condition and marketability are typical for the area.

The appraiser's description of the physical characteristics of the subject property is based on the drive-by inspection and what he or she believes to be reliable data sources. Such sources may include prior inspections, appraisal files, MLS data, assessment and tax records, information provided by the property owner, or other sources of information available to the appraiser.

If the appraiser does not have adequate information about the physical characteristics of the subject property, he or she must inspect both the exterior and interior of the property as in any normal appraisal.

Form 2055 consists of the same basic sections as the URAR:

1. Subject

2. Contract

3. Neighborhood

4. Site

5. Improvements

6. Sales comparison approach

7. Reconciliation

8. Additional comments

9. Cost approach

10. Income approach

11. PUD information

12. Definition of terms—scope of work, intended use, intended user, and market value

13. Statement of assumptions and limiting conditions

14. Appraiser's certification

15. Appraiser information block

16. Supervisory appraiser information block

If the drive-by inspection option is used, the only exhibits required are a photograph that shows the front scene of the subject property and a street map that shows the location of the subject property and comparables.

If both exterior and interior inspections of the property are required, the standard exhibits needed to support appraisal report forms such as the URAR must be included.

> ▸ **HUD/FHA** Fannie Mae forms that are used for streamlined appraisals, such as Form 2055, are not acceptable at this time.

Differences between Form 2055 and the URAR Form

In a normal appraisal using the URAR Form, the appraiser is required to perform both an interior and an exterior inspection of the subject property. In a streamlined or drive-by appraisal using Form 2055, the appraiser is required to do an exterior-only inspection. This is the key difference between the two forms.

Specifically, the two forms differ in the areas listed on the next page.

■ *Improvements Section.* Because Form 2055 requires an exterior inspection of the subject property only, there are no *interior* information blocks to be filled in. The URAR form, on the other hand, requires both interior and exterior inspections, and information blocks must be completed for both the outside and inside of the subject house.

In the first two lines at the top of the *Improvements* section of Form 2055, you are asked to fill in the source or sources used to collect information on the physical characteristics of the subject property. You won't find these lines on the URAR form.

■ *Reconciliation Section.* At the bottom of this section of Form 2055, the first line says that the appraisal was *based on a visual inspection of the exterior areas of the subject property from at least the street.* On the URAR form, that same line reads, the appraisal was *based on a complete visual inspection of the interior and exterior areas of the subject property.*

■ *Scope of Work Definition.* In an appraisal using Form 2055, the appraiser must   perform a visual inspection of the exterior areas of the subject property from at least the street. In an appraisal using the URAR form, the appraiser is required to perform a complete visual inspection of the interior and exterior areas of the subject property.

■ *Statement of Assumptions and Limiting Conditions.* In an appraisal using Form 2055, the appraiser is not required to provide a sketch to show the approximate dimensions of the improvements. A sketch is required for an appraisal using the URAR form.

■ *Appraiser's Certification.* The certifications in both forms are the same except for number 2. In an appraisal using Form 2055, the appraiser is required to perform a visual inspection of the exterior areas of the subject property only. In an appraisal using the URAR form, the appraiser must perform a complete visual inspection of both the interior and exterior areas of the subject property.

■ *Supervisory Appraiser.* Finally, in the URAR form, under *Subject Property,* the supervisory appraiser is asked whether he or she inspected both the interior and the exterior of the property. The same block of information on Form 2055 refers to an *exterior-only* inspection.

APPRAISAL 1

R E C O N C I L I A T I O N	Indicated Value by: Sales Comparison Approach $ 450,500 Cost Approach (if developed) $ 452,900 Income Approach (if developed) $

Because there are few rentals, the income approach is not considered applicable for properties in this area. There are no special financing considerations. The final value opinion is based on the sales comparison approach--a reasonable and supportable method for this type of property. The cost approach strongly suppports this opinion of value.

This appraisal is made [X] "as is," [ ] subject to completion per plans and specifications on the basis of a hypothetical condition that the improvements have been completed, [ ] subject to the following repairs or alterations on the basis of a hypothetical condition that the repairs or alterations have been completed, or [ ] subject to the following required inspection based on the extraordinary assumption that the condition or deficiency does not require alteration or repair:

Based on a complete visual inspection of the interior and exterior areas of the subject property, defined scope of work, statement of assumptions and limiting conditions, and appraiser's certification, my (our) opinion of the market value, as defined, of the real property that is the subject of this report is

$ 450,500   , as of   9-12-05   , which is the date of inspection and the effective date of this appraisal.

In Appraisal 1, the subject property is appraised "as is." There are no repairs or other on-going construction work to which the appraisal is subject. The appraiser has used the space in the RECONCILIATION section to begin the explanation of how the reconciliation process was carried out. The income approach was not considered applicable for properties in this area. There are no special financing considerations affecting market value.

The final value estimate is based on the sales comparison approach, because it is a reasonable and supportable method for this type of property and there were good comps to choose from. The market value opinion is $450,500.

E X E R C I S E : A P P R A I S A L 2

R E C O N C I L I A T I O N	Indicated Value by: Sales Comparison Approach $ Cost Approach (if developed) $ Income Approach (if developed) $

This appraisal is made ☐ "as is", ☐ subject to completion per plans and specifications on the basis of a hypothetical condition that the improvements have been completed, ☐ subject to the following repairs or alterations on the basis of a hypothetical condition that the repairs or alterations have been completed, or ☐ subject to the following required inspection based on the extraordinary assumption that the condition or deficiency does not require alteration or repair:

Based on a complete visual inspection of the interior and exterior areas of the subject property, defined scope of work, statement of assumptions and limiting conditions, and appraiser's certification, my (our) opinion of the market value, as defined, of the real property that is the subject of this report is $, as of , which is the date of inspection and the effective date of this appraisal. |

Complete the blank URAR RECONCILIATION section for Appraisal 2, using the following information. When you have finished, you can check your work against the completed Appraisal 2 in the Answer Key.

There is no ongoing or uncompleted construction work, repairs, or alterations to the subject property improvements. The property is appraised "as is."

The income approach is not considered a valid indicator of value for this appraisal, because few similar properties in the area are rented out. No new properties are being built in the area. The most reasonable and supportable conclusion of market value is reached by analyzing the sales prices of comparable properties.

The appraisal is subject to the market value definition, scope of work, and certifications and limiting conditions specified on the form. As of November 30, 2005 the indicated market value for the subject is $365,000.

SECTION 8: ADDITIONAL COMMENTS

This section of the URAR form is used to cover any information provided earlier that requires further explanation. If this space is insufficient, an addendum can be added to the form.

SECTION 9: COST APPROACH

COST APPROACH TO VALUE (not required by Fannie Mae)				
Provide adequate information for the lender/client to replicate the below cost figures and calculations.				
Support for the opinion of site value (summary of comparable land sales or other methods for estimating site value)				

ESTIMATED ☐ REPRODUCTION OR ☐ REPLACEMENT COST NEW	OPINION OF SITE VALUE .... = $			
Source of cost data	Dwelling	Sq. Ft. @ $	.... =$	
Quality rating from cost service Effective date of cost data		Sq. Ft. @ $	.... =$	
Comments on Cost Approach (gross living area calculations, depreciation, etc.)				
	Garage/Carport	Sq. Ft. @ $	.... =$	
	Total Estimate of Cost-New		.... = $	
	Less	Physical	Functional	External
	Depreciation			=$( )
	Depreciated Cost of Improvements.. =$			
	"As-is" Value of Site Improvements... =$			
Estimated Remaining Economic Life (HUD and VA only) Years	Indicated Value By Cost Approach .... =$			

An appraiser makes use of construction costs to determine value by the cost approach. The formula for the cost approach is:

$$\begin{matrix} \text{Reproduction or} \\ \text{Replacement} \\ \text{Cost of} \\ \text{Improvements} \end{matrix} \quad - \quad \begin{matrix} \text{Accrued} \\ \text{Depreciation} \end{matrix} \quad + \quad \text{Site Value} \; = \; \text{Property Value}$$

First the appraiser estimates the present reproduction cost to construct a duplicate of all the improvements on the subject property. If the improvements would be impossible or impractical to duplicate, the appraiser estimates replacement cost, the cost of constructing improvements with the same functional utility. The appraiser then subtracts any loss in value due to depreciation of the improvements. Finally the appraiser adds his or her opinion of site value. The resulting figure is the property's indicated value by the cost approach. The appraiser must provide the figures in the categories required by the form to determine the indicated value by the cost approach.

The URAR cost approach analysis requires the appraiser to

- develop an opinion of site value,
- compute the area of the dwelling,
- estimate the reproduction or replacement cost of the dwelling,
- estimate the reproduction cost of any garage, carport, or other structure,
- estimate the amount by which the structures have depreciated,
- estimate the "as-is" value of any other site improvements, and
- add site value to the depreciated cost of improvements to find the indicated value.

In addition, the appraisal usually will include an addendum showing a rough drawing of the perimeter of the subject structure(s), with dimensions given in feet.

It should be apparent from the list above that the cost approach requires a level of knowledge and experience beyond that of most beginning appraisers. For more technical information, courses in cost estimating and the proper use of available resources are available from appraisal organizations as well as Marshall and Swift and other cost estimating services.

▸ **Fannie Mae**   The cost approach assumes that a potential purchaser will consider building a substitute residence that has the same use as the property that is being appraised. This approach, then, measures value as a cost of production. The reliability of the cost approach depends on valid reproduction cost estimates, proper depreciation estimates, and accurate site values. Fannie Mae will not accept appraisals that rely solely on the cost approach as an indicator of market value.

Fannie Mae does not require the appraiser to use the cost approach for any appraisal documented on the URAR (Form 1004). Furthermore, the appraiser does not need to consider the cost approach when appraising a unit in a condominium or cooperative project because such units are integral parts of the total project, and the cost approach generally is impractical for determining the value of any given unit.

In the cost approach the indicated value of a property is reached by estimating the reproduction cost of new improvements, subtracting the amount of depreciation of the improvements from all causes and adding an opinion of site value as if it were vacant and available to be developed to its highest and best use.

As the effective age of a property increases, the reliability of the cost approach may decrease because the depreciation estimates may be subjective.

▸ **HUD/FHA**   For all new construction and existing properties less than one year old, both the cost and the sales comparison approaches must be used. If the appraiser does not have the plans, specifications, and construction documents as well as the completed builder's certification at the time the appraisal is to be performed, he or she may not complete the appraisal until such documentation is made available.

There should be a building sketch that includes all exterior dimensions of the house as well as patios, porches, garages, breezeways, and other "offsets." If there is a patio, indicate whether it has a roof by entering **COVERED** or **UNCOVERED.**

▸ **RHS**   Provide a sketch of the existing home on the reverse side of the Marshall and Swift Form 1007: "Square Foot Appraisal Form." ATTACH A RECENT PHOTOGRAPH OF THE EXISTING HOME IN THIS SECTION. [Sample Form 1007 is shown in Figure 10.]

▸ **VA**   A building sketch should be made only if necessary to illustrate unique features of the subject, the presence of functional obsolescence or other special property characteristics.

■ DEVELOP AN OPINION OF SITE VALUE

In appraisals of single-family residences, the sales comparison approach is most frequently used to arrive at an opinion of site value. Just as the value of a house

F I G U R E   10

Marshall and Swift form 1007: "Square Foot Appraisal Form"

SQUARE FOOT APPRAISAL FORM
For use with the RESIDENTIAL COST HANDBOOK

Appraisal for _____   Property owner _____

Address _____

Appraiser _____   Date _____

TYPE	QUALITY	STYLE	EXTERIOR WALLS	GARAGE TYPE
Single Family [X]	Low [ ]	No. Stories _One_	Hardboard/Plywood [ ]	Detached [ ]
Multiple [ ]	Fair [ ]	Bi-level [ ]	Stucco [X]	Attached [X]
Town House [ ]	Average [ ]	Split Level [ ]	Siding or Shingle [ ]	Built-In [ ]
Row House [ ]	Good [X]	1½ story - Fin. [ ]	Masonry Veneer [ ]	Subterranean [ ]
Manufactured	Very Good [ ]	1½ story - Unf. [ ]	Common Brick [ ]	Carport [ ]
House [ ]	Excellent [ ]	2½ story - Fin. [ ]	Face Brick or Stone [ ]	Garage Area

FLOOR AREA   **BASEMENT AREA**   2½ story - Unf. [ ]   Concrete Block [ ]   560 Sq. Ft.

1st _2,388 Sq. Ft._   Unf. _____   End Row [ ]   **MANUFACTURED**   **BALCONY AREA**

2nd _____   Fin. _____   Inside Row [ ]   Alum., Ribbed [ ]

3rd _____   **NUMBER OF PLUMBING**   Lap Siding [ ]   **PORCH BRZWY. AREA**

Total _2,388 Sq. Ft._   Fixtures _13_   **NUMBER OF MULTIPLE**   Hardboard [ ]   (a) _233 Sq. Ft._

Rough-in _1_   **UNITS** _____   Plywood [ ]   (b) _____

		Quan.	Cost		Extension
1.	COMPUTE RESIDENCE BASIC COST: Floor area x selected sq. ft. cost	2,388	$34.40		$ 82,147
2.	SQUARE FOOT ADJUSTMENTS:			+ −	
3.	Roofing _Wood Shingle (Base)_				
4.	Subfloor _Concrete Slab_	2,388	1.89	−	‹4,513›
5.	Floor Cover _80% Carpet @$2.23 = $1.78 20% Res. @ $1.93 = $.39_	2,388	2.17	+	5,182
6.	Plaster Interior				
7.	Heating/Cooling _Warm and Cooled Air (Mild Climate)_	2,388	.65	+	1,552
8.	Energy Adjustment _/Insulation: Mild Climate_	2,388	.19	−	‹454›
9.	Foundation				
10.	LUMP SUM ADJUSTMENTS:				
11.	Plumbing _11 Fixt + 1 R.I (Base) 2 Additional Fixtures_	2	755	+	1,510
12.	Fireplaces _Double, One Story_	1	2,900	+	2,900
13.	Built-in Appliances _R/O @$835 RH & E @$230 Dishwasher @$510_	1	1,575	+	1,575
14.	Miscellaneous (Dormers) _Garbage Disposal @$205, Exh. Fan @$110_	1	315	+	315
15.	SUBTOTAL ADJ. RESIDENCE COST: Line 1 plus or minus Lines 2-14				$90,214
16.	BASEMENT, UNFINISHED				
17.	Add for basement interior finish				
18.	Add for basement outside entrance				
19.	Add for basement garage: Single [ ] Double [ ]				
20.	PORCH/BREEZEWAY, describe _Open/Slab @$2.02 & Roof @$5.50_	233	7.52	+	1,752
21.	_& Ceiling @$1.52_	233	1.52	+	354
22.	SUBTOTAL RESIDENCE COST: Total of Lines 15-21				$92,320
23.	GARAGE OR CARPORT - sq. ft. area x selected sq. ft. cost _Use 600 Sq. Ft. Cost_	560	$13.06	+	7,313
24.	Miscellaneous (roofing adjustment) _Attached Garage −Deduct for com wall_	28	5,335	−	1,494
25.	SUBTOTAL GARAGE COST: Line 23 plus or minus Line 24				‹5,819›
26.	SUBTOTAL OF ALL BUILDING IMPROVEMENTS: Sum of Lines 22 and 25				$98,139
27.	Current Cost Multiplier _1.03_ x Local Multiplier _1.05_ 1.03 x 1.05 = 1.082			X	
28.	REPLACEMENT COST NEW: Line 26 x 27 _98,139 x 1.082_				$106,186
29.	Depreciation: Age _____ Condition _____ Deduction _____ % of Line 28 _____				
30.	Depreciated cost of building improvements: Line 28 less Line 29				
31.	Yard improvements cost: List, total, apply local multiplier and depreciate on reverse side				
32.	Landscaping cost: List and compute on reverse side				
33.	Lot or land value				
34.	**TOTAL INDICATED VALUE:** Total of Lines 30-33				

FORM 1007   *See back of page for sketch and computations*

is estimated by comparing the most recent sale prices of comparable houses in the neighborhood, an opinion of site value is usually developed through the same comparison technique. Site sales should be similar to the subject site in location and physical characteristics. Improvements included in the defined site may vary according to local appraisal custom. Be sure to avoid including any items valued in another part of the cost approach. For instance, if comparable sites in the area include all utilities as well as curbs and gutters, these items would be included in the site valuation here and not in the separate consideration of site improvements "as is."

Support for the opinion of site value (summary of comparable land sales or other methods for estimating site value)

Describe how you determined the value of the site; that is, how you analyzed, compared, and adjusted site sales to arrive at a supportable opinion of value. If you used a method other than sales comparison to develop site value, explain. If more space is needed, include additional comments in an addendum attached to the form.

Estimated, Reproduction, or Replacement Cost New

Estimate the cost to construct the subject improvements at current market prices. Check the appropriate box to indicate whether reproduction or replacement cost is used. All building components should be comparable in kind and quality to those used in the subject. If duplication of improvements, particularly in older structures, would be impossible or impractical (as may be the case with the elaborate exterior and interior trim work found in many Victorian-era homes), estimate the cost of a functionally identical replacement. Cost-estimating services, such as R. S. Means and Marshall and Swift, provide construction cost data that cover a wide range of property improvements in specific parts of the country, updated frequently to reflect current market conditions. Local builder surveys, used in conjunction with information from a cost-estimating service, help appraisers stay up-to-date on construction cost variables.

> ▸ **Fannie Mae** The reproduction cost estimate should reflect the cost of construction based on current prices of producing a replica of the property being appraised, including all of its positive and negative characteristics. Although construction materials used for the estimate should be as similar as possible to those used for the subject property, they do not have to be identical.

> ▸ **HUD/FHA** When using the cost approach, the square foot method must be used by completing Marshall & Swift Form 1007 (Figure 10). The pages from which the appraiser obtained the cost figures must be copied, the figures used in the calculations circled, and those pages attached to Form 1007. See HUD handbook 4150.1, REV-1 for more instructions.

Source of cost data

Enter the source of the cost data on this line. Current costs can be obtained from cost manuals and local builders and contractors.

Quality rating from cost service/Effective date of cost data

Enter the quality rating provided by the cost service used and the effective date to which the cost data applies.

Comments on Cost Approach (gross living area calculations, depreciation, etc.)

This space is used to enter any comments you feel are necessary to explain how the cost approach was applied. Appraisers may also show the measurement calculations indicating the total square footage of the structure in this area.

Comments on items such as the source of cost data, types of depreciation found, and how the site value was derived can be included here and/or in an addendum, as space constraints require. What is important is that you explain any significant factors affecting value. For instance, deductions for depreciation other than general wear and tear should be itemized separately, and items of functional or external obsolescence should be listed and explained.

As a general rule, in recent years federal property standards have deferred to local building codes. These codes typically follow the International Building Codes of the International Code Council (ICC), headquartered in Falls Church, Virginia. In the past, HUD/VA appraisals have relied on compliance with the minimum property standards that appear in Section 4905.1 of the HUD Handbook. Those standards are shown in Figure 11.

Estimated Remaining Economic Life (HUD and VA only)—Years

HUD and VA require that the remaining economic life of the property be estimated and included in this space. Remaining economic life is the estimated period during which improvements continue to contribute to property value, as opposed to estimated remaining physical life, which is the time period over which improvements may be expected to remain in existence, assuming normal maintenance. Economic life may be less than or equal to—but never more than—a property's physical life.

> ▸ **RHS**   Note the building code standard(s) used. Indicate the property's remaining economic life.

> ▸ **VA**   Remaining economic life is the estimated period of time until the improvements lose their ability to serve their intended purpose as a home. For VA loan Guaranty purposes, the remaining economic life of the security must be at least as long as the loan repayment term. A short remaining economic life estimate must be supportable and not arbitrarily established. This is to avoid depriving veterans of the home of their choice in an area where they can afford to live.

In estimating remaining economic life, the appraiser must consider

- the relationship between the property and the economic stability of the block, neighborhood, and community;
- comparisons with homes in the same or similar areas;
- the need for a home of the particular type being appraised;
- the architectural design, style, and utility from a functional point of view;
- the workmanship and durability of the construction, its physical condition, and probable cost of maintenance and/or repair;
- the extent to which other homes in the area are kept in repair; and
- in areas where rehabilitation and code enforcement are operating or under consideration, their expected results in improving the neighborhood for residential use.

If the estimate of remaining economic life is less than 30 years, the appraiser must provide a supporting explanation, based on either known economic factors or observed physical condition.

FIGURE 11
HUD Minimum Property Standards

REQUIREMENTS FOR EXISTING HOUSING ONE TO FOUR
FAMILY LIVING UNITS

Prepared by Program Participants and HUD Staff

Chapter 1—APPLICATION

1-1 *General.* These minimum requirements for housing were prepared by HUD and VA and apply to existing buildings containing one to four living units and to the sites upon which they are
located. The buildings may be detached, semi-detached, duplex, or row houses. These requirements also cover the immediate site environment for the dwellings, including streets, and
other services and facilities for the site.

1-2 *Proposed Additions and Alterations.* Any proposed additions to
an existing property shall comply with the requirements of
HUD Handbook 4900.1, MPS for one and two family dwellings.
This is only applicable to HUD programs.

1-3 *Compliance with Codes.* Enforcing, interpreting or determining
compliance with local codes and regulations is the responsibility of local authorities. When code compliance is required by
statute, responsibility to secure evidence of compliance rests
with the respective agency.

Chapter 2—GENERAL ACCEPTABILITY CRITERIA

2-1 General. These requirements for existing housing together
with appropriate administrative rules and regulations pre-
scribe the basic qualifications necessary for eligibility of existing properties.

2-2 *Real Estate Entity.* The property shall comprise a single plot
except that a primary plot with secondary plot for an appurte-
nant garage or for other use essential to the marketability of the
property may be acceptable provided the two plots are in such
proximity as to comprise a readily marketable real estate entity.

2-3 *Party or Lot Line Wall.* A building constructed on or to a property
line shall be separated from the adjoining building, or from the
adjoining lot, by a party or lot line wall. Party or lot line walls
shall extend the full height of the building.

continued

F I G U R E 11
HUD Minimum Property Standards (continued)

2-4 *Services and Facilities*

a. *Trespass.* Each living unit shall be one that can be used and maintained individually without trespass upon adjoining properties. Any easements granted shall run with the land to protect future owners.

b. *Utilities.* Utilities shall be independent for each living unit except that common services, such as water, sewer, gas and electricity, may be provided for living units under a single mortgage or ownership. Separate utility service shut-offs for each unit shall be provided. For living units under separate ownership, common utility services may be provided from the main to the building line when protected by easement or covenant and maintenance agreement acceptable to HUD. Individual utilities serving a living unit shall not pass over, under or through another living unit, unless provision is made for repair and maintenance of utilities without trespass on adjoining properties or legal provision is made for permanent right of access for maintenance and repair of utilities.

c. *Other Facilities.* Other facilities shall be independent for each living unit, except that common services, such as laundry and storage space or heating, may be provided for up to four living units under a single mortgage.

2-5 *Required Provisions.*

a. *Each living unit* shall contain each of the following:

(1) A continuing supply of safe and potable water.

(2) Sanitary facilities and a safe method of sewage disposal.

(3) Heating adequate for healthful and comfortable living conditions. The Field Office may determine that climatic conditions are such that mechanical heating is not required.

(4) Domestic hot water.

(5) Electricity for lighting and for equipment used in the living unit.

b. *When individual water supply* and sewage disposal systems apply, the following shall be required:

(1) Water quality shall meet the requirements of the health authority having jurisdiction. If the local health authority having jurisdiction does not have specific requirements, the maximum contaminant levels established by the Environmental Protection Agency (EPA) shall apply.

(2) Connection shall be made to a public or community water system whenever feasible.

continued

(3) Each living unit shall be provided with a water-carried sewage disposal system adequate to dispose of all domestic wastes in a manner which will not create a nuisance, or in any way endanger the public health. Individual pit privies are permitted where such facilities are customary and are the only feasible means of waste disposal, provided they are installed in accordance with the recommendations of the local Department of Health or, in the absence of such recommendations, with the requirements of the U.S. Public Health Service publication, "Individual Sewage-Disposal Systems."

(4) Whenever feasible, connection shall be made to a public or community sewage disposal system.

2-6 *Nonresidential Use.*

   a. *Design Limitations.*

   (1) Any nonresidential use of the property shall be subordinate to its residential use and character. A property, any portion of which is designed or used for nonresidential purposes, is eligible only if the type or extent of the nonresidential use does not impair the residential character of the property.

   (2) Areas designed or used for nonresidential purposes shall not exceed 25 percent of the total floor area. Storage areas or similar spaces which are integral parts of the nonresidential portion shall be included in the total nonresidential area.

2-7 *Access.*

   a. *Streets.*

   (1) Each property shall be provided with vehicular or pedestrian access from a public or private street. Private streets shall be protected by permanent easements.

   (2) The required street and provisions for its continued maintenance shall include a safe and suitable vehicular access to and from the property at all times.

2-8 *Access to the Living Unit.* A means of access to each living unit shall be provided without passing through any other living unit.

2-9 *Access to the Rear Yard.*

   a. Access to the rear yard shall be provided without passing through any other living unit.

continued

F I G U R E 11
HUD Minimum Property Standards (continued)

b. For a row type dwelling, the access may be by means of alley, easement, passage through the dwelling, or other acceptable means.

2-10 *Defective Conditions.* Existing or partially completed construction which indicates defective construction, poor workmanship, evidence of continuing settlement, excessive dampness, leakage, decay, termites, or other conditions impairing the safety or sanitation of the dwelling shall render the property unacceptable until the defects or conditions have been remedied and the probability of further damage eliminated.

2-11 *Space Requirements.* Each living unit shall be provided with space necessary to assure suitable living, sleeping, cooking and dining accommodations and sanitary facilities.

2-12 *Mechanical Systems.* Mechanical systems shall assure safety of operation, be protected from destructive elements, have reasonable durability and economy, and have adequate capacity and quality.

2-13 *Ventilation.* Natural ventilation of structural spaces, such as attics and crawl spaces, will be provided to reduce the effect of conditions which are conducive to decay and deterioration of the structure.

2-14 *Roof Covering.* Roof covering shall prevent entrance of moisture and provide reasonable durability and economy of maintenance.

2-15 *Hazards.* The property shall be free of those hazards which may adversely affect the health and safety of the occupants or the structural soundness of the improvements, or which may impair the customary use and enjoyment of the property by occupants. The hazards can be subsidence, flood, erosion, defective lead base paint, or the like.

If the estimate of remaining economic life is 30 years or more, the appraiser must state the estimate at its maximum (for example, 40 years).

Opinion of Site Value: $

Enter your opinion of site value on this line.

▸ **Fannie Mae**   If the opinion of site value is not typical for a comparable residential property in the subject neighborhood, comment on how the variance affects the marketability of the subject property.

▸ **VA**   Only this value must be completed in every case proposed or existing, *excluding* condominiums.

Dwelling

Enter the number of square feet of living space of the home. Be sure to measure square footage based on the form of measurement assumed by the cost service from which you receive cost data. Then enter the current construction cost per square foot of living space for a comparable new structure. Finally, multiply the number of square feet by the cost per square foot to determine a dollar value for the improvement. Additional lines are provided for

- calculating the cost of any areas or improvements (basement space or a secondary living structure, such as a guest house) not included in the figure derived on the first line;

- describing any special property features—such as an extra bathroom that is not part of the square foot estimate of the main living space, built-ins, special finishing materials, or other "upgrades"—not included in the base cost per square foot and providing a current construction cost estimate of that feature;

- identifying and entering the current construction cost of any energy-efficient item, such as a solar hot-water system; and

- describing a porch, deck, patio, or other exterior space by type and square footage and providing a current construction cost; for example, **500 SQ. FT. DECK = $5,000.**

Garage/Carport

If the property has a garage or carport, cross out whichever of the two structures is not present and enter the square footage of garage or carport space, the current construction cost per square foot of similar space and the dollar figure derived by multiplying those two figures.

Total Estimate of Cost—New

Add all the dollar amounts recorded in this column up to this point (except for opinion of site value) and enter the total here.

Less Depreciation

Enter your estimate of depreciation—physical, functional, and external—for the subject property,

Unless you are appraising a brand new property with no evidence of any form of physical, functional, or external deterioration, you will have to compute the amount by which the subject improvements have been reduced in value due to these factors. All property will physically deteriorate over time and may also suffer a loss in value due to changing market demands or the influence of economic factors or nearby land uses.

In the early 1990s, economic factors propelled property values in some parts of the country from all-time highs to dramatic lows over just a few years. As recent property values exceed historic high values and rates of appreciation in many areas of the country, it is even more critical for the appraiser to stay abreast of market conditions and their causes so that they are reflected where appropriate in the final opinion of value. It is important to remember that it is the reaction of buyers in the marketplace that determines the impact on value of any form of depreciation. A thorough understanding of the extraction of market values from the sales comparison analysis is vital for the appraiser's accuracy in the cost approach.

While there is not room here for a thorough analysis of each form of depreciation, the Fannie Mae requirements that follow provide a useful overview. Remember that, if a dollar amount for depreciation is recorded at the right, it must be broken down into the various depreciation categories to which it applies.

▸ **Fannie Mae** You must consider each of the three principal types of depreciation—physical, functional, and external.

Physical depreciation, traditionally referred to as *physical deterioration,* is a loss in value caused by deterioration in the physical condition of the improvements. Physical deterioration is classified as curable or incurable. *Curable* physical deterioration refers to items of deferred maintenance that are relatively easily and economically accomplished (for example, painting or repairing a broken stair rail). Items of *incurable* physical deterioration are impractical to correct because the cost to cure would not add commensurate value to the property; an example is extensive water damage to rafters and interior walls due to a roof that should have been replaced ten years ago.

Functional depreciation, traditionally referred to as *functional obsolescence,* is a loss in value caused by defects in the design of a structure. Design elements that may cause a degree of functional obsolescence include inadequacies in architectural style, floor plan, sizes and types of rooms, and style of fixtures. Functional obsolescence is caused by changing market preferences, as in the case of a home with a bedroom on a level that has no bathroom, and is generally incurable. An outmoded fixture, such as a wall-hung kitchen sink, is an example of curable functional obsolescence.

External depreciation, traditionally referred to as *external* or *economic obsolescence,* is a loss in value caused by negative influences outside the site. External depreciation is always incurable by the property owner over the short term, even though the cause of the depreciation (such as high interest rates) eventually may be alleviated. External depreciation can be caused by political factors, such as a change in zoning; economic factors, such as the loss in value that may result from high mortgage interest rates or a recession; or environmental changes, as when property is located next to a shopping center, expressway, or factory.

Depreciated Cost of Improvements

Subtract the total dollar amount of property depreciation from the estimated cost new on the line above to find the depreciated cost of the property improvements and enter this amount here. Note that what are considered "site improvements" (explained next) are not included in this calculation.

"As-is" Value of Site Improvements

Enter the present value of site improvements (in their current condition) that are not included in **your opinion of site value** above or any other cost valuation category. These could include items such as drainage systems, grading and landscaping, driveways, fences or walls, sidewalks, curbs, gutters, and so on. They could also include utility lines, sewer systems, and other items, if those items are not considered in developing your opinion of site value. As a practical matter, you should complete this entry after developing your opinion of site value so that the basis for the site valuation will be known and any site improvements not included in that category can be included here.

Indicated Value by Cost Approach: $

The entry here is the sum of

- the opinion of site value, plus
- the depreciated cost of improvements, plus
- the "as is" value of site improvements.

    ▸ **Fannie Mae**   In reviewing the appraisal report, the lender should make sure that the appraiser's analysis and comments for the cost approach are consistent with comments and adjustments mentioned elsewhere in the report. For example, if the NEIGHBORHOOD or SITE description on page 1 reveals that the property backs up to a shopping center, the lender should expect to see an adjustment for external depreciation in the COST APPROACH section on page 3. Similarly, if the improvement analysis indicates that it is necessary to go through one bedroom to get to another bedroom, the lender should expect to see an adjustment for functional depreciation.

    ▸ **RHS** Enter the indicated dollar value derived by the cost approach, as defined in Marshall & Swift Form 1007, "Square Foot Appraisal Form," line 34.

APPRAISAL 1

COST APPROACH TO VALUE (not required by Fannie Mae)					
Provide adequate information for the lender/client to replicate the below cost figures and calculations.					
Support for the opinion of site value (summary of comparable land sales or other methods for estimating sale value)					
Site value was determined by analyzing the most recent sale prices of comparable sites in neighborhoods similar to the subject neighborhood in location and physical characteristics.					

ESTIMATED [X] REPRODUCTION OR ☐ REPLACEMENT COST NEW	OPINION OF SITE VALUE		=$	90,000
Source of cost data Local builders	Dwelling 2,120 Sq. Ft. @ $ 147		=$	311,640
Quality rating from cost service Effective date of cost data	Entry 60 Sq. Ft. @ $ 50		=$	3,000
Comments on Cost Approach (gross living area calculations, depreciation, etc.)	Extras (porch, pool, fence)			38,450
See sketch for measurement analysis. Living area: 2120 SF. The	Garage/Carport 525 Sq. Ft. @ $ 30		=$	15,750
depreciation estimate reflects observed effective age. Cost	Total Estimate of Cost-New		=$	368,840
estimates are supported by builders in the area. Land value is	Less Physical	Functional	External	
based on area land sales. The land/value ratio of the subject	Depreciation 18,000	N/A	N/A =$ (	18,000)
property is supported by those for comparable properties.	Depreciated Cost of Improvements		=$	350,840
	'As-is' Value of Site Improvements		=$	12,020
			=$	
Estimated Remaining Economic Life (HUD and VA only) 54 Years	Indicated Value By Cost Approach		=$	452,860

In Appraisal 1, the subject property, as sketched in an addendum (shown on page 20), has 2,120 square feet of living area. The appraiser has determined that the property's value is well supported by its functional utility and its location's external influences. The depreciation estimate reflects observed effective age, based on area sales. The appraisal is based on a cash or equivalent sale, and no personal property is included in the valuation. Land value is based on area land sales. The land/value ratio of the subject property is supported by those for comparable properties.

The dwelling has a living area of 2,120 square feet; at an estimated current construction cost in this area of $147 per square foot, the cost estimate is $311,640. In addition, there is a covered entry area of 60 square feet, valued at $50 per square foot for an estimated cost of $3,000. Extras totaling $38,450 include a swimming pool enclosed in a bronze A-frame cage, an enclosed porch, and a wood fence that encloses the back yard area.

All energy-efficient items, such as wall and ceiling insulation, are included in the living area valuation.

The attached garage of 525 square feet is valued at $30 per square foot. The total estimate of cost-new of the subject dwelling is thus $368,840. Depreciation due to physical deterioration is based on the effective age of the subject in relation to other properties in the area. Because of its overall good condition, although the subject is 11 years old, it has an effective age of only about 5 years. The loss in value attributable to overall wear and tear is $18,000. There is no evidence of functional or external depreciation. The depreciated cost of improvements, then, is $350,840.

Site improvements, including the driveway and landscaping, are valued at $12,020. Site value, including all amenities commonly found in comparable sites (such as underground utilities, storm and sanitary sewers, and concrete curbs and gutters) is estimated by analysis of comparable properties at $90,000.

The indicated value of the subject property by the cost approach is thus $452, 860. This appraisal is not for Fannie Mae, HUD, RHS, or VA purposes.

EXERCISE: APPRAISAL 2

COST APPROACH TO VALUE (not required by Fannie Mae)	

Provide adequate information for the lender/client to replicate the below cost figures and calculations.

Support for the opinion of site value (summary of comparable land sales or other methods for estimating site value)

ESTIMATED ☐ REPRODUCTION OR ☐ REPLACEMENT COST NEW	OPINION OF SITE VALUE .... = $
Source of cost data	Dwelling Sq. Ft. @ $ .... =$
Quality rating from cost service Effective date of cost data	Sq. Ft. @ $ .... =$
Comments on Cost Approach (gross living area calculations, depreciation, etc.)	
	Garage/Carport Sq. Ft. @ $ .... =$
	Total Estimate of Cost-New .... = $
	Less Physical Functional External
	Depreciation =$( )
	Depreciated Cost of Improvements.....................................=$
	"As-is" Value of Site Improvements.................................=$
Estimated Remaining Economic Life (HUD and VA only) Years	Indicated Value By Cost Approach ....=$

Complete the blank URAR COST APPROACH section provided above for Appraisal 2, using the following information. When you have finished, you can check your work against the completed Appraisal 2 in the Answer Key.

The subject property is a rectangle, 75 feet wide and 150 feet deep. There is a center front entrance but no front porch. There is a rear sliding glass door to the left of the house, opening onto a deck that is 20 feet wide by 15 feet deep. There is a detached garage of 25 feet by 25 feet, directly behind and to the right of the house at the end of a concrete driveway. The energy-efficient items on the property are the same as those enjoyed by other homes in the neighborhood—well-insulated walls, ceilings, and floors. There are no special energy-efficient fixtures. A redwood board fence encloses the rear yard.

The appraiser gathered current costs from local contractors actively engaged in building similar houses in the area. These costs were then compared to known costs for a building of good quality published in the Anystate Cost Manual, September 2004.

Cost estimates are based on $145 per square foot for residential construction of this quality, $15 per square foot for decking, and $40 per square foot for a detached garage on a cement foundation. Basement finishing is valued at $6,000 using matched pair analysis.

The subject is 18 years old and in good overall condition. Depreciation due to physical deterioration is estimated at 20 percent. There is no evidence of functional or external obsolescence.

Site value, including all utilities, grading, and concrete curbs and gutters, is estimated by comparison with comparable properties, both sold and listed for sale at $94,000. The value "as is" of site improvements not considered in any other category (such as the driveway, landscaping, and fencing) is estimated to be $18,000.

The appraisal is not being performed for HUD, RHS, or VA purposes.

SECTION 10: INCOME APPROACH

INCOME APPROACH TO VALUE (not required by Fannie Mae)			
Estimated Monthly Market Rent $	X Gross Rent Multiplier	= $	Indicated Value by Income Approach
Summary of Income Approach (including support for market rent and GRM)			

The income approach can be the most technically complex method of appraisal when applied to large commercial properties. A far simpler method can be applied to single-family residences, however, based on the assumption that value is related to the market rent the property can be expected to earn.

Market rent is the rental income that a property would most probably command on the open market as indicated by current rentals paid for comparable space. To find market rent, an appraiser must know what rent tenants have paid, and are currently paying, on comparable properties. By comparing present and past performance of properties similar to the subject, the appraiser should be able to determine the subject property's rent potential. By analyzing sale prices of comparable properties, the factor, or gross rent multiplier, which represents the relationship between market rent and market value, can be determined. When the appropriate gross rent multiplier is applied to the rental income the subject property is expected to produce, the result is an opinion of market value. The steps in this method of applying the income approach are summarized below and explained in this section. The appraiser must

- estimate the subject property's monthly market rent;
- calculate gross rent multipliers from recently sold comparable properties that were rented at the time of sale;
- based on rent multiplier analysis, derive the appropriate GRM for the subject property; and
- develop an opinion of market value by multiplying the amount of the monthly market rent by the subject property's GRM.

■ GROSS RENT MULTIPLIER

The gross rent multiplier (GRM) is a number that expresses the relationship between the sale price of a residential property and its gross monthly unfurnished rental. This ratio can be expressed by the formula

$$\frac{\text{Sale Price}}{\text{Gross Rent}} = \text{GRM}$$

To establish a reasonably accurate GRM, the appraiser should have recent sales and rental data from at least ten properties similar to the subject that have sold in the same market area and were rented at the time of sale. The resulting GRM can then be applied to the projected rental of the subject property to develop an opinion of its market value. The formula for that step is

$$\text{Gross Rent} \times \text{GRM} = \text{Market Value}$$

Because even very similar properties rarely have the same rent or sale price, GRM analysis is likely to produce a range of multipliers. The appraiser must decide which multiplier is most appropriate for the subject property, in the appraiser's best judgment based on the property that is most comparable to the subject. No mathematical or mechanical formula can be substituted for careful analysis and judgment. Following is an example of the range of data that might be collected by an appraiser trying to determine an appropriate GRM for a single-family residence.

Sale No.	Sale Price	Monthly Rental	GRM (rounded)
1	$209,600	$1,400	150
2	209,500	1,400	150
3	212,200	1,425	149
4	210,000	1,420	148
5	211,700	1,450	146
6	210,300	1,420	148
7	208,200	1,375	151
8	213,000	1,465	145
9	210,900	1,425	148
10	212,500	1,450	147
11	211,100	1,435	147
Subject	?	1,420	?

In this example, the appraiser has determined that the market rent for the subject property is $1,420. The range of GRMs derived from recent sales of comparable properties is from 145 to 151. When applied to the subject's market rent estimate, the GRMs place value between $205,900 ($1,420 × 145) and $214,420 ($1,420 × 151). These comparisons bracket the estimate of value within reasonable limits. Because property sales 4, 6, and 9 are most comparable to the subject property, the appraiser concludes that the subject property's GRM should be 148. The GRM is applied to the subject's projected monthly rental: $1,420 × 148 = $210,000 (rounded), the indicated value of the subject property by the income approach.

The income approach can be a valid indicator of market value if the subject property is located in a rental-oriented neighborhood. In areas that are almost exclusively owner-occupied, however, rental data may be too scarce to permit the use of this approach. If the right kinds of data are available to develop valid market rent and GRM estimates, the income approach for single-family residences can be used, if only to serve as a check against the sales comparison and cost approaches.

■ INCOME APPROACH TO VALUE (Not Required by Fannie Mae)

Estimated Monthly Market Rent $_____ × Gross Rent Multiplier _____ = $_____ Indicated Value by Income Approach

Enter the subject property's monthly market rent estimate derived from the marketplace. Then enter the GRM applicable to the subject property. Finally, multiply the monthly market rent estimate by the GRM and enter the value opinion indicated by the income approach.

Summary of Income Approach (including support for market rent and GRM)

Explain the reconciliation process that supports your choice of market rent and GRM that most accurately reflects the market value of the subject property.

▸ **Fannie Mae**   Fannie Mae does not require the appraiser to use the income approach for any appraisal documented on the URAR (Form 1004).

The income approach to value is based on the assumption that market value is related to the market rent or income that a property can be expected to earn. Its use generally is appropriate in neighborhoods of single-family properties when there is a substantial rental market, and it is an important approach in the valuation of two- to four-family properties. However, it generally is not appropriate in areas that consist mostly of owner-occupied properties because adequate rental data generally do not exist for those areas. Fannie Mae will not accept an appraisal if the appraiser relies solely on the income approach as an indicator of market value.

To arrive at the indicated value by the income approach, multiply the estimated market rent for the subject property by a gross rent multiplier.

■ *Estimated market rent* is based on an analysis of comparable rentals in the neighborhood. After appropriate adjustments are made to the comparables, their adjusted (or indicated) values are reconciled to develop an estimated monthly market rent for the subject property.

■ The *gross rent multiplier* is determined by dividing the sales prices of comparable properties that were rented at the time of sale by their monthly market rent, which is then reconciled to create a single gross rent multiplier (or a range of multipliers) for the subject property.

When the property being appraised is a single-family property that will be used as an investment property, you must prepare a Single-Family Comparable Rent Schedule (Form 1007) in addition to the appropriate appraisal report form. This form is not required for a two- to four-family property because the Appraisal Report—Small Residential Income Property (Form 1025) provides substantially the same information. When you are relying on the income approach, you should attach the supporting comparable rental and sales data, and the calculations used to determine the gross rent multiplier, as an addendum to the appraisal report form.

▸ **HUD/FHA**   The income approach is rarely used to determine the value of a home that will be financed by an FHA insured loan unless it is an income producing property—such as a triplex or fourplex. When it is used, you must show the gross rent from each of the comparables on the Summary of Income Approach line, such as **COMP. #1 GROSS RENT = $1,000.00; COMP. #2 GROSS RENT = $1,200;** and so on.

If you do not use the income approach, the line items should be marked N/A.

▸ **VA** Complete this section only if applicable and a valid indicator of value (for example, if the subject property is a multiunit building).

APPRAISAL 1

	INCOME APPROACH TO VALUE (not required by Fannie Mae)			
Estimated Monthly Market Rent $	N/A X Gross Rent Multiplier	= $	Indicated Value by Income Approach	
Summary of Income Approach (including support for market rent and GRM)				

In Appraisal 1, the income approach was not considered applicable for single-family homes in this area.

EXERCISE: APPRAISAL 2

	INCOME APPROACH TO VALUE (not required by Fannie Mae)			
Estimated Monthly Market Rent $	X Gross Rent Multiplier	= $	Indicated Value by Income Approach	
Summary of Income Approach (including support for market rent and GRM)				

Complete the blank URAR INCOME APPROACH section for Appraisal 2, using the following information. When you have finished, you can check your work against the completed Appraisal 2 in the Answer Key.

The subject property is a single-family house located in a neighborhood that is predominantly owner-occupied, yet a small number of homes are rented out. Although the house being appraised has always been owner-occupied, current market information indicates that a potential rental income of $2,250 monthly is in line with recent comparable rentals in the area. A thorough rent multiplier analysis produced a GRM range of 138 to 192. The appraiser concluded that the median of the range, 152, was the appropriate GRM for the subject property.

SECTION 11: PUD INFORMATION

PUD INFORMATION	PROJECT INFORMATION FOR PUDs(if applicable)
	Is the developer/builder in control of the Homeowners' Association (HOA)? ☐ Yes ☐ No Unit type(s) ☐ Detached ☐ Attached
	Provide the following information for PUDs ONLY if the developer/builder is in control of the HOA and the subject property is an attached dwelling unit.
	Legal name of project
	Total number of phases Total number of units Total number of units sold
	Total number of units rented Total number of units for sale Data source(s)
	Was the project created by the conversion of an existing building(s) into a PUD? ☐ Yes ☐ No If Yes, date of conversion
	Does the project contain any multi-dwelling units? ☐ Yes ☐ No Data source(s)
	Are the units, common elements, and recreation facilities complete? ☐ Yes ☐ No If No, describe the status of completion.
	Are the common elements leased to or by the Homeowners' Association? ☐ Yes ☐ No If Yes, describe the rental terms and options.
	Describe common elements and recreational facilities

This section is completed if the property is a dwelling unit in a planned unit development (PUD) that includes a shared interest in recreational or open space, clubhouse, or sports or other facilities.

PROJECT INFORMATION FOR PUDs (If applicable)

- **Fannie Mae** A PUD is a project or subdivision that consists of individual units as well as common property and improvements that are owned and maintained by an owners' association for the benefit and use of the individual units within the project. Fannie Mae considers a project to be a PUD if the owners' association requires automatic, nonseverable membership for each unit owner and if it can establish mandatory assessments for the maintenance of the property.

  For condominium appraisals, use Appraisal Report—Individual Condominium or PUD Unit (Form 1073). The URAR (Form 1004) can be used in appraisals of detached condominium units, if the condominium project does not contain any common area improvements (other than greenbelts, private streets, and parking areas) and the appraiser includes an adequate description of the project and information about the homeowners' association fees and the quality of the project maintenance.
- **VA** You may use this form with *any* kind of PUD.

Is the developer/builder in control of the Homeowners' Association (HOA)?

A subdivision that is established as a PUD will conform with applicable state and local laws and regulations. Typically, until a certain percentage of units are sold (as specified by state law), the builder is responsible for administration of the shared elements of the PUD, as well as enforcement of rules regarding architectural and other standards that will apply to all property owners. When enough units have been sold, the homeowners are authorized to take over (or create, if it is not already in existence) the Homeowners' Association and carry on those responsibilities. An HOA is entitled to enforce the CC&Rs (deeded conditions, covenants, and restrictions) that impose limits on what can be done with an individual unit, such as by specifying architectural standards, permitted property uses, the level of upkeep required of each property owner, and other items. The CC&Rs typically also include by reference the requirements established in the bylaws of the HOA. Once it is under control of the property owners, an established, active HOA can be an effective way to help maintain the aesthetic appeal of a neighborhood.

Provide the following information for PUDs ONLY if the developer/builder is in control of the HOA and the subject property is an attached dwelling unit

This portion of the URAR form need not be completed if the subject property is a single-family detached home in a planned unit development.

Legal name of project

Enter the name of the subdivision or project in which the subject property is located. This will be found in the legal description of the property.

Total number of phases

A PUD will typically be built over a number of years, in segments called *phases*. As a practical matter, the builder will not want to incur financing costs for more than the number of units that can be built in a reasonable amount of time. Often, construction permits will be limited by governing authorities to control the rate of growth and resulting demand on local services.

Total number of units

What is the total number of living units comprising the PUD? Each unit is a separate legal entity, which may be one-half of a duplex, a patio home with walls shared with other units, or an apartment-style unit in a multilevel building.

Total number of units sold

As of the date of appraisal, how many units are no longer owned by the developer, or the developer's successor, if ownership of the project has been transferred to facilitate unit sales, or if the developer has defaulted on the construction loan?

Total number of units rented

A high number of units rented by owners may indicate that the PUD is less well-maintained than it might be if predominantly owner-occupied, or that payment of homeowner assessments may be more problematic. To avoid such problems, some PUDs prohibit rentals, or place restrictions on them (such as the ability to lease a unit for no more than one year upon approval of the HOA). Such a prohibition or restriction must appear in the CC&Rs that are part of all deeds to PUD properties, or may be made a part of the bylaws of the HOA upon vote of the required number of property owners—typically, a two-thirds majority—in conformance with state law.

Total number of units for sale

How many of the PUD units are currently listed for sale, or for sale by owner? The PUD itself is likely to be the best indicator of market activity for the unit being appraised. A high percentage of units being offered for sale may also indicate the need for further investigation by the appraiser.

Data source(s)

In addition to the lender, real estate agent, and property owner, another important source of information on a PUD will be the HOA and, if there is one, the property management company.

Was the project created by the conversion of an existing building(s) into a PUD? Yes or No. If Yes, date of conversion

The date of conversion of an existing building or complex of buildings to a PUD may explain the number of units on the market, as well as apparent discrepancies in purchase prices between preconversion residents and new homeowners.

Does the project contain any multi-dwelling units? Yes or No. Data source(s)

The PUD may be designed to accommodate the wants and needs of homebuyers by offering a variety of building types, including single-family detached homes, duplexes, and other multiunit buildings.

Are the units, common elements, and recreation facilities complete? Yes or No. If No, describe the status of completion.

Some units may be sold and occupied before the entire PUD is completed. This will usually be the case with larger complexes. State law should require the developer to set aside adequate funds for completion of common elements, if they are to follow completion of living units.

Are the common elements leased to or by the Homeowners' Association? Yes or No. If Yes, describe the rental terms and options.

The terms under which the common elements are managed should indicate a viable arrangement for ongoing maintenance and availability for homeowner use.

Describe common elements and recreational facilities

These may include greenbelts, clubhouses, swimming pools, and other meeting or recreational facilities. The extent of the common elements and shared recreational facilities should be reflected in HOA budget and dues that are adequate to maintain those parts of the PUD.

APPRAISAL 1

PROJECT INFORMATION FOR PUDs (if applicable)					
Is the developer/builder in control of the Homeowners' Association (HOA)? ☐ Yes ☐ No Unit type(s) ☐ Detached ☐ Attached					
Provide the following information for PUDs ONLY if the developer/builder is in control of the HOA and the subject property is an attached dwelling unit.					
Legal name of project					
Total number of phases	Total number of units		Total number of units sold		
Total number of units rented	Total number of units for sale		Data Source(s)		
Was the project created by the conversion of existing building(s) into a PUD? ☐ Yes ☐ No If Yes, date of conversion					
Does the project contain any multi-dwelling units? ☐ Yes ☐ No Data Source(s)					
Are the units, common elements, and recreation facilities complete? ☐ Yes ☐ No If No, describe the status of completion.					
Are the common elements leased to or by the Homeowners' Association? ☐ Yes ☐ No If Yes, describe the rental terms and options.					
Describe common elements and recreational facilities					

In Appraisal 1 the subject property is not part of a planned unit development.

EXERCISE: APPRAISAL 2

PROJECT INFORMATION FOR PUDs (if applicable)		
Is the developer/builder in control of the Homeowners' Association (HOA)? ☐ Yes ☐ No Unit type(s) ☐ Detached ☐ Attached		
Provide the following information for PUDs ONLY if the developer/builder is in control of the HOA and the subject property is an attached dwelling unit.		
Legal name of project		
Total number of phases	Total number of units	Total number of units sold
Total number of units rented	Total number of units for sale	Data source(s)
Was the project created by the conversion of an existing building(s) into a PUD? ☐ Yes ☐ No If Yes, date of conversion		
Does the project contain any multi-dwelling units? ☐ Yes ☐ No Data source(s)		
Are the units, common elements, and recreation facilities complete? ☐ Yes ☐ No If No, describe the status of completion.		
Are the common elements leased to or by the Homeowners' Association? ☐ Yes ☐ No If Yes, describe the rental terms and options.		
Describe common elements and recreational facilities		

Complete the blank URAR PUD Information section provided above for Appraisal 2, using the applicable portions of the following information. When you have finished, check your work against the completed Appraisal 2 in the Answer Key.

The subject property is located in a planned unit development called Meadow Green. Management of the Homeowners' Association passed to the homeowners 18 years ago, after the majority of the homes had been sold. There are 200 single-family detached residences in Meadow Green. All building lots were sold by the developer within the first year of construction. There are no multifamily buildings in Meadow Green. The common elements include a clubhouse, swimming pool, and tennis court and were completed at the time of initial construction of the development homes. The common elements, which are well maintained, are owned by the homeowners and are under the direction of the Homeowners' Association, which has hired Mills Property Management to carry on maintenance and other activities approved by the HOA.

## PART FOUR

Putting It All Together

APPRAISAL 3

Now that you have finished the discussion of the URAR form and practiced making entries in each section of the form, you should be ready to attempt a sample appraisal. Using the information supplied here for Appraisal 3, complete the three blank URAR form pages that appear on pages 162–164. Fill in as many items on the form as you can, then compare your entries against those in the completed Appraisal 3 in the Answer Key.

■ SUBJECT

The subject property is a single-family detached residence located at 582 Augustina Lane, Brandywine, Anystate 99999. The owners of record are Cindi and George Rattan, and this is the principal residence of Cindi Rattan. The property's legal description is

> Lot 58, Sunnyside Club Estates, as shown on page 36 of book 25, records of King County.

The appraisal of this fee simple interest is being made at the request of Ivers and Nussbaum, LLP, 4310 Frances Drive, Metro City, AN 99999, as part of a marital dissolution property settlement. The client has specifically requested that all three approaches to value be used in this appraisal.

The assessor's parcel number is 80808C8. The real estate taxes for the tax year 2004 (due in 2005) are $10,028.90. The map reference number is 95-2. The census tract number is 27.04.

This home is part of a suburban planned unit development designed around a shared recreational facility that includes four tennis courts, a swimming pool, and a golf course. The homeowners' association dues on this property (which do not include membership in the golf club) are $600 yearly. The HOA is under the control of the homeowners. There are no special assessments due or proposed.

The subject property is not currently for sale, and was last on the market six years ago, when it was purchased by the Rattans.

■ NEIGHBORHOOD DATA

The 20-year-old subject neighborhood is 100 percent developed with single-family residences ranging in value from $595,000 for the smallest one-story homes to $1,195,000 for the largest homes adjoining the golf course. Most are valued at about $840,000 and virtually all are owner-occupied with rare vacancies. Although most houses are 15 years old, they range in age from 12 to 20 years.

Sunnyside Club's neighborhood boundaries are well defined by an eight-foot concrete block perimeter fence, bounded by Willow Road to the west, Metro Highway to the north, Center Road to the east, and Sunnyside Avenue to the south. With most homes sited on cul-de-sacs, there are only two roads that lead into the neighborhood, on Center Road and Sunnyside Avenue, making the neighborhood quiet since there is no drive-through traffic.

There has been an adequate demand for housing in this subdivision, with a steady uptrend in values during the past few years. Although recent economic conditions have slowed overall demand in the metropolitan area, most houses in this desirable neighborhood are sold within 90 days of being put on the market.

The subject neighborhood is favorably affected by its proximity to the interstate highway and its convenience to area employment centers. Public bus transportation to the nearest commuter railroad station is somewhat limited and not as good as in competing areas. Except for this, all other subject neighborhood amenities meet expectations for the market area.

■ PUD DATA

There are 378 single-family detached homes in the subject's subdivision, Sunnyside Club Estates, and 6 of them, in locations scattered throughout the subdivision, are currently for sale.

■ SITE DATA

The subject lot has a frontage of 90 feet and a depth of 130 feet. It is rectangular in shape, level, and has a well-drained sandy subsoil. The lot size is typical of those found in the market area. Landscaping is good and typical of this area. The view from the subject house is of street, parkway, and surrounding houses—typical of most houses in the neighborhood, with the exception of the homes that adjoin the golf course.

The site has public electricity, gas, water, and sanitary sewers. The street is asphalt and is all publicly maintained. There are no alleys in this neighborhood. The driveway is concrete. The property is not located in a FEMA flood hazard zone, as indicated on FEMA map 123, dated 03/01.

The subject property is zoned R-1/Single-Family Residential and represents the highest and best use of the site. The zoning ordinance, which is strongly enforced, has many provisions controlling lot size and building dimensions. All special assessments for water, sewer, sidewalk, curb, gutter, and street surfacing have been paid in full by the developers of the property. There are no apparent adverse influences, easements, encroachments, or environmental conditions.

■ DESCRIPTION OF IMPROVEMENTS

All of the following have been verified by the appraiser through personal inspection.

The subject property has good market appeal and compatibility within the neighborhood. The dwelling is a two-story colonial-style house built in 1991, with foyer, living room, dining room, kitchen, family room, four bedrooms, and three full baths. Gross above-grade living area, based on outside dimensions, is 3,038 square feet. The effective age of the structure is estimated at 10 years.

Exterior: Poured concrete slab foundation with no apparent settlement or infestation problems; exterior finish is brick veneer; asphalt shingle roof with aluminum gutters and downspouts; wood-frame, double-hung windows with aluminum combination storm/screens.

Interior: All features typical of competing houses, including quality of construction (good), condition of improvements (good), room sizes and layout, adequacy of closets and other storage space, overall energy efficiency, plumbing and fixtures, electrical system, and kitchen built-ins.

Floors: Wall-to-wall carpeting in the living room, hallways and bedrooms; finished oak in the dining room and foyer; ceramic tile in the kitchen and family room; all floor coverings in good condition.

Walls/Ceilings: Drywall, taped, and painted; good condition.

Trim/Finish: Wood trim throughout the house; good condition.

Baths: Ceramic tile floor; ceramic tile wainscot around tub and shower area; good condition.

Attic: None.

Heating/Cooling: Central forced-air heating and cooling powered by electricity; the system is in good condition with adequate output.

Kitchen: Built-in range and oven, dishwasher, and garbage disposal; refrigerator and microwave not included in valuation process.

Amenities: Attractive masonry fireplace in family room; 20' × 20' concrete patio; redwood board fencing around rear yard.

Garage: Three-car, 25' × 40', detached; concrete driveway.

■ SALES COMPARISON DATA

There are six comparable properties currently on the market for prices ranging from $799,000 to $839,900. Ten comparable properties have sold in the last year at prices ranging from $780,000 to $832,000. The value of the subject property, as indicated by the sales comparison approach, was estimated after careful comparison with three recently sold similar properties. Neither the subject nor the comparable properties have been sold in the last three years according to the Assessor's Office. All sales data were verified by the listing and selling brokers involved in the transactions. Several other sales were considered but not included in this report because of a too-wide spread in cost, type of construction, location, or time of sale. All sales were of a fee simple interest. All of these properties have a view similar to that of the subject—the street and parkway.

Sale 1 is located at 205 Briarwood Drive—1/2 mile NW of the subject in the same subdivision. It sold for $815,500. The property is 14 years old and has a gross living area of 3,038 square feet.

Sale 2 is located at 570 Shanter Court, three blocks south of the subject in the same subdivision. It sold for $827,200. The property is 14 years old and has a gross living area of 3,000 square feet.

Sale 3 is located at 308 Crafton Street, one-half mile SE of the subject in the same subdivision. It sold for $791,000. It is 14 years old and has a gross living area of 3,150 square feet. Additional data are shown in the accompanying chart.

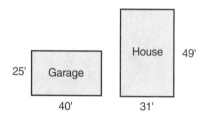

	Subject	Comp 1	Comp 2	Comp 3	Adjustment
Financing Concessions		None	None	None	
Date of Sale		10-14-05	8-26-05	7-19-05	
Site	11,700 – SF	11,500 – SF	12,000 – SF	8,800 – SF	$15,000
View	St/Pkwy/Avg	St/Pkwy/Avg	St/Pkwy/Avg	St/Pkwy/Avg	
Design (Style)	Colonial	Colonial	Colonial	Colonial	
Construction	Good	Same	Same	Same	
Actual Age	14	14	14	14	
Condition	Good	Good	Good	Good	
Above Grade Room Count	8/4/3	8/4/3	8/4/3	8/4/3	
Gross Living Area	3,018	3,100	3,100	3,150	
Basement	None	None	None	None	
Functional Utility	Good	Good	Good	Good	
Heating/Cooling	FA/Cent.	FA/Cent.	FA/Cent.	FA/Cent.	
Energy Efficient Items	None	None	None	None	
Garage/Carport	3-Car det gar	3-Car det gar	3-Car det gar	3-Car det gar	
Porch/Deck	Patio	Patio	Patio /Wood	Patio	–3,200
Fireplace	1	1	1	None	$4,000
Fence	Rear/redwood	Rear/redwood	Rear/redwood	Rear/redwood	
Other Improvements	None	None	None	None	

■ COST DATA

The square footage of the subject house can be computed from the diagram below. Cost figures were obtained from the Anystate Cost Service, revised March 2005, for a building rated as good quality.

House	$ 210 per square foot
Garage	$ 36 per square foot
Landscaping/driveway/ patio/fencing	$ 18,500
Site value, estimated by analysis of comparable properties	$240,000

■ DEPRECIATION

Overall, the house and garage are in good condition, with normal wear and tear. Based on an effective age of 10 years and estimated remaining economic life of 50 years, depreciation due to physical deterioration is estimated at 17 percent. There is no evidence of functional or external obsolescence.

This appraisal is not for HUD or VA purposes. The property has no construction warranties remaining in effect.

■ INCOME DATA

Current market analysis indicates that the subject property would rent for $3,300 per month with a GRM of 178. Properties in this area typically have a much lower rental value than sales prices would indicate. Properties reviewed have the following rental values/GRMs: $3,200/179; $3,000/178; $3,500/176.

■ CONCLUSION

The property has been appraised by the three traditional approaches, and the results indicated are:

Cost approach	$817,903
Income approach	$587,400
Sales comparison approach	$815,500

The cost approach is felt to reflect the upper limit of value; it has been given consideration because the cost data were sufficiently accurate and the depreciation factors reflect the actions in the market.

The income approach shows a lower value, which reflects the lower value of a like property if bought for investment purposes. The appraiser has given little weight to this approach, since homes in this neighborhood are predominantly owner-occupied.

The sales comparison approach is based on sales of similar properties in the immediate area. Sufficient sales data were available; because sales were made within a relatively short period, data were not influenced by a time adjustment. This approach is the most factual and accurate because it measures actions of buyers in the market.

Because the value range is fairly close and comparable 1 required no adjustment, it can be assumed that the subject property has a market value of $815,500. The date of appraisal is November 18, 2005.

EXERCISE: APPRAISAL 3

Uniform Residential Appraisal Report   File

The purpose of this summary appraisal report is to provide the lender/client with an accurate, and adequately supported, opinion of the market value of the subject property.

SUBJECT

Property Address	City	State	Zip Code
Borrower	Owner of Public Record	County	
Legal Description			
Assessor's Parcel #	Tax Year	R.E. Taxes $	
Neighborhood Name	Map Reference	Census Tract	

Occupant ☐ Owner ☐ Tenant ☐ Vacant   Special Assessments $ ☐ PUD HOA $ ☐ per year ☐ per month
Property Rights Appraised ☐ Fee Simple ☐ Leasehold ☐ Other (describe)
Assignment Type ☐ Purchase Transaction ☐ Refinance Transaction ☐ Other (describe)
Lender/Client   Address
Is the subject property currently offered for sale or has it been offered for sale in the twelve months prior to the effective date of this appraisal? ☐ Yes ☐ No
Report data source(s) used, offering price(s), and date(s).

CONTRACT

I ☐ did ☐ did not analyze the contract for sale for the subject purchase transaction. Explain the results of the analysis of the contract for sale or why the analysis was not performed.

Contract Price $ Date of Contract   Is the property seller the owner of public record? ☐ Yes ☐ No   Data Source(s)
Is there any financial assistance (loan charges, sale concessions, gift or downpayment assistance, etc.) to be paid by any party on behalf of the borrower? ☐ Yes ☐ No
If Yes, report the total dollar amount and describe the items to be paid.

NEIGHBORHOOD

Note: Race and the racial composition of the neighborhood are not appraisal factors.

Neighborhood Characteristics			One-Unit Housing Trends			One-Unit Housing		Present Land Use %	
Location ☐ Urban	☐ Suburban	☐ Rural	Property Values ☐ Increasing	☐ Stable	☐ Declining	PRICE	AGE	One-Unit	%
Built-Up ☐ Over 75%	☐ 25–75%	☐ Under 25%	Demand/Supply ☐ Shortage	☐ In Balance	☐ Over Supply	$ (000)	(yrs)	2-4 Unit	%
Growth ☐ Rapid	☐ Stable	☐ Slow	Marketing Time ☐ Under 3 mths	☐ 3–6 mths	☐ Over 6 mths	Low		Multi-Family	%
Neighborhood Boundaries						High		Commercial	%
						Pred.		Other	%

Neighborhood Description

Market Conditions (including support for the above conclusions)

SITE

Dimensions	Area	Shape	View
Specific Zoning Classification	Zoning Description		

Zoning Compliance ☐ Legal ☐ Legal Nonconforming (Grandfathered Use) ☐ No Zoning ☐ Illegal (describe)
Is the highest and best use of the subject property as improved (or as proposed per plans and specifications) the present use? ☐ Yes ☐ No If No, describe

Utilities	Public	Other (describe)		Public	Other (describe)	Off-site Improvements—Type	Public	Private
Electricity	☐	☐	Water	☐	☐	Street	☐	☐
Gas	☐	☐	Sanitary Sewer	☐	☐	Alley	☐	☐

FEMA Special Flood Hazard Area ☐ Yes ☐ No FEMA Flood Zone   FEMA Map #   FEMA Map Date
Are the utilities and off-site improvements typical for the market area? ☐ Yes ☐ No If No, describe
Are there any adverse site conditions or external factors (easements, encroachments, environmental conditions, land uses, etc.)? ☐ Yes ☐ No If Yes, describe

IMPROVEMENTS

General Description		Foundation		Exterior Description materials/condition	Interior materials/condition	
Units ☐ One ☐ One with Accessory Unit		☐ Concrete Slab ☐ Crawl Space		Foundation Walls	Floors	
# of Stories		☐ Full Basement ☐ Partial Basement		Exterior Walls	Walls	
Type ☐ Det. ☐ Att. ☐ S-Det./End Unit		Basement Area sq. ft.		Roof Surface	Trim/Finish	
☐ Existing ☐ Proposed ☐ Under Const.		Basement Finish %		Gutters & Downspouts	Bath Floor	
Design (Style)		☐ Outside Entry/Exit ☐ Sump Pump		Window Type	Bath Wainscot	
Year Built		Evidence of ☐ Infestation		Storm Sash/Insulated	Car Storage ☐ None	
Effective Age (Yrs)		☐ Dampness ☐ Settlement		Screens	☐ Driveway # of Cars	
Attic ☐ None		Heating ☐ FWA ☐ HWBB ☐ Radiant		Amenities ☐ Woodstove(s) #	Driveway Surface	
☐ Drop Stair ☐ Stairs		☐ Other Fuel		☐ Fireplace(s) # ☐ Fence	☐ Garage # of Cars	
☐ Floor ☐ Scuttle		Cooling ☐ Central Air Conditioning		☐ Patio/Deck ☐ Porch	☐ Carport # of Cars	
☐ Finished ☐ Heated		☐ Individual ☐ Other		☐ Pool ☐ Other	☐ Att. ☐ Det. ☐ Built-in	

Appliances ☐ Refrigerator ☐ Range/Oven ☐ Dishwasher ☐ Disposal ☐ Microwave ☐ Washer/Dryer ☐ Other (describe)
Finished area **above** grade contains: Rooms   Bedrooms   Bath(s)   Square Feet of Gross Living Area Above Grade
Additional features (special energy efficient items, etc.)

Describe the condition of the property (including needed repairs, deterioration, renovations, remodeling, etc.).

Are there any physical deficiencies or adverse conditions that affect the livability, soundness, or structural integrity of the property? ☐ Yes ☐ No If Yes, describe

Does the property generally conform to the neighborhood (functional utility, style, condition, use, construction, etc.)? ☐ Yes ☐ No If No, describe

Uniform Residential Appraisal Report

File #

There are _____ comparable properties currently offered for sale in the subject neighborhood ranging in price from $ _____ to $ _____ .

There are _____ comparable sales in the subject neighborhood within the past twelve months ranging in sale price from $ _____ to $ _____ .

FEATURE	SUBJECT	COMPARABLE SALE # 1		COMPARABLE SALE # 2		COMPARABLE SALE # 3	
Address							
Proximity to Subject							
Sale Price	$		$		$		$
Sale Price/Gross Liv. Area	$ sq. ft.	$ sq. ft.		$ sq. ft.		$ sq. ft.	
Data Source(s)							
Verification Source(s)							
VALUE ADJUSTMENTS	DESCRIPTION	DESCRIPTION	+(-) $ Adjustment	DESCRIPTION	+(-) $ Adjustment	DESCRIPTION	+(-) $ Adjustment
Sale or Financing Concessions							
Date of Sale/Time							
Location							
Leasehold/Fee Simple							
Site							
View							
Design (Style)							
Quality of Construction							
Actual Age							
Condition							
Above Grade	Total Bdrms. Baths	Total Bdrms. Baths		Total Bdrms. Baths		Total Bdrms. Baths	
Room Count							
Gross Living Area	sq. ft.	sq. ft.		sq. ft.		sq. ft.	
Basement & Finished Rooms Below Grade							
Functional Utility							
Heating/Cooling							
Energy Efficient Items							
Garage/Carport							
Porch/Patio/Deck							
Net Adjustment (Total)		☐ + ☐ -	$	☐ + ☐ -	$	☐ + ☐ -	$
Adjusted Sale Price of Comparables		Net Adj. % Gross Adj. %	$	Net Adj. % Gross Adj. %	$	Net Adj. % Gross Adj. %	$

I ☐ did ☐ did not research the sale or transfer history of the subject property and comparable sales. If not, explain _____

My research ☐ did ☐ did not reveal any prior sales or transfers of the subject property for the three years prior to the effective date of this appraisal.

Data source(s) _____

My research ☐ did ☐ did not reveal any prior sales or transfers of the comparable sales for the year prior to the date of sale of the comparable sale.

Data source(s) _____

Report the results of the research and analysis of the prior sale or transfer history of the subject property and comparable sales (report additional prior sales on page 3).

ITEM	SUBJECT	COMPARABLE SALE # 1	COMPARABLE SALE # 2	COMPARABLE SALE # 3
Date of Prior Sale/Transfer				
Price of Prior Sale/Transfer				
Data Source(s)				
Effective Date of Data Source(s)				

Analysis of prior sale or transfer history of the subject property and comparable sales

Summary of Sales Comparison Approach

Indicated Value by Sales Comparison Approach $

Indicated Value by: Sales Comparison Approach $ _____ Cost Approach (if developed) $ _____ Income Approach (if developed) $ _____

This appraisal is made ☐ "as is", ☐ subject to completion per plans and specifications on the basis of a hypothetical condition that the improvements have been completed, ☐ subject to the following repairs or alterations on the basis of a hypothetical condition that the repairs or alterations have been completed, or ☐ subject to the following required inspection based on the extraordinary assumption that the condition or deficiency does not require alteration or repair:

Based on a complete visual inspection of the interior and exterior areas of the subject property, defined scope of work, statement of assumptions and limiting conditions, and appraiser's certification, my (our) opinion of the market value, as defined, of the real property that is the subject of this report is $ _____ , as of _____ , which is the date of inspection and the effective date of this appraisal.

Uniform Residential Appraisal Report   File

ADDITIONAL COMMENTS

COST APPROACH TO VALUE (not required by Fannie Mae)

Provide adequate information for the lender/client to replicate the below cost figures and calculations.

Support for the opinion of site value (summary of comparable land sales or other methods for estimating site value)

ESTIMATED ☐ REPRODUCTION OR ☐ REPLACEMENT COST NEW	OPINION OF SITE VALUE .... = $
Source of cost data	Dwelling Sq. Ft. @ $ .... =$
Quality rating from cost service Effective date of cost data	Sq. Ft. @ $ .... =$
Comments on Cost Approach (gross living area calculations, depreciation, etc.)	
	Garage/Carport Sq. Ft. @ $ .... =$
	Total Estimate of Cost-New .... = $
	Less Physical Functional External
	Depreciation =$( )
	Depreciated Cost of Improvements .... =$
	"As-is" Value of Site Improvements .... =$
Estimated Remaining Economic Life (HUD and VA only) Years	Indicated Value By Cost Approach .... =$

INCOME APPROACH TO VALUE (not required by Fannie Mae)

Estimated Monthly Market Rent $ X Gross Rent Multiplier   = $ Indicated Value by Income Approach
Summary of Income Approach (including support for market rent and GRM)

PROJECT INFORMATION FOR PUDs (if applicable)

Is the developer/builder in control of the Homeowners' Association (HOA)? ☐ Yes ☐ No   Unit type(s) ☐ Detached ☐ Attached

Provide the following information for PUDs ONLY if the developer/builder is in control of the HOA and the subject property is an attached dwelling unit.

Legal name of project

Total number of phases   Total number of units   Total number of units sold

Total number of units rented   Total number of units for sale   Data source(s)

Was the project created by the conversion of an existing building(s) into a PUD? ☐ Yes ☐ No   If Yes, date of conversion

Does the project contain any multi-dwelling units? ☐ Yes ☐ No   Data source(s)

Are the units, common elements, and recreation facilities complete? ☐ Yes ☐ No   If No, describe the status of completion.

Are the common elements leased to or by the Homeowners' Association? ☐ Yes ☐ No   If Yes, describe the rental terms and options.

Describe common elements and recreational facilities

ANSWER KEY

■ **APPRAISAL 2**

■ **APPRAISAL 3**

APPRAISAL 2

Uniform Residential Appraisal Report   File # 05070001

The purpose of this summary appraisal report is to provide the lender/client with an accurate, and adequately supported, opinion of the market value of the subject property.

SUBJECT

Property Address 1053 Locust Lane	City Pleasantown State Anystate Zip Code 42555
Borrower Jack Morris and Hope Temple Owner of Public Record Frank and Mildred Justice	County Sunnyside

Legal Description Lot 5 of Block 32, Meadow Green Subdivision, page 997 of Book 438, Records of Sunnyside County

Assessor's Parcel # AL6857   Tax Year 2005   R.E. Taxes $ 4,344

Neighborhood Name Meadow Green   Map Reference D14   Census Tract 4499

Occupant [X] Owner [ ] Tenant [ ] Vacant   Special Assessments $ None   [X] PUD   HOA $ 80 [ ] per year [X] per month

Property Rights Appraised [X] Fee Simple [ ] Leasehold [ ] Other (describe)

Assignment Type [X] Purchase Transaction [ ] Refinance Transaction [ ] Other (describe)

Lender/Client State Savings Bank   Address 4312 State Street, Pleasantown, Anystate 42555

Is the subject property currently offered for sale or has it been offered for sale in the twelve months prior to the effective date of the appraisal? [X] Yes [ ] No

Report data source(s) used, offering price(s), and date(s). Listing agent reports property listed for $369,900 on September 30, 2005.

CONTRACT

I [X] did [ ] did not analyze the contract for sale for the subject purchase transaction. Explain the results of the analysis of the contract for sale or why the analysis was not performed.

Contract Price $ 365,000   Date of Contract 11-15-05   Is the property seller the owner of public record? [X] Yes [ ] No   Data Source(s) Listing Agent

Is there any financial assistance (loan charges, sale concessions, gift or downpayment assistance, etc.) to be paid by any party on behalf of the borrower? [ ] Yes [X] No

If Yes, report the total dollar amount and describe the items to be paid:

NEIGHBORHOOD

Note: Race and the racial composition of the neighborhood are not appraisal factors.

Neighborhood Characteristics			One-Unit Housing Trends				One-Unit Housing		Percent Land Use %	
Location [ ] Urban [X] Suburban [ ] Rural			Property Values [X] Increasing [ ] Stable [ ] Declining				PRICE	AGE	One-Unit	100 %
Built-Up [X] Over 75% [ ] 25-75% [ ] Under 25%			Demand/Supply [X] Shortage [ ] In Balance [ ] Over Supply				$(000)	(yrs)	2-4 Unit	%
Growth [ ] Rapid [X] Stable [ ] Slow			Marketing Time [X] Under 3 mths [ ] 3-6 mths [ ] Over 6 mths			325	Low	8	Multi-Family	%
Neighborhood Boundaries		Meadow Road to the North; Countryside Avenue to the				395	High	29	Commercial	%
East; Sunnyside Boulevard to the South; Pleasantown Avenue to the West.						360	Pred.	20	Other	%

Neighborhood Description Fully developed subdivision close to schools, shopping and services, and convenient to the downtown business and shopping district. Strong demand for close-in housing has resulted in short marketing times and consistent price increases for last 48 months.

Market Conditions (including support for the above conclusions) Metropolitan area has benefitted from expansion of state offices and local businesses. Strong, stable workforce supports current rising property values.

SITE

Dimensions 75Fx150LSx75Rx150RS   Area 11250 +/- sq. ft.   Shape Rectangle   View Hills

Specific Zoning Classification SF-1   Zoning Description Single-Family Residential

Zoning Compliance [X] Legal [ ] Legal Nonconforming (Grandfathered Use) [ ] No Zoning [ ] Illegal (describe)

Is the highest and best use of the subject property as improved (or as proposed per plans and specifications) the present use? [X] Yes [ ] No If No, describe

Utilities	Public	Other (describe)		Public	Other (describe)	Off-site Improvements--Type	Public	Private
Electricity	[X]		Water	[X]		Street Asphalt	[X]	
Gas	[X]		Sanitary Sewer	[X]		Alley None		

FEMA Special Flood Hazard Area [ ] Yes [X] No   FEMA Flood Zone   FEMA Map No. XX999   FEMA Map Date 03/97

Are the utilities and off-site improvements typical for the market area? [X] Yes [ ] No. If No, describe

Are there any adverse site conditions or external factors (easements, encroachments, environmental conditions, land uses, etc.)? [ ] Yes [X] No If Yes, describe

IMPROVEMENTS

General Description		Foundation		Exterior Description	materials/condition	Interior	materials/condition
Units [X] One [ ] One with Accessory Unit		[ ] Concrete Slab [ ] Crawl Space		Foundation Walls	Concrete/Good	Floors	Cpt/Ceram/Good
# of Stories 1		[X] Full Basement [ ] Partial Basement		Exterior Walls	Vinyl/Brick/Good	Walls	Drywall/God
Type [X] Det. [ ] Att. [ ] S-Det/End Unit		Basement Area 1,980 sq. ft.		Roof Surface	Mineral shingle/Good	Trim/Finish	Wood/Good
[X] Existing [ ] Proposed [ ] Under Const.		Basement Finish 75 %		Gutters & Downspouts	Alum/Good	Bath Floor	Ceramic/Gd
Design (Style) Ranch		[ ] Outside Entry/Exit [X] Sump Pump		Window Type	Wood dbl hung/Good	Bath Wainscot	None
Year Built 1987		Evidence of [ ] Infestation		Storm Sash/Insulated	Alum/Good	Car Storage	[ ] None
Effective Age (Yrs) 12		[ ] Dampness [ ] Settlement		Screens	Combination/Good	[ ] Driveway # of Cars	
Attic [ ] [X] None		Heating [X] FWA [ ] HWBB [ ] Radiant		Amenities	Woodstove(s)#	Driveway Surface Concrete	
[ ] Drop Stair [ ] Stairs		[ ] Other [ ] Fuel		[X] Fireplace(s) # 1 [ ] Fence		[X] Garage # of Cars 2	
[ ] Floor [ ] Scuttle		Cooling [X] Central Air Conditioning		[X] Patio/Deck [ ] Porch		[ ] Carport # of Cars	
[ ] Finished [ ] Heated		[ ] Individual [ ] Other		[ ] Pool [ ] Other		[ ] Att. [X] Det. [ ] Built-In	

Appliances [ ] Refrigerator [X] Range/Oven [X] Dishwasher [X] Disposal [X] Microwave [ ] Washer/Dryer [ ] Other (describe)

Finished area above grade contains: 8 Rooms   4 Bedrooms   2.00 Bath(s)   1,980 Square Feet of Gross Living Area Above Grade

Additional features (special energy efficient items, etc.) None

Describe the condition of the property (including needed repairs, deterioration, renovations, remodeling, etc.). The property is typical of others in the neighborhood and has been well-maintained though never remodeled. Heating and air-conditioning units are five years old, according to the property owner.

Are there any physical deficiencies or adverse conditions that affect the livability, soundness, or structural integrity of the property? [ ] Yes [ ] No If Yes, describe

Does the property generally conform to the neighborhood (functional utility, style, condition, use, construction, etc.)? [X] Yes [ ] No If No, describe

A P P R A I S A L 2 (continued)

Uniform Residential Appraisal Report   File # 05070001

There are _____ comparable properties in the subject neighborhood ranging in price from $ _____ to $ _____ .

There are _____ comparable sales in the subject neighborhood within the past twelve months ranging in sale price from $ _____ to $ _____ .

FEATURE	SUBJECT	COMPARABLE SALE # 1	+(-)$ Adjustment	COMPARABLE SALE # 2	+(-)$ Adjustment	COMPARABLE SALE # 3	+(-)$ Adjustment
Address	1053 Locust Lane Pleasantown	310 Minaqua Street Pleasantown		1091 Locust Lane Pleasantown		453 Chelsea Court Pleasantown	
Proximity to Subject		1/2 mile Northwest		Same block		3/4 mile Northeast	
Sale Price	$ 365,000	$ 340,000		$ 349,000		$ 362,000	
Sale Price/Gross Liv. Area	$ 184.34 sq. ft.	$ 170.00 sq. ft.		$ 188.65 sq. ft.		$ 182.83 sq. ft.	
Data Source(s)		MLS		MLS		MLS	
Verification Source(s)		Selling Agent		Selling Agent		Selling Agent	
VALUE ADJUSTMENTS	DESCRIPTION	DESCRIPTION	+(-)$ Adjustment	DESCRIPTION	+(-)$ Adjustment	DESCRIPTION	+(-)$ Adjustment
Sale or Financing Concessions		None		None		None	
Date of Sale/Time		8-26-05		7-22-05		8-22-05	
Location	Suburban/Gd	Suburban/Gd		Suburban/Gd		Suburban/Gd	
Leasehold/Fee Simple	Fee Simple	Fee Simple		Fee Simple		Fee Simple	
Site	11,250 +/- SF	11,000 +/- SF		10,880 +/- SF		10,500 +/- SF	
View	Hills/Good	Hills/Equal		Hills/Equal		Hills/Equal	
Design (Style)	Ranch	Ranch		Ranch		Ranch	
Quality of Construction	Good	Good		Good		Good	
Actual Age	18 yrs.	20 yrs.		18 yrs.		19 yrs.	
Condition	Good	Fair	+17,000	Good		Good	
Above Grade	Total / Bdrms. / Baths	Total / Bdrms. / Baths		Total / Bdrms. / Baths		Total / Bdrms. / Baths	
Room Count	8 / 4 / 2.00	8 / 4 / 2		7 / 3 / 2		8 / 4 / 2	
Gross Living Area	1,980 sq. ft.	2,000 sq. ft.		1,850 sq. ft.	+12,000	1,980 sq. ft.	
Basement & Finished	1,980 sq. ft.	2,000		1,850		1,980	
Rooms Below Grade	1,490 sq. ft.	1,600		1,400		1,490	
Functional Utility	Good	Good		Good		Good	
Heating/Cooling	FA/Central	FA/Central		FA/Central		FA/Central	
Energy Efficient Items	None	None		None		None	
Garage/Carport	2-car det.	2-car det.		2-car det.		2-car det.	
Porch/Patio/Deck	300 SF Deck	None	+3,000	360 SF Deck		300 SF Deck	
Fireplace	Masonry 1	Masonry 1		None	+3,000	None	+3,000
Net Adjustment (Total)		X + ___ -	$ 20,000	X + ___ -	$ 15,000	X + ___ -	$ 3,000
Adjusted Sale Price of Comparables		Net Adj. 5.90 % Gross Adj. 5.90 %	$ 360,000	Net Adj. 4.30 % Gross Adj. 4.30 %	$ 364,000	Net Adj. 0.80 % Gross Adj. 0.80 %	$ 365,000

I [X] did [ ] did not research the sale or transfer history of the subject property and comparable sales. If not, explain

My research [ ] did [X] did not reveal any prior sales or transfers of the subject property for the three years prior to the effective date of this appraisal.
Data Source(s)

My research [ ] did [X] did not reveal any prior sales or transfers of the comparable sales for the prior year to the date of sale of the comparalbe sale.
Data Source(s) County Assessor's Office

Report the results of the research and analysis of the prior sale or transfer history of the subject property and comparable sales (report additional prior sales on page 3).

ITEM	SUBJECT	COMPARABLE SALE # 1	COMPARABLE SALE # 2	COMPARABLE SALE # 3
Date of Prior Sale/Transfer				
Price of Prior Sale/Transfer				
Data Source(s)				
Effective Date of Data Source(s)				

Analysis of prior sale or transfer history of the subject property and comparable sales

Summary of Sales Comparison Approach   Of the comparable sales report here, comparable #3 is closest in features to the subject property, and required the lowest price adjustment. While the adjusted prices of all three comparables are very close, the adjusted price of comparable #3 is the best indicator of the market value of the subject property.

Indicated Value by Sales Comparison Approach $ 365,000

Indicated Value by: Sales Comparison Approach $ 365,000   Cost Approach (if developed) $ 370,100   Income Approach (if developed) $ 342,000

The lack of vacant lots available for building in the subject subdivision makes the cost approach less reliable as an indicator of value for the subject property. There are relatively few rentals, and rental prices have not kept pace with sales prices. The value indicated by the sales comparison approach most accurately reflects the actions of buyers in today's marketplace.

This appraisal is made [X] "as is," [ ] subject to completion per plans and specifications on the basis of a hypothetical condition that the improvements have been completed, [ ] subject to the following repairs or alterations on the basis of a hypothetical condition that the repairs or alterations have been completed, or [ ] subject to the following required inspection based on the extraordinary assumption that the condition or deficiency does not require alteration or repair:

Based on a complete visual inspection of the interior and exterior areas of the subject property, defined scope of work, statement of assumptions and limiting conditions, and appraiser's certification, my (our) opinion of the market value, as defined, of the real property that is the subject of this report is $ 365,000 , as of 11-30-05 , which is the date of inspection and the effective date of this appraisal.

Freddie Mac Form 70 March 2005   Page 2 of 6   Fannie Mae Form 1004 March 2005

A P P R A I S A L   2   (continued)

Uniform Residential Appraisal Report   File #   05070001

ADDITIONAL COMMENTS

COST APPROACH TO VALUE (not required by Fannie Mae)

Provide adequate information for the lender/client to replicate the below cost figures and calculations.

Support for the opinion of site value (summary of comparable land sales or other methods for estimating sale value)

Prices of vacant lots in nearby similar subdivisions, both sold and listed for sale, were considered to arrive at a value for the subject site of $94,000.

ESTIMATED [X] REPRODUCTION OR [ ] REPLACEMENT COST NEW	OPINION OF SITE VALUE..................................=$	94,000
Source of cost data Local builders/Anystate Cost Manual	Dwelling 1,980 Sq. Ft. @ $ 145 ....=$	287,100
Quality rating from cost service Good Effective date of cost data 09/04	Wood deck 300 Sq. Ft. @ $ 15 ....=$	4,500
Comments on Cost Approach (gross living area calculations, depreciation, etc.)	Basement finishing	6,000
The overall good condition of the subject indicates an effective	Garage/Carport 625 Sq. Ft. @ $ 40 ....=$	25,000
age of 12 years and an overall economic life of 60 years.	Total Estimate of Cost-New ....=$	322,600
	Less Physical Functional External	
	Depreciation 64,520 -0- -0- =$(64,520)	
	Depreciated Cost of Improvements.................=$	258,080
	'As-is' Value of Site Improvements.................=$	18,000
	.................=$	
Estimated Remaining Economic Life (HUD and VA only) 48 Years	Indicated Value By Cost Approach.................=$	370,080

INCOME APPROACH TO VALUE (not required by Fannie Mae)

Estimated Monthly Market Rent $ 2,250   X Gross Rent Multiplier   152   = $ 342,000   Indicated Value by Income Approach

Summary of Income Approach (including support for market rent and GRM)   Few rentals are available in this subdivision, but analysis of three such properties supports rent/GRM indicated: $1,970/172; $2,100/164; $2,500/138.

PROJECT INFORMATION FOR PUDs (if applicable)

Is the developer/builder in control of the Homeowners' Association (HOA)?   [ ] Yes [X] No   Unit type(s) [X] Detached [ ] Attached

Provide the following information for PUDs ONLY if the developer/builder is in control of the HOA and the subject property is an attached dwelling unit.

Legal name of project

Total number of phases   Total number of units   Total number of units sold

Total number of units rented   Total number of units for sale   Data Source(s)

Was the project created by the conversion of existing building(s) into a PUD? [ ] Yes [ ] No If Yes, date of conversion

Does the project contain any multi-dwelling units? [ ] Yes [ ] No Data Source(s)

Are the units, common elements, and recreation facilities complete? [ ] Yes [ ] No If No, describe the status of completion.

Are the common elements leased to or by the Homeowners' Association? [ ] Yes [ ] No If Yes, describe the rental terms and options.

Describe common elements and recreational facilities

APPRAISAL 3

Uniform Residential Appraisal Report   File # 05070001

The purpose of this summary appraisal report is to provide the lender/client with an accurate, and adequately supported, opinion of the market value of the subject property.

SUBJECT

Property Address 582 Augustina Lane   City Brandywine   State AN   Zip Code 99999

Borrower Cindi Rattan and George Rattan   Owner of Public Record Cindi and George Rattan   County King

Legal Description Lot 58, Sunnyside Club Estates, as shown on page 36 of book 25, records of King County

Assessor's Parcel # 80808C8   Tax Year 2004   R.E. Taxes $ 10,029

Neighborhood Name Sunnyside Club   Map Reference 95-2   Census Tract 27.04

Occupant [X] Owner [ ] Tenant [ ] Vacant   Special Assessments $ None   [X] PUD   HOA $ 600   [X] per year [ ] per month

Property Rights Appraised [X] Fee Simple [ ] Leasehold [ ] Other (describe)

Assignment Type [ ] Purchase Transaction [ ] Refinance Transaction [X] Other (describe) Marital dissolution property settlement

Lender/Client Ivers and Nussbaum, LLP   Address 4310 Frances Drive, Metro City, AN 99999

Is the subject property currently offered for sale or has it been offered for sale in the twelve months prior to the effective date of the appraisal? [ ] Yes [X] No

Report data source(s) used, offering price(s), and date(s).

CONTRACT

I [ ] did [ ] did not analyze the contract for sale for the subject purchase transaction. Explain the results of the analysis of the contract for sale or why the analysis was not performed. N/A

Contract Price $ Date of Contract   Is the property seller the owner of public record? [ ] Yes [ ] No   Data Source(s)

Is there any financial assistance (loan charges, sale concessions, gift or downpayment assistance, etc.) to be paid by any party on behalf of the borrower? [ ] Yes [ ] No

If Yes, report the total dollar amount and describe the items to be paid:

NEIGHBORHOOD

Note: Race and the racial composition of the neighborhood are not appraisal factors.

Neighborhood Characteristics			One-Unit Housing Trends				One-Unit Housing		Percent Land Use %	
Location	[ ] Urban [X] Suburban [ ] Rural		Property Values	[X] Increasing [ ] Stable [ ] Declining			PRICE	AGE	One-Unit	100 %
Built-Up	[X] Over 75% [ ] 25-75% [ ] Under 25%		Demand/Supply	[ ] Shortage [X] In Balance [ ] Over Supply			$(000)	(yrs)	2-4 Unit	%
Growth	[ ] Rapid [X] Stable [ ] Slow		Marketing Time	[X] Under 3 mths [ ] 3-6 mths [ ] Over 6 mths			595 Low	12	Multi-Family	%
Neighborhood Boundaries		*** See Additional Comments ***					1,195 High	20	Commercial	%
							840 Pred.	15	Other	%

Neighborhood Description   Consistent demand has kept prices in Sunnyside Club rising. Cul-de-sac streets neighborhood access from only two streets keep neighborhood quiet, with no through traffic. Only negative feature is limited public transportation.

Market Conditions (including support for the above conclusions)   Overall market area has seen a slight slump in prices, but Sunnyside Club has maintained its desirability.

SITE

Dimensions 90Fx130LSx90Rx130RS   Area 11700 +/- sq. ft.   Shape Rectangle   View Street/parkway

Specific Zoning Classification R-1   Zoning Description Single-Family Residential

Zoning Compliance [X] Legal [ ] Legal Nonconforming (Grandfathered Use) [ ] No Zoning [ ] Illegal (describe)

Is the highest and best use of the subject property as improved (or as proposed per plans and specifications) the present use? [X] Yes [ ] No If No, describe

Utilities	Public	Other (describe)		Public	Other (describe)	Off-site Improvements--Type	Public	Private
Electricity	X		Water	X		Street Asphalt	X	
Gas	X		Sanitary Sewer	X		Alley None		

FEMA Special Flood Hazard Area [ ] Yes [X] No   FEMA Flood Zone   FEMA Map No. 123   FEMA Map Date 03/01

Are the utilities and off-site improvements typical for the market area? [X] Yes [ ] No. If No, describe

Are there any adverse site conditions or external factors (easements, encroachments, environmental conditions, land uses, etc.)? [ ] Yes [X] No If Yes, describe

IMPROVEMENTS

General Description	Foundation	Exterior Description materials/condition	Interior materials/condition
Units [X] One [ ] One with Accessory Unit	[X] Concrete Slab [ ] Crawl Space	Foundation Walls Concrete/Good	Floors Cpt/wd/ceram/Gd
# of Stories 2	[ ] Full Basement [ ] Partial Basement	Exterior Walls Brk veneer/Good	Walls Drywall/Good
Type [X] Det. [ ] Att. [ ] S-Det/End Unit	Basement Area sq. ft.	Roof Surface Asph. shingle/Good	Trim/Finish Wod/Good
[X] Existing [ ] Proposed [ ] Under Const.	Basement Finish %	Gutters & Downspouts Alum./Good	Bath Floor Ceram/Good
Design (Style) Colonial	[ ] Outside Entry/Exit [ ] Sump Pump	Window Type Wd dbl-hung/Good	Bath Wainscot Ceram/Good
Year Built 1991	Evidence of [ ] Infestation	Storm Sash/Insulated Alum/Good	Car Storage [ ] None
Effective Age (Yrs) 10	[ ] Dampness [ ] Settlement	Screens Alum combo/Good	[ ] Driveway # of Cars

Attic	[ ] None	Heating [ ] FWA [ ] HWBB [ ] Radiant	Amenities	WoodStove(s)#	Driveway Surface Concrete
[ ] Drop Stair	[ ] Stairs	[ ] Other [ ] Fuel	[ ] Fireplace(s) # [ ] Fence		[X] Garage # of Cars 3
[ ] Floor	[ ] Scuttle	Cooling [ ] Central Air Conditioning	[ ] Patio/Deck [ ] Porch		[ ] Carport # of Cars
[ ] Finished	[ ] Heated	[ ] Individual [ ] Other	[ ] Pool [ ] Other		[ ] Att. [X] Det. [ ] Built-in

Appliances [ ] Refrigerator [X] Range/Oven [X] Dishwasher [X] Disposal [ ] Microwave [ ] Washer/Dryer [ ] Other (describe)

Finished area **above** grade contains: 8 Rooms   4 Bedrooms   3.00 Bath(s)   3,038 Square Feet of Gross Living Area Above Grade

Additional features (special energy efficient items, etc.) None

Describe the condition of the property (including needed repairs, deterioration, renovations, remodeling, etc.). The subject property is in good condition, with no apparent needed repairs, making it typical of most homes in this neighborhood.

Are there any physical deficiencies or adverse conditions that affect the livability, soundness, or structural integrity of the property? [ ] Yes [ ] No If Yes, describe
There are no outside conditions, or functional or physical deficiencies that would affect the livability or soundness of the property.

Does the property generally conform to the neighborhood (functional utility, style, condition, use, construction, etc.)? [X] Yes [ ] No If No, describe

APPRAISAL 3 (continued)

Uniform Residential Appraisal Report

File # 05070001

There are **6** comparable properties in the subject neighborhood ranging in price from $ **799,000.00** to $ **839,900.00**

There are **10** comparable sales in the subject neighborhood within the past twelve months ranging in sale price from $ **780,000.00** to $ **832,000.00**

FEATURE	SUBJECT	COMPARABLE SALE # 1		COMPARABLE SALE # 2		COMPARABLE SALE # 3	
Address	582 Augustina Lane Brandywine	205 Briarwood Drive Brandywine		570 Shanter Court Brandywine		308 Crafton Street Brandywine	
Proximity to Subject		.5 mile N/W		3 blocks South		.5 mile S/E	
Sale Price	$ N/A	$	815,500	$	827,200	$	791,000
Sale Price/Gross Liv. Area	$ sq. ft.	$ 268.43 sq. ft.		$ 275.73 sq. ft.		$ 251.11 sq. ft.	
Data Source(s)		Listing Agent		Listing Agent		Listing Agent	
Verification Source(s)		Selling Agent		Selling Agent		Selling Agent	
VALUE ADJUSTMENTS	DESCRIPTION	DESCRIPTION	+(-)$ Adjustment	DESCRIPTION	+(-)$ Adjustment	DESCRIPTION	+(-)$ Adjustment
Sale or Financing Concessions		None		None		None	
Date of Sale/Time		10-14-05		8-26-05		7-19-05	
Location	Suburban	Suburban		Suburban		Suburban	
Leasehold/Fee Simple	Fee Simple	Fee Simple		Fee Simple		Fee Simple	
Site	11,700 +/- SF	11,500 +/- SF		12,000 +/- SF		8,800 +/- SF	+15,000
View	Street/Pkwy	Street/Pkwy		Street/Pkwy		Street/Pkwy	
Design (Style)	Colonial	Colonial		Colonial		Colonial	
Quality of Construction	Good	Good		Good		Good	
Actual Age	14	14		14		14	
Condition	Good	Good		Good		Good	
Above Grade	Total 8 / Bdrms. 4 / Baths 3.00	Total 8 / Bdrms. 4 / Baths 3		Total 8 / Bdrms. 4 / Baths 3		Total 8 / Bdrms. 4 / Baths 3	
Room Count							
Gross Living Area	3,038 sq. ft.	3,038 sq. ft.		3,000 sq. ft.		3,150 sq. ft.	
Basement & Finished Rooms Below Grade	None	None		None		None	
Functional Utility	Good	Good		Good		Good	
Heating/Cooling	FA/Central	FA/Central		FA/Central		FA/Central	
Energy Efficient Items	None	None		None		None	
Garage/Carport	Gar 3 det.	Gar 3 det.		Gar 3 det.		Gar 3 det.	
Porch/Patio/Deck	Patio	Patio		Patio/Wd deck	-3,200	Patio	
Fireplace	1	1		1		None	+4,000
Fence	Rear/redwd	Rear/redwd		Rear/redwd		Rear/redwd	
Net Adjustment (Total)		[ ] + [ ] -	$	[ ] + [X] -	$ -3,200	[X] + [ ] -	$ 19,000
Adjusted Sale Price of Comparables		Net Adj. % Gross Adj. %	$ 815,500	Net Adj. -0.40 % Gross Adj. 0.40 %	$ 824,000	Net Adj. 2.40 % Gross Adj. 2.40 %	$ 810,000

I [X] did [ ] did not research the sale or transfer history of the subject property and comparable sales. If not, explain

My research [ ] did [X] did not reveal any prior sales or transfers of the subject property for the three years prior to the effective date of this appraisal.
Data Source(s)

My research [ ] did [X] did not reveal any prior sales or transfers of the comparable sales for the prior year to the date of sale of the comparalbe sale.
Data Source(s) County assessor

Report the results of the research and analysis of the prior sale or transfer history of the subject property and comparable sales (report additional prior sales on page 3).

ITEM	SUBJECT	COMPARABLE SALE # 1	COMPARABLE SALE # 2	COMPARABLE SALE # 3
Date of Prior Sale/Transfer				
Price of Prior Sale/Transfer				
Data Source(s)				
Effective Date of Data Source(s)				

Analysis of prior sale or transfer history of the subject property and comparable sales   N/A

Summary of Sales Comparison Approach   The number of recent sales of comparable properties in the subject neighborhood makes this the most reliable indicator of value for the subject property. Of the comparables included in this report, comparable #1 is most like the subject and required no price adjustments, making its sale price the best indicator of value of all of the comparables studied.

Indicated Value by Sales Comparison Approach $ 815,500

Indicated Value by: Sales Comparison Approach $ 815,500   Cost Approach (if developed) $ 817,900   Income Approach (if developed) $ 587,400

This appraisal is made [X] "as is," [ ] subject to completion per plans and specifications on the basis of a hypothetical condition that the improvements have been completed, [ ] subject to the following repairs or alterations on the basis of a hypothetical condition that the repairs or alterations have been completed, or [ ] subject to the following required inspection based on the extraordinary assumption that the condition or deficiency does not require alteration or repair:

Based on a complete visual inspection of the interior and exterior areas of the subject property, defined scope of work, statement of assumptions and limiting conditions, and appraiser's certification, my (our) opinion of the market value, as defined, of the real property that is the subject of this report is
$ 815,500 , as of 11-18-2005 , which is the date of inspection and the effective date of this appraisal.

Freddie Mac Form 70 March 2005   Page 2 of 6   Fannie Mae Form 1004 March 2005

APPRAISAL 3 (continued)

Uniform Residential Appraisal Report   File # 05070001

Neighborhood boundaries defined by eight-foot concrete block perimeter fence, bounded by Willow Road to West, Metro Highway to North, Center Road to East, Sunnyside Avenue to South.

ADDITIONAL COMMENTS

COST APPROACH TO VALUE (not required by Fannie Mae)

Provide adequate information for the lender/client to replicate the below cost figures and calculations.

Support for the opinion of site value (summary of comparable land sales or other methods for estimating sale value)

Analysis of sales prices of comparably sized property in similar neighborhoods indicates a value for the subject site of 240,000.

ESTIMATED [X] REPRODUCTION OR [ ] REPLACEMENT COST NEW	OPINION OF SITE VALUE.................................=$	240,000
Source of cost data Anystate Cost Service	Dwelling 3,038 Sq. Ft. @ $ 210 ....=$	637,980
Quality rating from cost service Good Effective date of cost data March, 2005	Sq. Ft. @ $ ....=$	
Comments on Cost Approach (gross living area calculations, depreciation, etc.)	Garage/Carport 1,000 Sq. Ft. @ $ 36 ....=$	36,000
	Total Estimate of Cost-New ....=$	673,980
	Less Physical	Functional	External	
	Depreciation 114,577 =$ (114,577)	
	Depreciated Cost of Improvements...........................=$	559,403
	'As-is' Value of Site Improvements.........................=$	18,500
	...............=$	
Estimated Remaining Economic Life (HUD and VA only) 50 Years	Indicated Value By Cost Approach.........................=$	817,903

INCOME APPROACH TO VALUE (not required by Fannie Mae)

Estimated Monthly Market Rent $ 3,300   X Gross Rent Multiplier   178   = $ 587,400   Indicated Value by Income Approach

Summary of Income Approach (including support for market rent and GRM)   Rents typically less than sales prices would indicate; comp property rentals have rents/GRMs of $3,200/179; $3,000/178; $3,500/176, supporting a rent of $3,300 and GRM of 178 for subject.

PROJECT INFORMATION FOR PUDs (if applicable)

Is the developer/builder in control of the Homeowners' Association (HOA)? [ ] Yes [X] No   Unit type(s) [X] Detached [ ] Attached

Provide the following information for PUDs ONLY if the developer/builder is in control of the HOA and the subject property is an attached dwelling unit.

Legal name of project

Total number of phases   Total number of units   Total number of units sold

Total number of units rented   Total number of units for sale   Data Source(s)

Was the project created by the conversion of existing building(s) into a PUD? [ ] Yes [ ] No If Yes, date of conversion

Does the project contain any multi-dwelling units? [ ] Yes [ ] No Data Source(s)

Are the units, common elements, and recreation facilities complete? [ ] Yes [ ] No If No, describe the status of completion.

Are the common elements leased to or by the Homeowners' Association? [ ] Yes [ ] No If Yes, describe the rental terms and options.

Describe common elements and recreational facilities

INDEX